JONESTOWN
An American Family Tragedy

JONESTOWN
An American Family Tragedy
By H.J. Jones

Author: H. J. Jones
Designer: Kelly Ludwig
Cover design: M. Beckman

Readers are encouraged to go to www.MissionPointPress.
com to contact the author or to find information on how to
buy this book in bulk at a discounted rate.

Published by Mission Point Press
2554 Chandler Rd.
Traverse City, MI 49696
(231) 421-9513
www.MissionPointPress.com
ISBN: 978-1-961302-11-2
Library of Congress Control Number: 2023914697
Printed in the United States of America

JONESTOWN

An American Family Tragedy

H. J. Jones

MISSION POINT PRESS

This book is dedicated to:
Mary, Steve, and Mac

TABLE OF CONTENTS

Prelude ix

Author's Note xi

Part I: Uprooted
    Chapter 1: The New Land 3
    Chapter 2: Love and Death 15
    Chapter 3: Dead Ends 27
    Chapter 4: Orphans and Misfits 39
    Chapter 5: Slipping Away.. 49

Part II: Transplanted
    Chapter 6: A Temple in the Valley 73
    Chapter 7: Crossing the Golden Gate..................................... 93
    Chapter 8: Exodus.. 103

Part III: Sowing Lies
    Chapter 9: An Unpromising Land 121
    Chapter 10: The Jungle Wins 141
    Chapter 11: It Was Murder... 153

Part IV: Lethal Harvest
    Chapter 12: Courage and Compassion.................................. 201
    Chapter 13: A Slow Agony 209
    Chapter 14: No Rest, No Peace 221

Part V: Paying Tribute
    Chapter 15: Hooked, Dismembered 235
    Chapter 16: Telling the Story.. 247
    Chapter 17: Revelations... 261

Acknowledgments 273

Notes 279

PRELUDE

It was late fall. The summer crowds were gone, and I had Lake Michigan's shoreline all to myself — until the world came crashing into it. While driving down a country road one Sunday morning, I had the car radio on without really listening to it. I was thinking, instead, about the freshly baked cinnamon rolls I was planning to buy. But when I overheard the word "Guyana" during a newscast, I snapped to attention: my sister was living in that country at the time. After moving there with her church, she was working in some kind of hippie, agricultural commune there. Or so I thought.

AUTHOR'S NOTE

"The past is never dead; it's not even past." William Faulkner

For me to tell this story, I needed a safe distance from it, in fact, decades. It is terrible, sad, and true. But it is also about a kind and generous young woman who had a great sense of humor, my sister Mary Wotherspoon. Her death occurred in an infamous world event, and as such, it has been misunderstood or even dismissed by too many.

Throughout most of our childhood, she and I endured a private misery and hidden emptiness. Since she can no longer speak for herself, I hope to illuminate the family that shaped us, and her passage from our early years to her catastrophic death. In the beginning, I wrote solely about my own childhood, which she shared, albeit as my younger sister. I cannot speak for all of her experiences back then, but I trust that mine will shine a light on hers as well.

I begin.

PART I

UPROOTED

CHAPTER 1

THE NEW LAND

NIGHT FELL EARLY THERE IN ONE OF THE WILDEST PLACES ON EARTH. Large boa constrictors rested on tree limbs, and jaguars silently wove through the night hunting their prey. In this primordial Guyanese jungle unscarred by humans, save for machete-carved footpaths, my sister died, the light fading from her life forever. In the following dark, only the occasional snarl of jungle cats, or the mutterings of cuckoos and parrots, penetrated the dank night air before silence gave way to the dawn. Then, a choir of bird songs descended from the jungle canopy. Sunshine warmed the earth below, and a soft mist floated above hundreds of bodies — piles and rows of them — as if to blanket them in slumber.

My sister Mary had not died there alone. Among the bodies lay her beloved daughter, Mary Margaret, who had just celebrated her eighth birthday, and Mary's husband, Peter. All dead. Believing they would be rising together as a soul-cloud entering their next incarnation, some who died had consoled each other with, "See you in the next life." They had been infected by fear, lies, and the promise of a better life by a madman, who then fed them cyanide — his final dose of poison. Now their cruel deathbed, hacked from this remote paradise, has come to symbolize a festering wound for humanity, one whose power continues to this day: Jonestown.

Other people's tragedies are interesting, in part because they did not happen to you, but if you become one of those "other people," it is a different story. Tragedy marks you for life. You become a target. In your small-town grocery store, a stranger leaves her cart to inform you of the latest gruesome detail as if she knows you, as if you did not already know it. A new acquaintance's mother invites you in for some of her homemade pie, only to press you for details. Forty years on during a chance encounter, someone from elementary school days skips "hello" and goes straight to "why." Why did it happen? Your real friends just want to know that you are OK. You are not. You can still get stabbed by random references when someone utters, "drinking the Kool-Aid." Tragedies don't end.

Often, it's only in hindsight that you can clearly see tragedies forming. Jonestown "began" for my family long before cyanide or socialist utopias entered the picture; it began after an earlier tragedy left my father dying at home, tied to his bed while cancer ate his brain. Offering no medical help or support, his doctors had refused to medicate his pain, fearing he might become an addict during the three years they predicted he had left. They were wrong on all counts: he had only three months.

OUR FATHER WAS a Dutch immigrant, sailing to the United States aboard the first ship transporting troops back home from World War I. Soldiers had crowded their requisitioned luxury steamship, the Rotterdam, which carried 3,575 passengers, where our dad, age 11, mingled with the officers and nurses in its first-class lounge. His oldest sister, Margaret, an accomplished pianist, entertained them on the ship's piano during their two-week voyage.

When the Rotterdam, filled with these returning troops, entered New York harbor on April 11, 1919, a ceremonial Water Salute from fire boats welcomed it by spraying tremendous arcs of water. Clouds of confetti descended, and an armada of smaller boats tooted with patriotic fervor as the Statue of Liberty reigned over the jubilant welcome. At the dock, paper streamers, candy, and flowers were tossed up at the passengers, and Margaret was so excited that she accidentally left all her sheet music behind on the ship. Due to their first-class status, the family was spared an Ellis Island examination. Instead, they were examined on board by a doctor, and then immediately freed to disembark. America was a wonderful place.

Our grandfather, a wealthy man, held patents for some of the first commercially produced baby food, Kindermeel, and the first self-rising flour, Bakmeel, in the Netherlands. He also owned a thriving business buying bulk spices and food from the East India Company for resale in his grocery store. As such, the family had eaten well during the recent war, but in their small town near the North Sea, others had not. Food rationing and coupons had complicated everything. The Netherlands stayed neutral during the war while hosting thousands of refugees from war-torn Belgium and France. My father's town of Dokkum in the Netherlands province of Friesland had its share living inside the local schools.

With an eye to the future, our grandfather became restless. At age 53, he longed to expand his business opportunities, as well as spare his five sons and four daughters from any future wars. Against all their wishes, he had taken his 42-year-old wife, their nine children, and eldest daughter Margaret's fiancé, to this new country, America. After transferring his money to Wall Street, he wired it to their destination in Hull, Iowa. Thus began his grand venture's slide from high hopes to a hard landing.

While traveling west by train to join other Dutch settlers in Iowa, the family spent one night in Chicago, where some of their well-meaning fellow travelers coaxed the family into seeing a vaudeville show. The performance shocked my grandparents' Calvinist, old-world sensibilities, but their children loved it. Later, the cloudy, rainy weather that greeted them in Iowa felt more familiar. Yet its muddy, unpaved streets were a far cry from the clean-swept brick streets they were used to back home.

Meeting them at the train, Grandpa's brother loaded the family into a horse-drawn wagon, and then scattered them among welcoming families until proper housing could be found. After only a few weeks in this strange new country, Margaret's unhappy fiancé returned to the Netherlands. For Margaret, it was a hard landing indeed.

Back in their home province of Friesland, it was the farmers — not businessmen — who occupied the highest rung on the social ladder. In addition, vast tracts of land were hard to come by, as land was handed down through families and rarely sold. As a result, our ambitious grandfather looked to America, where land was both plentiful and relatively cheap. He could own land here and become a wealthy, respected farmer. To that end, the family moved to Rock Valley, a small town near the South Dakota border, and lived in a small wood house there. It was a novelty. Trees were plentiful in Rock Valley, unlike Friesland, where bricks made from its abundant clay were used for all buildings, including their barns.

Pursuing his American dream, Grandpa hired out to work on a farm so as to get the hang of it, but the coarse, dirty experience quickly banished his farming ambitions forever. This elegant businessman who once paraded in carriages through Parisian parks, smoking fine cigars, and sporting an ornate cane, suffered a crash landing. Along with Margaret, he would now have to find another way.

He abruptly moved the family to Orange City, named after the Dutch Prince, William of Orange. In the Dutch enclave here, he bought a former jailhouse and converted it into a grocery store. Then he bought a bigger store, which soon became a gathering place for other immigrants, smoking their pipes and sitting around its coal-burning stove. According to Margaret, they talked about business, the "Indians," and the "old country." But commerce here was a bit different, with poor farmers sometimes paying for their groceries with eggs.

By now, the family was once again living with their Delft blue porcelain, fine oriental rugs, Chinese ceramics, and prized antique Frisian clock — all shipped to Iowa despite the expense. Even so, our grandmother no longer had a seamstress or a maid to help with her large brood of nine children. Nor did she have the time to sit around and chat about the old country like the men. There was no daily bread from the neighborhood baker here, and without preservatives, it had to be made every day using dried corn cobs to fuel the oven. Cooking for her large family was an endless chore. Clothes no longer came from their dressmakers, but from the Sears mail-order catalog, and were delivered by train. Grandma never learned to speak English despite the private tutor our grandfather had hired to teach the family before emigration. It was said that she never stopped crying after leaving her homeland — she wept Dutch, not American, tears.

Her many children were a different story, however. Discovering popcorn, fruit pies, and ice cream cones was pleasure enough to keep the glow of their new country alive. The boys continued with the same mischief they had enjoyed back in the "old country," as it came to be known. Now they jumped naked into rivers instead of canals; their after-school fights occurred between town and country boys, not Catholics and Protestants, as before.

But it was different for the girls. Replacing grandma's former servants, they were now commissioned to work in the kitchen and do housework, all except for Margaret. She had paid attention to their English tutor and was now proficient in English. Before immigration, she had traveled to France and Belgium with Grandpa on business, and she continued to be his assistant now in their new country. As his right hand, she translated English to Frisian (a separate language) and Dutch for him.

Margaret was regarded as a beauty. But when another young man, also a recent immigrant, wrote to her father for permission to court her there in Orange City, Grandpa warned her not to get serious. He said the family would be returning to Friesland. If so, his children would be traveling with the Anglicized first names they received at school. Among others, the tongue-twisting Tjeerd became Ted, Jelte softened to Jack, Trijntje transformed to Catherine, and Grietje became Margaret. The children were fast outpacing their parents' assimilation.

COMING FROM THE northernmost part of the Netherlands, Frisians were an amphibious lot by necessity. They lived at the mercy of the ferocious North Sea, whose waters sustained them with plentiful fish and international connections, but also killed them with its catastrophic floods. Its give-and-take was legendary. It made highly skilled sailors of them, and deposited fertile soil for lush grasses and happily grazing cows. But it could also destroy and kill everything and everyone, leaving behind thousands of bloated corpses. Consequently, Frisians' survival depended on their wits and hard work. They built canals that became ice-roads for horses and skaters in the winter, and waterways for boats and swimmers in the summer, all while connecting eleven separate towns. Frisians lived in partnership with the water, erecting dykes to hold back the sea, excavating drainage ditches around croplands, and leaping over those ditches between fields using long poles to vault them to the other side. It eventually became a sport known as "fierljeppen."

Now as landlocked Frisians in dry Iowa, our father's family began to splinter. The oldest son, Sid, held no illusions about country life and left for the big city of Chicago, but not for its vaudeville. He sold vacuum cleaners there to other Dutch immigrants. Two of his younger sisters soon followed him, never to return to Iowa. Like sea turtle hatchlings emerging from the sand, everyone in the family eventually followed them back to water — The Great Lakes.

Restless and rootless, our grandfather first visited his children in the Windy City, and then ventured further east to the Dutch settlement of Holland, Michigan, on the eastern shore of Lake Michigan. He may have felt right at home here while walking its shoreline dunes. They resembled the windswept dunes of Ameland, an island in the North Sea where the family owned a vacation cottage in the dunes. These large "American" dunes, beach grasses, and vast waters may have called to him, and like a seabird, he began circling for a landing.

Further east, the larger city of Grand Rapids beckoned to him as well. Smitten by its booming furniture industry and business opportunities, he wrote to our grandmother back in Iowa, telling her to sell everything, pack up, and come to Grand Rapids. She did. However, with each successive move, his wealth was rapidly decreasing.

He worked in a furniture factory for a while, but temperamentally unsuited to work for others, he opened yet another grocery store. It was doomed almost from the start. First threatened by the advent of chain stores, and then later by a bitter doctrinal battle between the local Calvinist churches, it failed, and so did Grandpa along with it. Fiercely devoted to his side of the schism, he refused to wait on customers from the "wrong" side of it, shooing them out with his broom. After closing this, his last store, he went to work briefly as a janitor at the local YWCA in a spectacular fall from his Dutch riches to American rags.

PROPELLED BY AMBITION and safety concerns, Grandpa had joined a steady migration of Europeans to the "Promised Land" in America.

But once there, he became a small fish in an exceptionally large pond; his wealth drained, his offspring grown, his hopes dashed. However, in the summer of 1939, our Frisian grandparents made a visit to the Netherlands, reconnecting with their beloved hometown of Dokkum.

Just twenty years earlier, the whole town had seen the family off at the train station when they emigrated, and now our grandparents were welcomed back again. But unfortunately, they had to leave early due to rumblings of yet another war, just as our grandfather had feared back in 1919. And this time the Netherlands would not be spared. Only weeks after they left their native land, Hitler invaded Poland and then bombed Rotterdam. The "old country" suffered a brutal German occupation that lasted for five years. Daughter Catherine, a U.S. Army nurse, would follow American troops across Europe, from D-Day to concentration camps, now as an American.

Safely back in their adopted country, the family continued the European tradition of Sunday gatherings at the grandparents' house. Now with many grandchildren, the large family grew even larger. When they gathered, the men would stand around talking while haloed by wreaths of cigar and cigarette smoke. The women drank coffee around the kitchen table, while grandchildren tried to stay out of the way. Yet no matter where we went, we grandchildren could overhear the adults' loud voices as these stubborn Frisians seemed to argue even when they agreed.

Despite his financial demise, our grandfather would still dress like the dandy he had once been. One of his neighbors reported that on Sunday mornings, people would come to their windows just to see him out on the walk. Reliving a bygone era, he would be wearing spats and brandishing a fancy cane, apparently revisiting the "peacock" days of his youth, the days before wars, before emigration, and before all enterprise and wealth had escaped him. In the end, our Frisian grandparents were supported in their last house by their children, who, of course, argued over that as well.

Unlike our Frisian grandfather, we never got to know our humble grandmother. She never talked to us. Instead, she just smiled while handing out candy as we left her house. She never learned to speak English, and she died quietly, too, forever silenced by a stroke.

On the other hand, our larger-than-life grandfather was a widower for the next 20 years, complaining that almost no one spoke his native language. Frisians were a minority among his fellow Dutch immigrants in this new country. Nonetheless, he still had company, his daughter, Catherine, the former Army nurse who reportedly drove an ambulance in London during the Blitz. If so, she certainly had the right mindset for that job — you did not want to cross her. After working for decades as a head nurse in a large Chicago hospital, she was forced to leave for a new position with only one patient to order around; she cared for our grandfather during his last years.

Now isolated, lonely, and blinded by cataracts, Grandpa would sit at the window next to a large radio, which he listened to all day, every day. As a boy, he had been fascinated by the story of President Lincoln's assassination, and he remained fascinated by American history even now as it was being made. He fed his hungry brain with current events until he quietly died in bed at the age of 102.

OUR MOTHER'S FAMILY emigration story was far different. There were no bands playing for her Dutch parents when their ship docked in Hoboken, New Jersey, in 1900. This grandmother had a baby on her lap with another one on the way, and she had been seasick during their rough voyage from the Netherlands. They had not sailed in first class, nor were they seeking riches in America's "Promised Land." Instead, this grandfather, Jake, would be joining his brothers — a butcher, and a baker — in Michigan. He had been a baker himself in Utrecht, but due to an abundance of bakers in his Oud Kamp neighborhood there, he decided his bread might be more appreciated in Michigan, and it was.

Grandfather Jake was perhaps descended from Norwegians who had fled mass starvation in Norway by crossing the North Sea to settle in Rotterdam. He was a brilliant but humble man. His parents worked in that port city as cheese mongers, and he delivered their cheese by taking the train to market in Amsterdam. It was there that he met his future wife — and our grandmother — Hendrieke, admired for her fair skin and dark eyes.

She was a real beauty, but she was also educated, which was

uncommon for women at the time. Back then, wealthy families educated their children at home using private tutors and governesses, and Rieke, as she was called, worked for one such family. As a governess, she taught her young wards French along with several other subjects. Our grandfather, Jake, was also a scholar at heart, although his parents could not afford to send him to college. Despite their differences in social class, he and Rieke fell in love, but being too shy to propose in person, Jake proposed in a letter instead. Rieke's parents opposed the union, believing that their daughter would be marrying beneath her. Nevertheless, she accepted Jake's proposal. The newlyweds were the same age, 26, and no doubt hoped to escape the entrenched class snobberies of the Netherlands when they emigrated to America at the turn of the new century.

Once in Michigan, Jake worked with his brother Bill at his wholesale bakery, rising at 3:00 a.m., and returning home later to sleep. But there was little sleep to be had. The din and uproar of the growing brood inside his family's little house kept him awake. By then, they had lost two children, including one who died in 1906 after being prematurely induced by an incompetent doctor over our grandmother's objections. No neonatal care was available. Our grandmother returned from the hospital heartbroken, but her pain only worsened when her 13-month-old toddler, Gerard, died too. It was said that Gerard sang "like a bird" before he could even talk, but he had contracted diarrhea, known as "summer complaint." Both children were buried in a potter's field.

AFTER HIS WIFE died, and four of his five children were living in America, Grandfather Jake's own father pined for his absent family. But Great Britain and Germany were at war, and great peril threatened even the ships flying under non-combatant flags, including those of the U.S. and the Netherlands. Between 1914 and 1918, almost fifty large passenger ships were hunted down and destroyed by the German navy. Prospective passengers were duly warned by Germany of the danger. Despite the risk, in 1915 our great grandfather made the voyage to the United States by himself at age 77. But once safely there, he found America too foreign, and he soon recrossed the Atlantic again.

However, with the war now rumbling much closer to his native land, he braved the dangerous ocean voyage one last time. Three voyages during a war at sea was enough, and this time he stayed put. He died in America two years later, his grave in a cemetery not far from the crowded little house where his son Jake was trying to get some sleep.

WARNED BY THE family doctor to stop working through the night, our exhausted grandfather was forced to give up baking to find a healthier occupation. Accordingly, on October 22, 1918, Jake signed the mortgage for a large farm. At the stroke of his pen, his oldest sons, aged 15, 17, and 20, now became farm hands. His daughters Mary and Helen were just five and three years old, respectively, but everyone now had to pitch in to make it work.

Their new farm was located at the corner of two country roads, and they named it Hillcrest Dairy. Its brick two-story farmhouse was perched upon a gentle hill surrounded by stately horse chestnut trees. They owned 23 milk cows, two teams of workhorses, chickens, and pigs, plus corn and oat crops. The family had to milk, plant, harvest, cook, and can, as well as breed their stock.

Sisters and best friends Mary and Helen were born exactly two years apart. During harvest, their job included standing in the dirt road looking out for the threshers. By putting their ears to the ground, they could hear the distant rumble of the machines, and then run back to the house to tell their mother who was busy cooking for the crew. The girls' "playground" stretched across railroad tracks to the back pasture, then to a pond with a rope swing, and back again to a wondrous barn and several outbuildings. Mary once broke her arm slipping in the ice house. Later, she contracted lockjaw from stepping on a rusty nail, because, as it was said, she could not keep her shoes on. As the youngest children and only girls, these two little scamps free-ranged much like their chickens.

To keep the barn cat population in check, their father would drown newborn kittens, as was the custom. Then Mary and Helen would find the lifeless little creatures on the manure pile. They would try to warm them in their hands, then dress them in little rags, and wheel them about in a doll carriage. When they discovered that their father actually loved cats and would not kill a kitten with its eyes open, they took to hiding kittens in the barn until their eyes opened.

During the school year, these two hooligans alternately walked and ran down their country lane to their Christian elementary school two miles away. When passing a cemetery, Mary liked to scare Helen by mentioning ghosts, and they would quickly run past, their braids and lunch pails flying. They were country girls with almost no parental supervision, and they did as they pleased. They drove an old Model T car around the farmyard and out on their road. Its reverse gear no longer worked, so with Mary, age 12, at the wheel, they navigated with care. When Mary milked cows, she would squirt the warm milk at city cousins who complained about barn odors, holding their noses. Meanwhile, the girls' older brothers were known for being "wild," and local mothers warned their daughters to steer clear of them. Apparently, our grandparents could run a farm or supervise their children, but not both at the same time. Plus, Grandpa Jake was known for having a soft touch. But Grandma Rieke was a different story.

Two more babies would be born and die on the farm, one buried there in a shoe box. There were eleven children but five died sometime after birth. When Helen once remarked that their mother was "always pregnant," she spoke the truth. With no effective birth control, high infant mortality rates, and the need for many hands to support families, 15 to 17 children were not uncommon back then, yet many also died. But all those losses took a toll, including for our grandmother.

Upon hearing a baby cry in church, Grandma Rieke would walk out to escape the painful memories of her dying babies. Over time, she built a protective wall around herself by withdrawing from her surviving children, too. As a little girl, our own mother never forgot being dumped off her mother's lap after she tried to sit on it: she grew up without her grief-stricken mother's care and affection. Yet as busy as he was farming and doing family chores, her affectionate father filled in. He taught young Mary how to bake as she stood right beside him.

When the older boys went off to college, they were so cash-strapped as students that they hauled their dirty clothes home on weekends, unable to afford the laundry fees at school. The family was hard-pressed, and it was Mary who would suffer the consequences. Although an excellent student, she was pulled out of school to work in the barn, haul silage for the cows, and milk eight of them by herself. She used to milk before school in the morning, but now there was no more school for her.

She enjoyed working with her father, whom she adored, but she dearly missed school. When her teacher came out to the farm to beg her father to send her back, arguing that Mary was her brightest student, he refused. Back then, educating a girl was considered a waste of money, and their Christian school cost money, as did the boys' college. With three of her brothers in college, Mary was needed in the barn. She was only thirteen and never returned to school. She worked for one year in the barn and then left home to work for a wealthy family with eight children. At age fourteen she was still a child herself, but one now doing childcare and housework. On Thursdays, her day off, her father would pick her up and bring her back to the farm, where a hired hand had taken her place in the barn.

It may have been during one of those home visits when their father caught teenagers Mary and Helen "riding around" with older boys in a car. He roundly ordered the girls out of the car, mortifying the rambunctious sisters. Even so, the girls were undeterred.

CHAPTER 2

LOVE AND DEATH

THOUGH LIVING APART, THE SISTERS STILL STUCK TOGETHER, AS DATING IN THOSE DAYS WAS FRAUGHT WITH DIFFICULTY, ESPECIALLY OUT IN THE COUNTRY. It was easier in the city where girls would stroll the sidewalks, and boys would slowly cruise by in their cars. With luck, they would wind up riding together, and Sunday evenings after church were popular times for these roving romances. And that is when Helen found Mary's husband for her. He was a Frisian immigrant and his Anglicized name was Jack.

Although it was considered risqué at the time, feisty Helen smoked cigarettes, and at age 18, she radiated a mischievous charm. On the other hand, her equally independent sister was more reserved. After church one Sunday evening as Helen was going to visit Mary at her domestic post, she was approached by an older man on the sidewalk. Using a ploy straight out of the movies, and movie-star handsome himself, he asked Helen for a light. Helen obliged him and as they walked along together, she told him that she was going to visit her "pretty sister." He asked if he could accompany her.

By now, 20-year-old Mary had been working for the same doctor's family for six years. When she answered the door there that evening, there stood Helen with this stranger. At the time, it was joked that our mother had so many boyfriends she had to shove one out the back door when another one came to the front. But upon seeing the man who would become our dad, her parade of boyfriends came to a halt.

Social propriety still discouraged marrying beneath yourself, even if family standards were often maintained by deceit or carefully guarded secrets. Now, just as our Grandmother Rieke's parents had disapproved of her marrying beneath herself, Jake, the man she had defiantly married — and who was now a father himself — was standing up for his "pretty" daughter. But Jake was up against a stubborn Frisian, Jack's father. Our parents, Jack and Mary, were expecting their first child before making it to the altar. In this conflict between class snobberies and their love, love won out: love for one another, and love for their unborn child.

Social snobbery combined with the lack of birth control made private dramas like theirs a common occurrence. While our two grandfathers originated from the same country, they came from culturally diverse regions with separate languages, and now they stood toe to toe. One was a scholarly farmer radiating kindness and grace, the other a stern patriarch bristling with pride and privilege. Mary's father would not stand for his daughter's worth to be challenged, while Jack's father was trying to save his son from a "mistake," as well as protect his family's social status.

Without sex education — when even the word "sex" had to be spelled out, if mentioned at all — unplanned pregnancies were common. As it was, one of Jack's own sisters had been forced by her upper-crust family to relinquish a baby born "out of wedlock." It is said that she would stand pitifully at the window of her baby's adopted home just to see the little girl that she lost. Our mother would be spared that cruelty.

It was 1935, the middle of the Great Depression, when large formal weddings were rare. Hence, couples often married at home. Brides wore their best dresses, and men suits, if they had them. Honeymoons were an extravagance when even paid work was hard to come by. Our parents married quietly without formality or fuss. Our mother was 21, and our dad, a seasoned playboy, was settling down at 27.

THE NEWLYWEDS WERE welcomed at the farm, living there in a small house-trailer where their first child, a son, was born. The little boy played in a meadow that served as their front yard. His father Jack had spent two years in college before marrying, but in the country's current financial crisis, he drove a milk truck. When he later moved on to sales, the little family moved to an apartment in town. As the country climbed out of its economic woes, he turned into a consummate salesman, selling windows and siding in the construction business, which he eventually joined. The young family's fortunes expanded rapidly as, apparently, Jack had inherited his father's head for business.

Spared serving in World War II because he had three children, Jack built a large house for his growing family in 1945. Wisely anticipating a pent-up housing demand from returning GIs, he built tracts of small houses that qualified for their G.I. Bill home loans. And he could not build them fast enough. Hiring Dutch immigrants like himself, his crews were raising roofs around the county, their native language mixing with the pounding of hammers.

Eventually, there would be six children in our family, with the last three "boomers" arriving after the war. My little sister, Mary, and I arrived in that batch. Our father had been content with four children, but our mother won out with two more. I was fortunate to be number four, but as numbers five and six, Mary and Steve would miss out on too much to feel lucky. Back then, fathers in our Dutch culture did not cuddle their children until they were out of diapers. Owing to that, last-born Stephan missed out on his dad. Mary may have been held by our dad, but did she remember him?

He was gone a lot. His financial success freed him to explore more of his new homeland, from California to Florida, and north into Canada. A natural-born hunter who thrived in the wild, he hired indigenous guides in Canada and slept in tents, sometimes with his two oldest sons and a lucky nephew. He also rode a Canadian freight train, signaling the engineer when to stop, and then jumped off to fish for days at a time by himself. Soot-belching car ferries then transported him across the Straits of Mackinac back home again. His hunting trophies included a bearskin rug and a deer draped over the car hood, its tongue dripping blood. He also arrived bearing gifts. We were given dolls, deerskin gloves, and slippers, while our mother added to her collection of duty-free china from England.

Our dad never really stopped fishing — he did it year-round. While he angled for lake perch, I would bob around in our rowboat with him at our Lake Michigan cottage. Then I watched fish scales fly as he cleaned his catch, with the occasional fish head still flopping after it hit the ground. Those scared me, but not as much as a marlin's huge eye staring at me as it hung from a hook on a Florida pier. Mary was still a toddler in those days, safe with our mother instead of witnessing dead-fish horrors.

Our family spent winters in Florida because concrete for housing construction could not be poured in the frozen north. Florida also offered year-round fishing. I was happy to play in the wet sand digging up coquina shells, keeping watch while my dad fished in the surf. Apparently, the only time he stood still was when he held a fishing pole, although when a seagull once pooped on his head, he just dove into the water to wash it off. I thought he was invincible. And people said he was a natural athlete, good at golf, volleyball, and softball. At the YMCA, he made friends in the steam room, no doubt making business deals as well.

He had a large personality and seemed to fill the house when he was at home. Leading family singalongs while our mother played the piano, he made anyone refusing to sing then sing a solo. Or he lay on the floor while we little kids would crawl all over him getting tickled, or wrapped inside his strong arms. I adored him. While sitting on the children's step stool in the bathroom, I would gaze up at him in the morning, a giant wiping soap suds on his face and then scraping them off again.

When I was five, I was his sidekick, riding on his shoulders while swimming in the "Big Lake." Shoreline summers there were sublime: picking blueberries, riding horses on the beach, and living barefoot every day. My hair whipped at my face as we soared over the lake in our mahogany Chris-Craft speedboat, my dad at its red steering wheel. I would spin around next to him on a bar stool while he had a beer at the marina. In his long, green Buick, I stood on the seat next to him, my hand on his shoulder as we zoomed over low dunes, winding through shoreline forests with deer occasionally leaping across the road. From our cottage atop a high dune, we could watch clouds bedazzled with color as the sun set "into" the lake. By the time the stars came out to play, we little kids were already sleeping.

Life was far slower and more tangible before all things digital.

Children wore sweaters hand-knitted by mothers and grandmothers. Food was not fast, and the word "virtual" was just an adjective. Clothes were made from cotton or wool, while polyester might have been mistaken for a girl's name. Plastic was in its infancy. Our cars lumbered along two-lane highways like wheeled tanks, and before seat belts and child seats, kids knocked out their front teeth on metal dashboards. I once watched my older sister, Marcia, roll out onto the pavement when our heavy car door flew open rounding a corner. Life was much slower then, but also more perilous.

At our big house, I would sit on my dad's lap in his office, fascinated as he rolled out blueprints for his business. Large photogravures of Presidents Theodore Roosevelt and Lincoln hung on the wall, with President Lincoln peering mournfully down at us. My dad and I would also sit together in front of our new television set — a wondrous thing in the early 1950s — waiting for the test pattern to give way for the programs. Yet those times were rare; he was busy, and not one to sit around much.

Due to a devastating post-WWII famine back in the Netherlands, thousands of Dutch were immigrating to the U.S. Many came to the established Dutch communities in Michigan, often with little more than what they could carry. My dad secretly bought groceries for some of these new arrivals, directing our older brothers to leave the bags on their doorsteps, ring the bell, and dash back to the car. Compared to these newcomers, we were "real Americans," although we lived among Dutch-speaking relatives and other immigrants, like our dad.

In those days of the late 1940s, three of our fathers' Frisian siblings were also our neighbors. Margaret lived right next door, and a few doors down, their oldest brother, Sid, lived with his family. These two brothers were not only best friends, they also hunted together, and supported each other in business. In fact, just before I was born, Uncle Sid borrowed and repaid the $300 saved to pay for my birth: they trusted each other. They also built their summer cottages close together, and it was that uncle who would be the first to arrive at our house when troubles came.

During a weekend at our cottage in October, my father coughed so loud one night that it woke me up. I had just turned six that week, and I was terrified hearing such roaring from him. I started to cry. My older brother, Herm, woke up too. He was sleeping in the bunk above me, and leaning down from there, he comforted me by saying, "It's OK." But it wasn't. Our dad had lung cancer. A few weeks later, I was standing outside on a hospital lawn; children were not allowed inside hospitals back then. I was holding my mother's hand, and from there I looked up to see my dad, a small figure waving down at me from a window high above.

I had been listening to my mother telling people that the surgeon had "opened and closed him right up again because there was too much cancer to treat him." I did not know or understand how people could be "opened and closed." My sister Mary had just turned four and must have sensed trouble, too, but we were both too young to understand it. I just knew something was terribly wrong.

Then our dad came home. At first, he sat in his favorite chair by the large front window in the living room. Visitors would come and go, while I wondered why he wore his bathrobe all the time, and worse, did not go to work. One day when he complained about the smell of bacon frying in the kitchen, I told him if he did not like it, we would just have to get a new dad. I was surprised to see tears filling his eyes: I did not know dads could cry. I was ashamed, but I was also mad at him for not getting dressed, going to work, then coming home and playing with me, like he was supposed to.

Instead, he was moved to an upstairs bedroom where I visited him every day when I got home from first grade. I showed him my new doll still in its box, wanting him to like it with me, and was happy when he said he did. But on another day when I went up to visit him, he was in trouble. I found him with his hands tied to the bed. One arm stretched behind him, the other reached almost to the floor, with only the ropes holding him as he hung over the floor. He looked surprised to see me, staring at me as if I were a stranger. As if he did not know me. And that scared me more than flopping fish heads, or dead deer, or anything I had ever seen before. He terrified me.

He had become dangerous to himself, and to us. Untreated, the cancer that filled his lungs had begun to eat his brain, and with no medication to ease his pain, he suffered terribly. Meanwhile, our mother was caring for her, him, and the rest of us by herself. Our oldest brother was already married, while the youngest, baby Steve, was still in diapers. Mary was four. Our mother needed sleep to manage her overwhelming load, so it fell to Herm, the next oldest child, to take the night shift to watch over our dad. At age 15, Herm got almost no sleep, instead doing his best to comfort and care for "Pa." With no hospice care available to ease our father's suffering, death began to fill our house and all our lives.

And so it was that I watched our father leave our house forever on an overcast winter's day, his maroon bathrobe flapping in the wind, his leather slippers dragging through the snow as he leaned heavily on two of his brothers. His arms hung over their shoulders as they guided him to a waiting car. I was worried because he was not supposed to wear his bathrobe in the snow, and worse, that he was unable to walk by himself.

He died just two weeks later at a psychiatric hospital, locked inside a secure room, driven mad by unmitigated pain. He had attacked our mother who had to shout for help when she visited him one last time.

On the day he died, Mary and I were playing together on the floor of our living room. It was midafternoon after school when our mother came in and told us to, "Get on your knees and thank God your father has died." Without understanding, we did so while the scratchy sofa upholstery we leaned on rubbed against our arms and folded hands. Then people started coming into our house. I saw our Uncle Sid from down the street comforting and hugging our mother. I was confused — only my dad did that. And why were they all crying? Grownups were not supposed to do that, either.

On that gray January afternoon in 1954, our lives were turned upside down. Our father had left us forever. He was 46.

There followed much discussion about who should attend his funeral. Mary and Steve were considered too young, but was I? I had been my father's favorite child at the time, so it was decided I should attend both the visitation and the funeral. It was a mistake. At the funeral home, I was forced to look at my father lying in a silver box lined with pink satin and carnations. My oldest brother held me up over his body even though I struggled to break away. After that, the pungent scent of carnations would forever smell like death to me. Yet at the time, I was embarrassed to see my first-grade teacher, Miss Ryskamp, in the crowded room there. Like my dad, she was in the wrong place, too. She belonged at school where teachers lived.

Life was all mixed up. Mary and Steve were definitely too young to witness this horror, but as it turned out, so was I.

The world was covered with snow on the day of the funeral. It was cold, but I refused to wear my scratchy wool leggings, and I created a ruckus as I was strong-armed into them. I kicked, I screamed, and this time, I won. At the church, I sat between my mother and my sister Marcia, who, at age 13 was crying aloud in church. To make matters worse, we were sitting in the very front row and everyone could hear her. Ours was a stern Calvinist denomination, where people neither laughed nor cried during its austere services. Even the occasional cough would be hushed with embarrassment, so I asked my mother to please make her stop crying. They both ignored me.

To make matters worse, it was not even Sunday, yet our church was full; the mayor was there, and our neighbors, too. What was going on? They were in the wrong church — they had their own churches and this one was ours. Later, I sat on a foldout bench in a long black car near Herm and Marcia who were sitting with our mother in the very back. At the cemetery, we all stood together beneath some bare trees by a large hole in the ground. I wanted to get back to the warm car, and was glad when we got home again. But now our house was full of strangers, too.

I wandered there among a forest of legs, with men jangling change in their pockets, and women's purses staring at me from at eye level. There was no room for me anywhere. A neighbor who was cutting pieces from a flat cake in another room let me stand by her as she worked. She wore a hearing aid on top of her head, and she bent to talk with me as she was slicing up the biggest cake I had ever seen. When I went to bed later that night, I could hear Marcia sobbing herself to sleep in her bedroom.

After that, the house felt empty. It was deathly quiet. Every day I stood at the front window watching the road, waiting for my dad to come home. Maybe he was hunting, or fishing, or playing golf. He was always going somewhere. While Mary played with Steve on the floor near me, I kept a lookout, hoping to see his car drive up our long driveway. During those bleak days, our father's elderly parents would walk two miles from their house to care for us when my mother was busy. As immigrants from the old country, they did not drive, and without speaking English, our grandmother could only pat our heads and smile.

But one afternoon, she held me back as our mother was trying to leave the house. I had grabbed at my mom's red purse, hanging on to it like a lifeline, preventing her from leaving. I screamed and kicked, but this time I lost. I watched her drive away through tears streaming down my face. What if she did not come back either?

For the rest of that winter, my father's favorite chair by the window sat empty, waiting for him to return, like me.

OUR FAMILY FALTERED as our 39-year-old mother sorted through the shards of the catastrophe. There would be no more winters in Florida for us. And the cascade of our losses continued: Our oldest brother had dropped out of college and married young. Then, our mother escaped the painful memories of our father's death that she associated with the beautiful house he had built for us. She sold it soon after he died, and then she sold our cottage on Lake Michigan, too. By that time, she knew how to get a house built herself, so she had a new one built on the hill directly behind our house. We owned a number of lots in our developing suburb of open fields, scattered farmhouses, and gravel roads.

So, from our backyard that spring, we could watch this new house rise up from the ground. In early June, it was finished, only five months after our dad's death. Now in our mother's flight from grief, she uprooted us, and we moved into it immediately, hostages to her pain. At first I thought we just had two houses now: the one our dad built and the one our mother did. But a few weeks after our move up the hill to this new house, I was outraged to see another family move into what I believed was still my dad's house down there — our house.

It was a warm day when this crime occurred. I was in our new back yard, gazing down at the white picket fence that separated our two houses. Unaware that our dad's house had been sold, I was shocked to see a group of trespassing strangers walk right into it as if they owned it. Which they did. Seven intruders: five children and their two terrible parents. As I sat up on the hill, I stared at them and their car in the driveway. That was our driveway! Everyone knew it was waiting for my dad to return, and we would live there again, wouldn't we?

I was crushed, but no one else seemed to care about losing our dad's house. A short while later when Marcia received a pink plastic radio for her birthday, I smashed it on our new driveway. As it broke into pieces, everyone, including me, was shocked. I felt even worse when I then went unpunished for it. Instead, the cruel silence that followed shamed me. I was six years old, with no words for the feelings that were overwhelming me, and no place to put them. Yet I was ignored — lost — with no idea how anyone else felt. No one talked. So, without warning, postmortem storms began destroying our family tree, dropping leaves, branches, and wreckage everywhere.

Our brother Herm, haunted by caring for our dying father by himself all those nights, turned 16 a few months after his death. Herm then seemed to self-destruct, flunking out of his Christian high school, and then getting expelled from a public one for riding a motorcycle through its halls. A few months after that, he ran away with some of his friends, selling their spare car tire for gas, getting as far as Arizona before running out of money. Thus chastened, Herm returned home to work in a gas station. We brought him a hot meal there every evening, and it was my job to hold his plate on my lap, then hand it to him through our car window. I was proud of that.

He was my favorite brother, but when he enlisted in the Navy on his 17th birthday, I had no idea how much I would miss him. Life used to be much better when our two older brothers and their buddies would spend afternoons bent under car hoods, tinkering with engines in our driveway. I would hang around them savoring the smell of gas and the clank of metal tools hitting the driveway. Now they were all gone, too.

Our mother had been a quiet, reassuring presence in our lives, but she changed after our father died. At first, her scornful glares silenced me if I said anything about "daddy." At other times, she would invoke his memory to discipline me by scolding, "Your father would not like that!" Nevertheless, we were not to talk about him, or tell stories to try and keep him alive if only in memory. As a result, I was happy when I overheard the older kids occasionally say the word, "Pa." I used to hear it every day when he was alive. Now it was a secret pleasure.

One evening, when our oldest brother stopped by our new house, my mother asked him to help her. I was in trouble again. I was being punished for refusing to eat my spinach, and was sitting on the basement stairs by myself. He used to be a fun brother, but now he had to be the man in the family, the only one left, and I overheard her warn him, "Careful — she was the apple of his eye." She was talking about my dad and me, but where was he now? He was gone and I wanted him back. I was mad at the whole world, and I did not want to be an "apple," either.

After our cottage was sold, we returned to the Big Lake just once, but this time, we had to use a public beach. This was new. Who were all those other people on the beach? Standing there at the water's crowded edge, I encountered a drowned body that had just rolled up on to the shore. The dead man was purple, and I ran away crying. I was afraid that my dad might have turned purple, too, while he was being dead.

We never returned to any more public beaches. As a result, we lost not only our dad, and his house, but Lake Michigan, too.

CHAPTER 3

DEAD ENDS

AS A CHILD, OUR MOTHER HAD WITNESSED HER OWN MOTHER HOBBLED BY GRIEF. As an immigrant in a strange land, with no real support, or anywhere to run, that grandmother had turned inward. But her daughter — our mother — did have the resources to run from her own grief, and run she did.

Our first Christmas without our dad passed quietly. There was no joy to be had in it. But soon after, Steve, Mary, and I climbed into our mother's new car, a Ford Fairlane convertible, heading for California. Marcia stayed behind for high school. A friend of our mother's accompanied us as we drove west for days and days. This friend and her baby sat in the front seat, where, much to my disgust, the baby pooped in his pants the whole way. After we finally got rid of them at their relatives' house in California, we went on to our mother's favorite brother, Uncle John, and he soon became a favorite of ours, too. He was kind, and he was also a lot of fun.

Laughter had always been part of our mother's family, and our Uncle John spread it wherever he went. Those who knew him regarded him as a "Dutch Will Rogers" in his day. He had a chicken ranch from which he delivered fresh eggs, house to house, with an old black hearse. A born comedian, he was regularly welcomed with his eggs into the kitchens of Hollywood chefs and beyond, in Pasadena and Beverly Hills.

We stayed with him and our Aunt Habe, who, as a Norwegian, was a rather exotic addition to our Dutch family. She also had a glass eye, which made her a little scary. But Mary and I had free rein on their chicken ranch, and it was a paradise — except for one day. I watched in horror as the ranch dog, Tippy, killed a chicken by grabbing its foot and pulling the whole bird through the chicken wire. It was shredded to death, accompanied by ear-splitting squawks. We had also seen these weird birds laying eggs, muttering their chicken-speak until the job was done. Now I lost my appetite for breakfast eggs, knowing that they had been "pooped" by chickens. But I still ate "chicken" at dinner, even when it was actually rabbit. When others around the dinner table commented on their tasty rabbit, however, I immediately stopped eating. Nor would I continue until I was assured that the meat on my plate was not rabbit but chicken.

One afternoon when all the grownups were gone, Mary and I played in our uncle and aunt's bedroom. We were not supposed to be there, so we quickly hid under their bed when they suddenly returned. From under there, we overheard our aunt complain that we were "brats," and then our uncle exonerated us by reminding her that we had been through a hard time. But when we had to crawl out from under the bed, we sort of proved our aunt's point.

Whatever the case, we "brats" were having a California adventure, bedazzled by Disneyland and Marineland of the Pacific. Then came a trip north to see our brother Herm, who was stationed at Bakersfield. A Navy jet engine mechanic, he wore a white uniform when we picked him up; he was a man now. And he was quiet, as usual, as we ate dinner at Fisherman's Wharf in San Francisco. I was the only one to order a hamburger because dead fish reminded me of my dad, and they smelled terrible.

Back home in Michigan again, we continued to move into new houses built on our "lots" in the neighborhood. And once, we even moved to California to live near our Uncle John. That year, we left Michigan just before Christmas, and as before, Marcia, a high schooler, stayed behind with relatives. But for this trip, there were no pooping babies in the front seat, just Mary, Steve, our mother, and me — and I got the front seat. From there, I served as lookout for motels with vacancy signs. I loved my job, spying motels with teepee rooms, and one with a two-story cowboy boot out front. For two long days, we could see mountains ahead, but they took a long time to get to us.

Once in California at our uncle's chicken ranch again, Mary and I were cut loose on our own. At six and eight years old, we would climb a fence trying to ride a neighbor's donkey which bared its teeth whenever it saw us coming. So, we mostly stuck with the noisy chickens. But then we moved to a small rental house in Riverside. We were waiting to move into what we were told would be our new house in Redlands. It was in a vast area of orange groves, and the house was beautiful. In fact, our Uncle John joked that he felt like burning his own house after seeing it. It seemed exotic by our midwestern standards: a white stucco, mission-style ranch with a red tile roof. It had a brown chicken coop, a green-tiled swimming pool, and twelve orange trees all our own. In spite of all that, it did not look or feel like home to me. But we were staying.

When it was time for school to start after the Christmas holidays, Mary somehow escaped it, but not me. There I was, riding a school bus for the first time, to a new school, in a new state. When the bus driver once threatened to take off his belt to beat the noisy students in the back, I sat there terrified, keeping very still. I hated everything about my new school, even though my teacher tried to welcome me by showing my artwork to the class. It was a drawing of our old house, my dad's house, to which I had added apple trees in the front yard.

I do not remember playing with anyone on the playground there, either. I was miserable. After a few torturous days, I told my teacher that I was sick. The school nurse then took me home, but when she asked which house was ours, I pointed to a different one, hoping she would let me walk the rest of the way myself. Seeing right through me, the nurse insisted on walking me to our rental house. So when my mother answered the door, there I was begging her to please not send me back. It worked.

None of us wanted to live in California — except our mother. Finally realizing this, she sold the new house back to its previous owner, but at a great expense. We left the oranges, the chickens, and our uncle, and headed back to Michigan. On the return trip, we stopped to stretch our legs by climbing a foothill next to the road. From the top of it, I could see far into the distance, but suddenly felt rootless and afraid. I feared that we no longer had a real home anywhere. Home kept changing.

Back in Michigan, the house we had left behind was now filled with family when Marcia joined us again. From that house, Mary and I could walk to our old school together as usual, and I felt much better. She and I were a "pair," close in age and doing most everything together. This particular house was located at the dead end of a street, and next to the terminal of some old railroad tracks. We lived there for only a short time, but Mary and I managed to explore every off-limit place we could find, including an abandoned brick factory, and "bums'" hideouts.

There was a pond where boys would throw cherry bombs at frogs just to see them explode. There were dragonflies which we called "sewing bugs" because we believed they could sew our lips together, and we always ran from them. Near the train tracks, the "hobos" empty campsites lent our forbidden playground a sense of danger, but the overgrown fields around them were a great place to wander.

We lived in that house of forbidden adventures for only a short time, but for one summer weekend, I was left there alone. My mother had announced at bedtime that she and the other kids would be going to Chicago the next day. While they visited one of her brothers and his family there, I was to stay behind. I protested loudly. I wanted to go, too. Nonetheless, the next morning, I awoke to the sound of car doors slamming shut. Looking out my bedroom window, I saw my family driving away up the street. They had waited to close the doors so as not to awaken me, but I heard them through the screen window anyway. My dad had left me, but now I knew that my whole family could leave me, too. And I never forgot it.

I found a note in the kitchen instructing me to call my favorite aunt and stay at her house, but I did not want to. I would have to sleep with my cousin, who was my age, but she wet her bed and it stank. Plus, I was afraid of her father. He once laughed at me after he told me he shot kittens for target practice. So instead, I called my brother, who took me to his house for the weekend. While sitting by myself in his living room, I overheard a loud argument between him and his wife. She already had three children and did not want me there. It seemed nobody wanted me. And I never forgot that, either.

But no matter where we lived, it was always close to our church, which is where I realized that my siblings and I were orphans. Every Sunday morning, we would hear our minister pray for all the "widows and orphans," and since our mother called herself a widow, I realized that we were the "orphans" part of that prayer. By now, I already knew the word "deceased," which was about my dad. Because of that, when people prayed, "Our father, who art in heaven," I thought of him stuck up there, and I started to resent heaven. Adults would reassure me by saying he was there, yet I wanted him back home again with us. I hated church, and for that matter, heaven, too. But we still had to keep going to church.

Worse yet, our mother made us arrive early for Sunday morning services to sit in the very back by ourselves, before everyone else came. From there, we could see where everyone else would then sit, who was late, and who was missing. Afterward, we had to be the first out the door, too, never getting to run around outside while the men smoked and the women talked. Instead, we were hurried to the car, and all because our mother was a sinner. But we already knew that.

It happened one evening right after supper when two church "elders," which was something like church police, came to our house. The men were wearing their Sunday clothes and they had come to punish our mother for sinning. Someone had told on her; it was our mailman's mother. She and her son, who lived at home with her, were both members of our church, and the mother had reported our mother to the church police. But I already knew something was wrong at our house because that mailman was not my dad.

The following night, one of the church police secretly returned, demanding that our mother now sin with him. She refused, but was frightened and ducked into the nearest bedroom in our small house. Mary and I were there in our bunk beds, sleepy but awake. We sensed that our mother was afraid, but we were no help. After she left our bedroom, I told Mary our mother needed to go to the hospital for crazy people. This frightened Mary, who began to cry.

The next day when Mary asked our mother if she was going to the hospital for crazy people, I was punished for what I thought was the truth, the kind of truth that adults try to hide from children. And now because of those church police, our family were outcasts — rejects refusing to leave while sitting in the back of the church. From there, every Sunday I could see our mailman and his mother righteously sitting in the center of the church, acting as if they belonged there.

If our mother's faith remained unshakeable, mine was not. Mary and I soon learned to hate church and everything that went with it. And the church made it so easy. When a new minister requested that she and I meet with him one Sunday afternoon to check on our "faith," it did not go well. We both knew by now that he was not God, and we also knew from experience that church people were mean. I went into his office first, sitting in a large chair across from his desk where he demanded in an accusatory voice, "What is your personal relationship with Jesus Christ!?"

I was only nine or ten, but I knew what "personal" meant, so I responded equally loudly with, "Personal!" Then about to cry, I ran out the door. Mary was up next, but she shot out of his office even faster, equally upset. Would we be punished? We did not care. We walked home together, hating all ministers, and all church people. But for all that, I did not dare to hate God, even though he had taken our dad away. That would have been a really big sin.

By now, I had given up on my dad returning from heaven, and I missed him terribly. Our little brother, Steve, never really knew him, and Mary, only a little, but our dad had been a huge part of my life. And now there was a giant hole in it. No more hugs or special times together, and to make matters worse, we were not allowed to even talk about him at home. If we did, our mother would shut it down.

OUR MOTHER KEPT building new houses for us every year, then sold them to move on to the next one. Located in new housing plats from our dad's business, our new houses were always at the dead ends of new streets, yet all were within walking distance of our Christian school and church. Only our addresses changed. Overhearing talk of FHA, permits, excavators, carpenters, setbacks, plasterers, electricians, concrete, and land contracts, was common for us kids.

After the "railroad tracks" house, the next two were built back in our old neighborhood near my father's house, the one with the interlopers still living there. These two new houses were located down a long sloping hill on the same block. The first of these two was the best of all the new ones, and the one our mother called "her dream house." It was brick, had four bedrooms, a finished basement, two fireplaces, a flagstone entry, and a roomy upstairs where the kids had their own bathroom. This wonderful house was surrounded by open fields of wild asparagus, and pheasants wandered through our front yard. We could watch the sunset in the west, and we loved everything about it. We even built a treehouse in a field behind it, and a photo of us perched up inside it on a rainy day wound up in the *Detroit Free Press*. It felt really and truly like our home, perhaps because it was similar to our dad's house. But it was also the last time our mother would spend time at home with us.

As such, it was the last time we could have fun together, including the sin of seeing a movie, which was forbidden by our church. All the better. Movies were considered "worldly" and therefore dangerous. We went anyway, risking the fires of hell in our convertible with the top down at a drive-in movie. We watched *Bambi*, which had nothing wicked in it — no naked ladies, or swear words of any kind — but we still had to keep this movie sin a secret. It was wonderful.

While living in our good new house, Mary wound up playing with one of the interlopers living in our father's house up the street. She played there in its knotty pine basement, where long before, the piles of our toys had been the envy of our cousins. That was then. Now Mary and her new friend would be repeatedly molested by her friend's grandfather there. Mary told me about it one night as we were about to fall asleep. When I told our mother about it the next day, she warned us not to talk about it. It was shameful. The molester turned out to have a brain disease and was soon dead, yet both Mary and I felt somehow guilty for telling on him.

WHEN OUR MOTHER's "dream house" was sold after only one year of living there, I was sad. Did we have to keep moving? We did. Money was getting tighter, and some missionaries needed it right away. After an offer on it from our church's Board of Missions was accepted, we had to vacate it in a hurry. Undaunted, my mother built another house, but this one on the lot right next door, which we also owned. It would be our last move, and there was no time to waste.

We watched the hole for the basement dug and the concrete poured. Then our carpenter, Gerrit, a trusty Frisian who spoke with a heavy accent, built a platform to cover the newly built basement. The platform would eventually become the floor of this new house, but for now, it was also our roof. We spent the whole summer living in the basement underneath it while this new house was built right over our heads.

We went to sleep each night with crickets chirping close by, and awakened in the morning to builders clomping around overhead. Our living quarters were comfortable, if dark. One corner served as a rustic kitchen and bathroom with a shower. Our beds were stationed in rows across the middle next to the laundry, and a living area of sorts nestled in another corner near a future fireplace. Along another wall, Gerrit had built large storage cabinets and closets for us. From this underground burrow we could see the world through narrow windows up at ground level, and we had everything we needed, including stairs up into the daylight, and a door to lock at night. It was summer camp without the counselors.

From our basement windows up at ground level, we could see our new neighbors' feet and car wheels on what was now their driveway. Yet we did not feel close to them. They turned out to be a strict, churchy family with too many rules, and they let us know when we were breaking them, too. They would have five children in all, one of whom caught us watching television on Sunday. In our church, this was a sin. We also played outside on Sunday: more sin. When I wore red nail polish, it was yet another strike against us. Consequently, we never told them we had seen *Bambi*, having been told too many times that movies and Hollywood were the "devil's playground." Their oldest boy, who was about Mary's age, won a big contest for memorizing the most Bible verses, while our family sometimes skipped church.

To make matters worse, their mother was writing a book about John Calvin, and their father was a chaplain in the Army. You did not want to mess with these people. They were on the road to heaven, while we, as sinners, were risking the one to damnation and hell. Yet we all walked to the same Christian school in the morning. On rainy days, they might ride right past in their car without giving us a ride. But this was no surprise. We already knew that church people were mean.

We adjusted, making the best of it until the day some of us kids were playing outside in a large mud puddle. A road excavation crew had thoughtfully left it for us on our dead-end gravel road. While standing near the oldest neighbor boy, the one with all those Bible verses stuffed inside his head, I grabbed some of the mud with both hands. Then I smeared it all over his head until it was completely covered. He ran home crying. Lucky for me, our mother was usually too easygoing, or too busy, to discipline us, and we took full advantage of it. I was never punished for my mud crime, although she did let me know that covering someone's head with mud was not very smart.

According to our church, we were the "elect," specially designated for heaven, which was a much better place than this "vale of tears," the earth. I already knew all about the tears. Anyway, if we did not sin too much, we would be spared burning up in hell, so we had to be careful to live "in the world, but not of the world." Anything "worldly" was dangerous, and because of that, some of the elect felt compelled to make sure that no one broke the rules by sinning. As a result, with missionaries now living right next door, our Sundays were under special scrutiny: no television, swimming, playing, homework, or housework. We were supposed to read nothing but the Bible, or the church magazine which had a children's page. Accordingly, we had a lot to hide from these spying neighbors, especially after we moved up above the ground again.

We did so just in time for school in the fall. Steve was in first grade, I was in fifth, and Mary in third, but Marcia was a senior in high school with all the other big kids. She and her friends were cool, so I took notes. What did they wear? What music did they listen to? Did they have boyfriends? And what were dates, anyway? Now I became a spy, too.

I wondered if her friends sinned by dancing. In 1957, the music on the radio made it impossible not to, as far as I was concerned. I loved Jerry Lee Lewis's "Great Balls of Fire," and Elvis Presley's "Jailhouse

Rock." Because of that, this particular category of sin bothered me. Accordingly, at an afterschool catechism class at our church, I asked our minister exactly why dancing was a sin. Judging from the look on his face he was shocked by my question. As the other kids in the class shifted in their seats, now paying close attention, he reluctantly said, "If a married couple danced in private with their window shades pulled down, it would be OK."

Well, this was absolutely no comfort to me while I watched teenagers dancing like crazy on *American Bandstand* on TV, so I danced along with them in our basement, but in secret.

MARY AND I were born exactly two years and one week apart, and due to frequent moving, we often had only each other to play with. After finally staying in the same house for more than just a year, we could make neighborhood friends of our own ages now. One of Mary's friends from way back before our dad died, Carol, reconnected with her after we returned to our old neighborhood. They had stayed buddies at our Christian school, but now this older Mary was a good swimmer, a strong bike rider, and a ready adventurer. She and Carol could now explore what was still our rural suburb, and Mary had a new partner for mischief.

At home, domestic mischief included running through the house chasing each other, or trying to get away. With only one parent, we had more free range than most kids, and soon, we would have far more.

After our final house move, our mother decided it was time to realize a dream deferred. She had lost out on countless opportunities by being pulled out of school to work in the barn while her brothers were in college. Now it was her turn. She had always wanted to be a nurse. So after Steve started first grade, and all her children were in school, so was she — in nurses' training. When we ate dinner together, she would excitedly tell us about what she was learning in her classes. Nutritional labeling was still decades away, but we learned from her that broccoli was good for us, which was not good news. It tasted terrible. But the good news was that there would be no more drying the dishes after washing them. Dish towels spread germs, so the dishes had to air-dry instead.

As a student in her 40s, our mother was by far the oldest in her class of young women. In a colossal mistake with long-term consequences, she dropped out of training just weeks before graduating. Her nursing instructor had openly mocked her for using reading glasses. That was the story we heard, but perhaps her lack of a high school diploma had undercut her confidence; she had missed both junior and senior high school. Whatever the reason, the consequences of her hasty decision were far-reaching. She would be working at the lowest wage scale as a nurse aide, even though she was a fully trained, but not licensed, practical nurse.

While our mother was busy with school, and then work, our sister Marcia often functioned as our second mother, and we felt safe with her. Like Mary, she was both gentle and funny, but unlike Mary, she could also supply me with great spy material. Marcia had a boyfriend, and he spent a lot of time at our house, as did her other friends. She was popular and sang soprano in her school's Honors Trio, which practiced at our house. In view of all that, when Marcia left for the University of Michigan, life at our house became far less interesting. And soon, much harder as well.

Our mother beamed with pride with Marcia heading off to college. The summer before she left, we pinched pennies to buy her a bicycle to get around on campus, and it was not just any bicycle. A shiny new Schwinn with chrome fenders stayed hidden in our garage, waiting to surprise Marcia. We gave it to her the day before she left for Ann Arbor. She was so excited, as we were for her. On the big day, we all squeezed into our car already stuffed with luggage, and the bike strapped into the trunk, for the pilgrimage to the University of Michigan.

After unloading everything at her dormitory, I looked back as we drove off to see her standing at the curb, smiling and waving goodbye. I was sad, but our mother was happy! She had never finished sixth grade, but her daughter was going to college. And not just any college — one of the best. Even better, Marcia would attend nursing school there, following in our mother's footsteps. I could hear the pride in her voice whenever she talked about Marcia and "U of M." But for us "little kids," our big sister was now gone. No more spying, no more boyfriends, and no more cool big kids at our house.

CHAPTER 4

ORPHANS AND MISFITS

WITH MARCIA GONE, THE THREE OF US LEFT BEHIND BEGAN TO LIVE LIKE THOSE ORPHANS I HAD ONCE MISTAKEN US FOR. Without her, and with our mother working, we were pretty much on our own now. When our mother changed hospital shifts from day to second shift, she would leave our house at 2:30 p.m. and return after 11:00. As such, we saw her only at breakfast, and then came home from school to an empty house. She had two days off a week, but even then, she was often away, so we learned to manage by ourselves. Our family ties were unraveling, and our mother would frequently remind us, "My job is to put a roof over your heads!" The rest was up to us.

There seemed to be little connection even when we did see our mother. For me as the oldest now, there were no hellos, goodbyes, or even interest from her. Instead, it was mostly announcements or instructions, as in "the lawn needs mowing," or "take the clothes off the line before it rains." I did not feel cherished, only useful, or in the way. For me, school provided a reliable refuge where grownups were in charge, and as far as I could tell, none of them were sinning. Not like the two that were at our house.

Our first intruder lived behind us with his mother in a small cottage without a garage. With only one car, our two-stall garage was always half empty, so this neighbor asked if he could rent the extra spot for his car during the winter. His name was Don. I suspected Don was also the man who once frightened me one night by peeping into my bedroom window, and also the one who had scared me so badly, I wet myself one evening. I was alone in the previous house next door when I noticed the figure of a man through the front door side window, testing the lock on the door. It terrified me, and my felt poodle skirt paid the price.

After parking in our garage, Don would knock at our back door, then stand there so red-faced, even his bald head was red. He never chatted with us kids — he was there to see our mother, and we had to stay out of the way. Just like that mailman from our church, Don was creepy, and I hated him. Plus, I desperately hoped that the missionary spies next door didn't notice his visits, which continued after the winter.

WHEN MARY WAS in about 6th grade, she developed what our mother called a tic. She would blink nervously and pull out her eyelashes, and I thought it was strange. It bothered me. In those days, psychological problems were silenced by shame, and if any help was to be had, it came from either the family doctor or the clergy. However, our mother was not worried. She dismissed Mary's behavior as just a phase, and she was right. In time, Mary recovered her good humor and easygoing nature, never being one to complain much. You hardly knew what she was thinking, even though she could make us laugh. Once when she had a bad stomach ache, she absurdly insisted that our mother call the doctor because it was "worse than cancer!"

Mary was smart, too, but for some reason, she had been placed in the slow-learner group in 7th grade. Aptitude tests the previous year may have caught her on a bad day, or during her "tic" phase. In a short-lived experiment, the school divided her class the following year into groups of slow, average, and bright. It was a foolish move with far-reaching harm for some. When a school chum asked Mary why she seemed to like being in the slow group, Mary surprised her by saying, "Because they are more honest." Was Mary more comfortable on the sidelines, or was she actually struggling with schoolwork? Whatever the case, her answer packed a lot of wisdom.

Middle school was three years of misery for many, if not most, students. Perhaps Mary felt left out of the mean-girl cliques that formed during that time. I was two years ahead of her there, and probably one of those mean girls myself. She, on the other hand, got by on the sidelines with her quiet ways. Even so, those years were hard on both of us, if for different reasons. It stank, but we had to get through it on our own.

Fortunately, Mary found a new friend, a newcomer at school. Her name was Barb. The two of them walked part way home together after school every day, commiserating, comparing notes, and laughing. They secretly enjoyed hating the teachers, the school, and the mean girls; they were "outcasts" together.

They rode bikes together near and far: speeding down hills, goofing off, and getting into fun trouble — that is until the police got involved. After parking their bikes on a highway overpass once to wave at truck drivers, they thought that sprinkling gravel on their trucks might be fun, too. The highway patrol cops thought otherwise, and showed up at Barb's house, where her parents agreed with the cops. But there were no adults at our house for the officers to contact, so Mary's escapade went unnoticed, much like the rest of her life back then. At least she had a great sense of humor, which was a basic survival skill in our family.

It was around this time that Mary began making up names for herself, and special friends. She went by "Farina," from the Little Rascals movies, and Barb soon became "Baboola." Mary also began to speak "chicken," which she must have picked up at our uncle's chicken ranch. Now as a teenager, she spoke it freely, even on the phone. I would overhear her release a loud, "Bega-a-a-wk! Buck-buck-buck…." and had to smile. It was her all over.

On the other hand, Mary was often quiet at home with just us kids. She kept her head down, spending time alone with her special cat, Peter, and she found other animals for company, too. Sometimes we would find strays that she had "rescued" wandering in our basement.

As MONEY PROBLEMS began to haunt us at home, the word "payday" became increasingly relevant. It was feast or famine for us, with steak or a drive-in restaurant on payday, followed by an increasingly empty refrigerator and cupboards. At times, our mother even borrowed my babysitting money to make it to the next payday, although she always paid it back.

Things changed at school, too. Though never a "room mother" like other moms, our mother now missed our parent-teacher conferences and school functions. She barely glanced at our report cards, and was nowhere to be seen after school when it rained, either. On those days, I walked past cars lining the curb as moms picked up their kids, while I grew wetter and more embarrassed with every step. No one picked us up: we were the oddballs, and in more ways than one.

Even though ours was the largest Christian elementary school of its kind in the country, there were no single-parent families in it. Back then, divorce was almost unheard of, perhaps because matrimony was believed to be holy. On account of that, our single-parent-family was highly unusual, so much so that when another student's father was killed in an accident, I felt secretly relieved. Now there was at least one other family like ours with no father. When the newly widowed mother remarried the following year, our family continued its status as "that poor family."

Since we only saw our mother before school in the morning, I left her messages in the evening while she was at work: lists of what we ran out of, and forms that needed her signature. I also took phone calls from angry parents complaining about Steve, who was becoming rather rebellious. He would then get angry when I did not defend his behavior, but how could I? He ran wild, and our mother was no disciplinarian even when she was at home.

On her days off, when not running errands, our farm-girl mother was the happiest when she was outside. Summers were for getting outdoor work done, not vacations. One summer she painted the whole house during the day before she left for work in the afternoon. Fearless, she stood on ladders and seemed to enjoy it. She tended her rose bushes with devotion, and planted Kentucky wonder beans, which grew up the side of the house. Clinging to our kitchen window screens, the beans could then watch in horror as we ate their brethren for dinner.

Our summers felt endless without the routine of school. Most families we knew seemed to be either on vacation or at their cottages, which meant no friends around to play with. We were stuck. Home felt like a boarding house with an absentee landlord as I juggled feelings of shame, and a near constant sense of abandonment. A week at a friend's cottage or summer camp helped, but other than that, war would sometimes break out at our house. The three of us, Mary, Steve, and I, often fought; yet as the oldest, it fell to me to keep order while Mary and Steve formed coalitions. I once threw scissors at Steve, which lodged into his arm and bled. I feared I would be arrested like the people on television were for their crimes. So, I bribed Steve not to tell on me. Mary, on the other hand, was usually quiet and escaped overt trouble. Or was she so good at it that no one noticed?

Occasionally, a grouchy aunt or a mean friend of our mother's would stop by while she was at work. One scolded us for the mess in our house, while another one criticized me for being too skinny. As "orphans," we were easy targets. When other grownups admonished me to help our beleaguered mother, I resented it. We did feel sorry for her, but we also had to pretend that we were OK. I was not. None of us were. And I dreaded first meeting friends' parents, especially their fathers, who routinely asked who my father was. When I said he was dead, they would invariably turn away without a word. In our Dutch culture, this may have been a sign of respect, but I felt ashamed and guilty for making them uncomfortable.

Over time, our family came to embody the widows, orphans, and poor that we prayed for in church. We were shamefully living from paycheck to paycheck, and rarely brought friends home. Staying away as much as possible, we never knew where the others were, or what they were up to.

At home, we sometimes scrounged through the cupboards for lunch, lucky to find stale crackers and maybe some peanut butter. Our mom was usually out somewhere running errands, and our back door was always unlocked. Except for one day when it had been accidentally locked. A kind neighbor noticed us sitting forlornly on our front steps and fed us at her house that day. I was as grateful as I was embarrassed. Over time, we watched our friends' families become increasingly wealthy, their mothers always at home, and none of them ever going hungry. Thankfully, I would soon "join" one of them.

In 6th grade, I began walking home from school with a new friend, Valerie, who often invited me to her house for lunch. I looked forward to that not only for the good food, but also to see her mother, Mrs. A. She treated me as if I belonged there, and I wished I did. In fact, Valerie's family seemed to live in a different world, a wonderful world, and I jumped at every chance to spend time in it. I became a regular there.

Eventually, I was even included in their family outings. During one of their beach picnics, I ate five hamburgers as Mr. A, who was grilling them, kept handing them to me with an amused smile. Another time, during a quiet Sunday afternoon at their house, a fire engine went screaming past, and everyone went running out the back door toward the garage. As I ran with them, I asked where we were going. Valerie shouted back, "Fire!" in reply. Her dad was already backing the car out as everyone piled in, closing car doors on the way. I adored these crazy people. They not only chased fire engines, but they did it on Sunday when we were not supposed to have any fun!

I felt safe and happy with them in their perfectly managed household. Their bathroom towels matched, and the kitchen dishes did, too. Their carpets were vacuumed daily, and each child had a special drawer of their very own in the family room. During sleepovers there, I slept on Mrs. A's freshly ironed cotton sheets. But best of all, I could just be a kid there.

I became a regular there after school, too. Mrs. A would greet Valerie and me at the back door, smiling and asking how school went. We often had stories to report, and she took the time to listen. She cared. Then we would feast on her freshly baked cakes, including second helpings, and all the milk we could drink. I would stay until dinner time. Then I walked the two long blocks home to my real family, passing by my father's old house where the interlopers still lived.

Unlike the A house, ours was always dirty, which bordered on scandalous in our Dutch culture. Our kitchen floor was usually sticky, and unwashed dishes often covered the kitchen counters. If you needed something to wear, you might find your clothes still soaking in the old wringer washing machine in the basement. Even our kitchen clock was cockeyed, always set between 10 and 15 minutes fast. When a schoolmate once called our house a junkyard, she was being mean, but she was not wrong, either. After that, I stopped inviting friends over.

Dried-up cat or dog poop might be "lounging" on our basement floor next to a pile of dirty clothes. At night, darkened rooms sometimes waited for light bulbs we could not afford. We became experts at finding substitutes for toilet paper when it ran out, and at times, utility shut-off notices would threaten. But we never let on to our friends. Valerie used to envy our freedom, but she never knew that that freedom sometimes included hunger.

Yet our mother was known for her great cooking, and having learned from her father, she was also an excellent baker. It was a treat sometimes to be surprised by freshly baked bread, or chocolate eclairs, when we came home from school. When she was working, our dinner was left warming in the oven, and Mary, Steve, and I would eat it while watching television. I took the nightly phone calls from the hospital, answering our mother's routine questions: Had we eaten? Did you bring in the laundry from the clothesline? Then came the one I dreaded: "You know I love you kids, right?" I dutifully said yes but felt like a liar. She seemed to be gone all the time at work, or just gone. We came home to an empty house, and went to bed alone. I felt as if we had been discarded. And there were times when she worked a double shift, returning home the next morning as we were getting ready for school. Then she would be gone again when we got home from school. But she never complained. She loved her job.

As it was, we were too young to realize that our childhood must have been fortunate compared to hers: pulled out of school at age 13, working on the farm, and then a servant for a wealthy family. She could not — or would not — see how abandoned and cheated we felt. Especially when compared to the small, orderly Dutch world of "our kind." Consequently, I alternated between the home I had, and the one I wished I had at the A's.

When Mr. A came home from work, he would always smile at me as he read the newspaper in his white, sleeveless undershirt after shedding his suit. Over time, I secretly adopted him as my own father. By then, the black-and-white photo of my real dad hanging on our mother's bedroom wall felt more like a mug shot. I avoided looking at it. Too young to realize he had been unable to say goodbye because of his fast-moving cancer, I was mad at him for abandoning us. Being mad felt better than missing him, and it was best just to forget him.

By around 8th grade, I developed what our mother called "a big mouth." I complained, talked back, and questioned both her and our lifestyle at home. Mary, on the other hand, was too smart, or too humble, to do so. I was temperamentally unsuited to rolling with our punches. So, I used to get yelled at in Dutch, with our mother shouting, "Hou je bek!" at me. It means, "shut your trap." I did not speak Dutch, but I knew from the sound of her voice that she was extremely angry with me, and I heard it often.

Because of her increasing frustration with me, after helping out at our brother's house one summer, I stayed there at his invitation. He had five children by then, and his wife was glad to have me — this time. My relieved sister-in-law no longer had to search for babysitters, and she actually had free time. She even took flying lessons. It was the summer before 9th grade, and my mother now had one less mouth to feed back home. Here, I had my own room with a canopied, four-poster bed. I lived in a clean house, with regular meals, and adults in charge. They even bought me clothes, and I felt safe and wanted there.

After about six weeks there, I got a phone call from Mary one day. She was speaking for our mother when she told me I had to come home now. I was needed there. I refused by repeating what my sister-in-law had drilled into me by then: my mother was not a good mother. All the while, I thought I was loved at my brother's house, when, in fact, I was merely useful.

That fall, 9th grade went into full swing for me. We were the oldest class now, the big kids in our combined elementary and middle school. Most of my class had been together since kindergarten and they almost felt like cousins. I was not an athletic student—I was afraid of balls, bats, and other weapons—but I did make the cheerleading team. My "big mouth" was finally an asset. Then, without seeking it, I was also elected to the student council, and then president of it. My sister Mary's friend, Carol, who was also on the council, cast the deciding vote. This position meant that I could have Valerie work with me in the school bookstore, and we could steal gobs of the candy sold there.

As it turned out, I became so busy with after-school activities that I was no longer useful to my sister-in-law. One day I was told to pack up, then driven back home without a word, where I was also received without a word. I felt like a spare part, moved wherever I was useful, and then dumped when I was not. Mary was probably the only one who noticed enough to even care, but as usual, we never talked about our lives together. Plus, with me back home, she was no longer the oldest left in charge. So now it was back to being lonely survivors of what had once been a real family.

Later in that same school year, my science teacher summoned me to stay after school one day. When he reported that I had scored high on a recent aptitude test, it meant nothing to me: it was just another test. It was his attitude that I remembered. Meeting with him turned out to be my mean minister's Sunday afternoon interrogation all over again. My teacher now spoke resentfully, wanting to know why I was not doing well in his class, given that I had the aptitude to do so. Stung by his accusatory manner, I defiantly replied that I did not like science, and I left his room, wounded. By the end of 9th grade that year, I was in full rebellion, and I suspect that Mary was not far behind.

SINCE OUR FATHER's death, our mother had had several boyfriends, but then she found one that she wanted to marry. She met him while working at the hospital, and like our father, he was another Romeo. His name was Art, and they planned to marry after all of their children were grown. He was a widower, also with six children and two still at home on their farm, while our mother had three of us "impediments" holding her back. While waiting for all of us to grow up, our mother and Art just had "dates" at our house.

We already knew about staying out of the way when our mother's boyfriends were around, but now we were hounded to grow up as fast as possible so she could remarry. She would often sigh, "I wish you kids would just grow up!" We stood in the way of her happiness.

Art visited her on Sunday nights after his evening church service in town. When she was not at work, she would have his favorite cake and fresh coffee waiting. If he happened to catch sight of us kids before we did our disappearing act, he would loudly exclaim, "I hate kids!" Then he would laugh at us; our mom would flash angry looks as we melted away, leaving them alone for the evening. Once during a rare weeknight when he visited, I happened to be the only child at home, and was ordered to leave the house, even though I had nowhere to go. It was cold and dark outside, so I hid in a small depression in a newly built park across the street. I was afraid the whole time, and then ran back home after seeing Art's car finally leave our driveway. It was close to midnight.

On another evening when I was 16, Valerie happened to be at our house where she witnessed my mother kicking me out yet again: Art was on the way. To get rid of me, she gave Valerie the keys to her car. Claiming that her car was her lifeline, she had never trusted me with it, but now she was giving my best friend the keys. I was used to being kicked out, but Valerie was shocked. She could not imagine her own mother doing that to her. Nor could I. Regardless, the two of us took advantage of having a car for the night, and Valerie taught me how to drive a stick shift; once again, she was the best friend ever.

I hated it when Art stopped over, which he did sometimes even when he knew our mom was at work. During those times, he might sit next to me on the couch, reach over to feel my bare legs, and then run his hands over them. I would be too afraid to stop him. I later learned that he did the same with Mary, and even Marcia, when he had the chance. One afternoon when he arrived as I was about to leave for a friend's house, he offered me a ride there. I took it, but on the way, he ordered, "Watch this!" as he sped down a residential street with the speedometer reading 80 mph. Then he laughed at me as I climbed out of his car, shaking. He was that kind of man.

Our home life had been difficult before, but now with Art in the picture, it became downright hostile. Its worsening dysfunction and disorder ate at me, and I stubbornly pushed back. When I did so, my mother would become infuriated, calling me a "big mouth." I was her "worst kid." For emphasis, she might add, "Why don't you just leave!" and once, "You don't deserve to live." But I had nowhere to go, or to put the hurt. Who could I tell? Who would care? I suspect that we all felt like a burden to her by then, but I was the only one foolish enough to rebel.

CHAPTER 5

_____

SLIPPING AWAY

EVEN THOUGH SHE MADE THE DEAN'S LIST AT THE UNIVERSITY OF MICHIGAN, MARCIA HAD TO DROP OUT AFTER ONLY TWO YEARS THERE. She left college and returned home, working as a waitress to earn her own tuition money. We were all glad to have her back again. Then she disappeared.

Through her work at the restaurant, she met, and then became engaged to, a man twenty years her senior: Howard. This was shocking enough, but then one night she did not come home from work. Or the next day, or the next night. Howard hired a private detective to find her, and we all were extremely worried about her, jumping each time our phone rang. Finally, it was her. She was alive. She was in Florida. She was married!

Hanging out after work with coworkers from the restaurant, she had met another man at a bowling alley: Frank. Frank convinced her to run away with him and get married, even though she was engaged to someone else. She did. They were married in Georgia by a justice of the peace.

At the time, I was a freshman in high school, and Mary was still in middle school. During our spring break that year, our shrinking family made a hurried road trip to Florida to see Marcia. I sat in the front seat holding the map, while Mary and Steve kept a lookout from the back seat. We were used to cross-country trips together, but this was no vacation, and Miami was a long way down on the map. During our first night on the road, rain was falling in blinding torrents, and — of course — all the motels were filled. Northerners were heading south for spring break. As we drove deeper into the night, I kept a keen lookout for vacancy signs, finally finding one in Horse Cave, Kentucky. I darted through the rain to secure the last room in that lone roadside motel.

The next day went better, although we did get lost in rural Georgia. We stopped three times to ask for directions, but none of us could understand the locals' answers, although they were delivered with friendly smiles. Their accents were so thick, it felt as if we were in a different country. We drove on wondering what language they spoke, and no doubt, they must have wondered the same about us. What a relief it was, then, finally to turn into a driveway in Miami, lay eyes on Marcia, and meet Frank. He introduced himself by saying, "This is what a husband looks like." He was not wearing a shirt, confident of his good looks.

After we returned to Michigan again, I let my friends think we had simply vacationed in Florida like normal families did. I did not tell them we had slept on the floor of a shabby little duplex, or shared a primitive bathroom with people we could hear, but not see, in its other half. I also did not mention that our new brother-in-law kept pigs in a vacant lot. I told no one about hiding in the car there, petrified while his pigs were fed garbage thrown over the walls of their overcrowded pen. Their squeals tore through me like gunshot, and I covered my ears as the poor things fought desperately for food. Who would treat pigs like that?

Yes, Frank was handsome, and yes, he spoke several languages. He was also a biology teacher, just as Marcia had reported. She was working here as a waitress again, but this time at the famed Fontainebleau nightclub in Miami Beach. While hearing the likes of Tony Bennett and Frank Sinatra performing, she was raking in huge tips. She appeared to be radiantly happy, and after three crowded days at her little place, we headed back north, somewhat dazed, but glad to know she was OK.

BACK HOME, WE bemoaned our new normal without Marcia. And we struggled in other ways, too. Our church-mandated Christian educations from kindergarten through college were expensive. Our mother paid for ours up through middle school, even though doing so could mean significant shortages at home, and for us, sometimes learning on an empty stomach. Hunger followed us right into high school, where each of us had to pay for our tuition. During my first semester, Mr. A faithfully picked me up every day, taking Valerie and me to school on his way to work. When he noticed that I often left our house without a lunch bag, he offered to have Mrs. A make lunches for me. It was torture turning him down, but shame demanded it. Even so, getting through the day without lunch was hard.

On the other hand, the shame that stopped me from accepting lunches from Mrs. A did not stop me from pilfering food from other students. Lunch bags stored on open shelves in our old school building were easy pickings, and I was a hall monitor during fourth hour just before lunch. A small bag of chips from a nearby convenience store could not get me through the day. Thankfully, the free dinners that came with my afterschool job at a hospital kept me going, although bouts of hunger continued to hound us at home.

When I returned home after work each evening, I had no idea what, or how, Mary and Steve had been doing. We did not talk much. In fact, I only learned that Mary was in a car accident by overhearing my mother telling someone else about it. Mary was unhurt, but afraid of riding in cars after that. During the short time the three of us kids were home together, it would be homework, then lights out, almost always by ourselves.

In the morning, I sometimes had to search for my schoolbooks, only to find them in our mother's bedroom. She would borrow them to read late at night after work, still hungry to learn after missing so much school herself. But did she ever wonder how we kids managed? About times without milk, or bread, or her? She complained that we were "eating her out of house and home." Deep down, it probably was not so much about the food: We were hungry for a parent at home, but her heart was in her work, not our home.

At the Catholic hospital where she worked, I was once confronted by the hospital president, an imposing nun who lurked under a long black habit and white wimple. I was there to pick something up from my mother, and wound up standing next to this fearsome woman in an elevator. It was summertime and I was wearing shorts, which was strictly forbidden attire there. Even worse, hospital visiting hours had not yet begun. The stern administrator glared at my bare legs and asked what I was doing there. When I revealed my mission, she asked for my mother's name — I was in trouble now for sure. But upon hearing my mother's name, she smiled! And she kept smiling, saying that my mother was one of the best nurses in the whole hospital, and that she was given some of their most difficult patients to care for.

WE PLOWED THROUGH those difficult years by hanging out with friends. Mary gave hers names like "Rooster" and "Baboola," or sometimes addressed them as "Vegetable." And she continued to "speak" chicken, too. Our uncle's chickens had taught her well. Reportedly she even spoke chicken in public, causing her friends to double over with laughter. I knew very little about her life then, or that she joined the Camp Fire Girls with her pal, Carol. The two of them worked in hospitals, and also at a nursing home, as Horizon Girls. Carol reported that Mary's "lively imagination, good judgment, and positive attitude" made her good with patients. She made their volunteer work more fun, and it would be no surprise if Mary spoke chicken to her patients there, too. It came naturally.

Humor ran in our family. As a handy coping mechanism, it was far more useful than tears. Marcia, too, could be very funny, even in the hardest of times — and she had plenty of them. Mary was no different. Given half a chance, and the right company, my irrepressible sisters found ways to have fun. But for all that, we laughed far more outside of our house than in.

As Mary blossomed into a pretty teenager, she showed little, if any, interest in boys. She did not date, but rather cruised with friends downtown, as teenagers did back then. Flirting with boys consisted of splashing them with squirt guns out the car window. That was it. She preferred, instead, the relaxed company of her girlfriends, and increasingly, those she worked with at her afterschool job. Working as a tray girl at the same hospital where I had worked in high school, Mary and her co-worker, Sue, would put Black Jack gum over their front teeth so patients thought they were missing teeth: Mary's idea.

They also raced empty tray carts down the halls together, breaking as many rules as they could get away with, just as I had done with Valerie when we worked there together.

And shy Mary could be surprisingly bold. On a ten-dollar bet with friends, she once donned our brother's ratty flight suit from the Navy, added a frumpy wig, and then walked barefoot into a dicey, inner-city bar. She was supposed to stay there for ten minutes, but she was hustled right back out again when a patron feared she was going through delirium tremens, and used a pool stick to poke at her bare feet. My crazy sister lost the bet, but had a good story, one our family never heard at home.

Allegedly, few places were safe from her mischievous ways. She and Sue did jumping jacks in front of a bar named Jumping Jack's, no doubt amusing those sober enough to get the joke. I missed out on that Mary. At home, she was often subdued, but then our lives there were not conducive to light-hearted fun. Because of that, our small, teenaged shenanigans were an important rebellion against the adult world that was failing us. We could feel momentarily powerful by breaking their rules, and Mary was smart enough to hide it when she did.

Working to pay for our high school tuition kept us busy. We earned just over a dollar an hour at the hospital, and on weekends, she and I babysat for 50 cents an hour. School tuition was $300 a year, plus we had to buy all of our schoolbooks and clothes. For us, there were no afterschool clubs, events, or sports. Tuition payments loomed over everything. However, I was extremely lucky to have a friend like Valerie, who knew I was paying for my own tuition. She secretly made several payments on it herself. Valerie was that kind of friend.

High school was a busy time for me, working hard while also keeping up with my schoolwork. It was no different for Mary, but she had a stubborn streak that we were about to encounter. She astounded me when she made a break from almost everything we had been taught. For her last semester of high school, she left our Christian high school for a public one. This was no small thing. From our church's point of view, she risked contamination from the "sinful" world found in public schools, and as kids growing up, this doctrinal bondage had been accepted as truth.

Thus, believing the lie that our Christian schools were better, I tried to talk her out of leaving. I argued that she would get into a better college if she stuck it out at her Christian school. But Mary was not thinking of college. She simply walked away, leaving that school's "sanctimonious staff" and condescending classmates behind. And in doing so, she escaped tuition bondage, too. It was a daring move, and perhaps even a smart one, but we never saw it coming.

1967 TURNED OUT to be a pivotal year for our family. Mary graduated from her new high school, while I still lived at home, working my way through college. It was also the year when our sister Marcia lost vision in one eye, sending her to the doctor. On March 24, Good Friday, she underwent surgery for a brain tumor in her hippocampus, the part of the brain important for memory and learning, among other functions. This threat hit our family like a bombshell.

At the time, brain surgery was in its infancy, and it was unclear if she would even survive the operation. The night before her surgery was excruciatingly hard. As we gathered around her bed, we struggled with our goodbyes. Even though she could be leaving an adorable little son behind, Marcia continued to be her sweet, uncomplaining self, saying she would either see us later the next day, or in heaven.

I sat alone with our mother the next morning during the long procedure. In essence, she was reliving another surgery long before, when a surgeon had reported our father's fatal lung cancer. When Marcia's surgeon finally emerged to report that it was not cancer, our mother almost fainted with relief. But unfortunately, the surgeon was unable to completely remove Marcia's tumor due to its critical location. He predicted that Marcia would not regain normal functioning, and because of that, it was particularly important to spare her undue stress.

Back at the hospital that evening, our mother was given a sedative to protect her from what she was about to see. We had to wait 20 minutes for it to take effect, but there was no sedative for Mary, Steve, or me. Marcia's head was grotesquely swollen to almost the size of a soccer ball. Her eyelashes were all but buried, and I was horrified to see her lying there, trapped in total darkness. But she could hear us, so we sat at her bedside. While I gently stroked her hand, she smiled a little even though she was in unimaginable and undermedicated pain.

Having worked in a hospital for years, often transcribing doctors' orders, I now felt confident asking the charge nurse on duty about pain relief for Marcia. Surely there had to be more than she was getting. But no. Her neurosurgeon, one of only two in the city at the time, had left town for the Easter holiday weekend without orders for pain medications. We were stunned, and I was furious. When a nurse suggested that Marcia could have an aspirin, I demanded that the resident on duty immediately write orders for her pain relief. Had our nurse mother not been so sedated herself, she would have been right there with me to demand the same.

Marcia recovered slowly; her face turning black and blue, her shaved head reluctantly regrowing hair. At the same time, our family tried to make up for her spouse's shocking neglect. Even under these circumstances, he seemed to be too inconvenienced by her ordeal to show much concern, but by then, we were not surprised. She had made a terrible mistake by marrying him, and we needed no reminders. Her tumor and its sequelae would completely change her life; stress, which she was supposed to avoid, was instead a constant companion. Our precious sister, once a reassuring presence in our wobbly family, was now in dire need of support herself. We had relied on her when we were kids, but now she needed us to do the same for her. She was only 26, with a little boy to care for at home.

It was hard for doctors to pin down the exact cause of her tumor, although an over-the-counter drug was a prime suspect. It was recalled for being implicated in brain tumors, and had been popular on college campuses; Marcia had gobbled plenty during her exams. And in fact, one of her tumor's first symptoms may have been impaired thinking: marrying a complete stranger while also engaged to a man 20 years her senior.

OUR LEAKY BOAT of a family managed to stay afloat during the summer after Marcia's surgery. Mary graduated from high school during the "Summer of Love." It was a pivotal time, not just for the country, but also for Mary. All things California would soon dominate much of the youth culture, with songs even written about it. "California Dreaming" and "San Francisco" were big hits, and Mary was listening.

At the same time, her friends, both old and new, were heading off in different directions for college. While recovering in bed from a tonsillectomy that June, Mary was feeling adrift. Her good friend Meredith was spending the summer in California where Mary wrote to her. In a letter dated June 19, she addressed Meredith as, "You booger!" She also refers to her as "Fafoofnik." After salutations like these, no signature was ever needed to identify the sender.

Back when Mary left her old high school, she had left behind many classmates she had known since kindergarten. At her new school, she had only one friend — Meredith. In her letters to Meredith, she now thanked her for being a lifesaver among the bewildering new crowd there. Mary had been lonely, feeling lost in hallways filled by strangers between classes. And apparently, she was lonely again now, too.

In a second letter to Meredith, dated July 5, Mary talked about moving to California, referring to it as a "lifetime goal." She also wrote about a "hippy boy" that she had recently met. She seemed to both admire and feel sorry for him: he was down on religion, found no meaning in life, traveled a lot, and used drugs. But the encounter with him also made her think about her own life. She wondered if Meredith would ever "take LSD." In the same letter, she referred to herself as "born dumb," a mistaken notion that no one else believed. Then on a lighter note, she tells Meredith about a new hat with images of a roadrunner and chickens on it. It was perfect for Mary's chicken-squawking wit, and in fact, she drew a chicken right below her signature.

As Mary now struggled to find her place in the world, San Francisco's blossoming counterculture was transforming countless young lives. But it took a while to make its way across the country to the Midwest, and marijuana was its calling card. Apparently, Mary began smoking it before I had even smelled it. I was busy working, studying, and taking care of things at home that summer. As a result, I did not have a solid sense of who Mary was, or what she did away from home. Or even at home.

At the time, I was shocked and disappointed to hear that the Beatles were using drugs, but I had no idea that Mary was, too. She "dropped" LSD, which she also shared with Steve, age 14, at our house. After that, it was pot at the beach and at parties in town. Meanwhile, my summer could not have been more different.

Our mother had surgery and needed care and rest for six weeks. I was working the overnight shift at a hospital, taking a college biology class in the morning, and then sleeping during the day. Consequently, I had to divvy up care for our mother, as well as make sure we had groceries at home. I became the enforcer, and the job stank. I hardly saw Steve, and Mary was often uncooperative, which was new for her. She was working at her summer job when I was sleeping, and I was working when she was either sleeping, or apparently gone. I leaned on other family members to help, but our unwieldy home situation prevailed.

When race protests then erupted in our city, I was frightened. Working the overnight shift at a neighborhood hospital, I walked to work in the dark hearing sirens. The glow of distant fires in the night sky hurried me along. I would quickly climb a fence that surrounded the hospital's parking lot, and then run to its back door. But these so-called riots, or protests, had the opposite effect on Mary. She did not run from them; instead, she called her friend Sue, exclaiming, "Let's go!" And according to Sue, they went.

That summer would be the last time that we all lived together. In the fall, Mary started community college while living at home; I worked as a live-in nanny for a wealthy family while in school. Mary's friend Meredith moved to a different city, and then later to another one, also for college. It was said, however, that Mary was interested only in her college's art classes, and because of that, she was easily persuaded to drop out during her second semester. After that she just worked as a waitress and hung out with friends. She would soon become part of a different "freshman class," this one belonging to the growing antiwar, anti-establishment movement sweeping the country. In fact, she already had one foot out our door.

After her friend Meredith married later that year, they lost touch. Then Sue left college to marry young as well, although she stayed in touch with Mary for a while. Their correspondence often concerned issues relating to Sue's difficult marriage, with Mary offering encouragement. Yet Mary was searching, too, and over time, her letters became more philosophical as she wondered about the meaning of life.

ADDING TO THE rolling cultural upheavals of 1967, 1968 sent further shock waves across the county. It was a year like no other. It brought the sharp rise of the Black Panther Party, the assassination of Dr. Martin Luther King Jr., and the murder of Bobby Kennedy — all in close succession.

Our family endured its own trauma when our mother suffered a betrayal and loss so deep she could not run from it this time. After seven years of working hard and waiting to marry Art, he dumped her for a friend of hers with no warning. He was still that kind of man. My sisters and I already knew that and were glad to be rid of him, but even so, it was hard to see our mother so unfairly wounded. She was a strong person, but now, totally devastated.

Meanwhile, cultural shifts continued to upend our country. Adding to the tumult, rebel Harvard psychologist Timothy Leary was encouraging our generation to "turn on, tune in, and drop out." It appears that Mary decided to do just that. In late August, she and a friend hitchhiked to Chicago.

While on the road, the girls were picked up by two men in a semi-truck. But soon after the girls had stuffed themselves into the sleeping compartment behind the driver, they sensed the threat of sexual violence. One of the girls strategically feigned a bathroom emergency, and the driver let them out at a rest stop. There the frightened girls stayed hidden inside as the truck driver kept the engines running outside. The men were waiting for them. Desperate, the girls appealed to an older man also using the facilities. Appreciating their situation, he bundled them into his car and drove them to a different rest stop, where the two put their thumbs out for Chicago. Again.

I was not at home that summer, but working for the Upward Bound program, and living comfortably in a college dorm. I was thus unaware that Mary was anything but comfortable once she and her friend made it to Chicago. Along with others, she was sleeping under the bushes in

Grant Park, there to protest the Democratic National Convention. She was shoplifting food to eat.

At the same time, the convention delegates at their headquarters in Chicago's Hilton Hotel were undoubtedly eating well, and sleeping comfortably. The luxurious hotel stood right across Michigan Avenue from Grant Park, where the dramatic anti-war protest soon superseded national convention coverage. Television cameras turned away from the convention inside to the protest outside.

Outside, an estimated 10,000 mostly peaceful protesters from across the country were stealing their story, and the spurned delegates and politicians inside were outraged. The Chicago police were deployed, soon to be labeled "pigs" by the surging throngs of protesters, who were brutally beaten, most armed with only their voices.

The National Guard was called in, some with machine guns mounted on jeeps, but the protesters carried on, chanting, "The whole world is watching!" It was true. They were demonstrating against the Vietnam War, the draft, and the military. In the meantime, some of the very men who were sending the protesters' generation to war were inside the convention hall, a powerful elite now facing a backlash of historic proportions.

Attracted by the message of social justice and "Make Love Not War," Mary was actively searching for her place in this exciting new movement. And she suffered for it, bashed in the head by one of the reportedly thousands of Chicago's club-wielding cops under Mayor Daley's command. The streets literally ran with protesters' blood, and the air was clouded with tear gas for five days. The brutality of the authorities' unrestrained force shocked the nation.

Six thousand National Guard troops flooded the scene, while intelligence agents from the FBI, CIA, Army, and Navy, numbered in the hundreds, standing ready to assist. Another 6,000 U.S. Army were put on standby. In the meantime, Joan Baez showed up to help care for the wounded, and our cousin, a medical student living nearby, joined her with triaging and bandaging. Mary managed to survive her head wound without medical help, and when the convention ended, she made a brief visit back home. But she was not alone — she brought a boyfriend.

Who was this new Mary? She was in a hurry, focused, and apparently in love. Never suspecting that she had been in the bloody mayhem we had seen on television, we were shocked to learn that she had just come from it. Yet typically for her, she said very little about the protest, staying only long enough to raise bail money for some of the protesters. She never said anything about that, either. Our quiet, unassuming Mary had just been publicly protesting nationwide in front of television cameras. After years of seeing my "big mouth" getting me in trouble at home, she had now found hers, but used it to help others and got beaten for it. And who was this boyfriend of hers?

Peter Wotherspoon was born a British citizen in Valparaiso, Chile, and also held dual U.S. and Chilean citizenships. Compared to our family, he was a man of the world. His parents had lived in an enclave of British citizens while residing in post-World War II Chile. However, when Peter was a toddler, they emigrated to York, Pennsylvania, to further his father's career with the Caterpillar corporation. There, Peter grew up an only child in a bilingual household, and later lived in Chile once again while serving in the Peace Corps. He possessed a dazzling intellect, but had dropped out of Penn State to be close to his mother in Illinois. His father had succumbed to injuries sustained in a car accident there. But Mary never revealed any of this at the time, nor did he. He was a stranger. And Mary? She was becoming one, too.

Quiet, unpretentious, and likeable Peter seemed perfect for Mary. On the other hand, our mother was skeptical, declaring that Peter was not "our kind." He had "lace on his underwear," she said, implying that he was gay. Furthermore, he was not Dutch, or Christian Reformed, and it did not help that he was short compared to the 6'4" men in our family. But none of that mattered for Mary. The parochial trap that was our Dutch community had been sprung, its cage door opened. She had found her voice, had a partner, and she was free. She moved to Chicago.

PETER'S THREE-BEDROOM APARTMENT in Chicago's Old Town had been made available to visiting protesters during the convention. It remained open for some who stayed on, still cluttered with mattresses on the floor, where a stray cat named Elvis lounged about. Mary and her friends stayed there with Peter. She landed a job in the art section of the University Book Exchange on Wabash Street, a perfect job for a talented artist.

Only a few months later, Mary and Peter left Chicago, moving 50 miles north to a small commuter town near Crystal Lake, Illinois. They could see the lake from their cozy, two-bedroom rental house. Open fields around the house afforded them privacy in their hippie lifestyle. Sharing the rent with another couple, they were still somewhat crowded, but at least there was room to decompress outdoors. After tiring of her train commute to work, Mary soon quit her bookstore job, and Peter became the breadwinner by stocking shelves in a local grocery store. They were "dropping out."

Street drugs, political protest, and communal sharing became the new norm. Mary and Peter were appreciated for their hospitality as friends, and even stray hitchhikers, were welcomed to their little house. Peter played guitar and sang, while Mary cooked for everyone. She was content to draw and paint, often using social justice themes. However, only our brother Steve was aware of their new lifestyle after visiting them there several times. Given our strict upbringing, Mary did not want our mother to know about her new living situation. Cohabitation between the sexes was still shameful, and of course, according to our church, an egregious sin.

Despite living with others, Mary was lonely after precipitously leaving family and friends back home. She philosophized in letters to friends, wondering what life was all about. Perhaps she should return to college? At other times she called herself "lazy and dumb." The harmful legacy of being placed in her 7th grade's "slow class" seemed to stick, for she was neither lazy nor unintelligent. She even mentioned suicide in one letter, but then rejected the idea, believing that she was here to help out in the world.

In another letter to a friend, she described our brother Steve as a good listener, and said that she needed one. Leaving home to land in a street-drug culture without a bottom or guardrails was unsettling. Now uprooted, she struggled to find her bearings. Smoking pot and taking LSD did not help. A potent drug, LSD affects the brain, emotions, mood, and perceptions. Its long-term effects could include anxiety, depression, flashbacks, and for some, serious disability. Its therapeutic effects had not yet been scientifically explored, although many of its users made great claims about its benefits.

Adding to the dizzying rate of change in her life, Mary was now in love. She could hardly believe it. Perhaps downplaying it, she wrote to her friend Barb that, "…well I guess I love him cause I get butterflies in my stomach." In other letters she writes more seriously about her surprisingly deep love for Peter.

The new couple did not stay in Crystal Lake for long. Cut loose from both college and family moorings, Mary headed for California with Peter. Apart from its new mystique as a hippie mecca, the state may also have felt familiar from our family's time there. Whatever the reason, the two idealists wanted breathing room, and the West Coast promised exactly that, as well as a freer lifestyle. Mary's pet cat Oogie was sent howling in the trunk of our mother's car, headed for a new home.

Mary and Peter landed in beautiful Santa Barbara, with its Mediterranean climate and spectacular coastline. As an enclave for the rich and quietly famous, it was also known for its art festivals. From their cozy rental house near the ocean, Mary and Peter could walk to the public beach near the end of their street. Peter took a job working for the Post Office, while Mary tried selling her artwork.

I visited her there in December 1969, spending only an hour or so during a quick trip west on my Christmas break from graduate school. Peter's mother, Margaret, was also visiting at the time. Peter was at work, so it was just the three of us, and a friendly cat. Mary rarely lived without cats if she could help it, and Margaret cuddled one of hers under her neck as we chatted.

The English-born Margaret Wotherspoon still spoke with a clipped British accent despite her many years in Chile and Pennsylvania. Had I known that she had worked in British Intelligence during World War II, I would have been even more frustrated with the short time of my visit. Peter's father had been a pilot with the Royal Air Force and Margaret was his "war bride." So, our mother had been right: Peter was definitely not "our kind." It was refreshing. I thought there would be plenty of time to get to know him and his mother in the years to come.

While in Santa Barbara, Mary kept up her correspondence with Sue. In those letters, she encourages Sue to work through her difficult marriage, but she also writes about her ongoing search for the meaning of life. She describes this quest while venturing deeper into the hippie drug-culture. She sent Sue a list of the street drugs that she and Peter were using: psilocybin, mescaline, acid [LSD] and pot. Mary writes about feeling at one with the universe, declaring that "We are all one in God."

MEANWHILE, DURING THAT same 1969–70 academic year, pandemonium reigned on many university campuses, as it did on mine. My oldest and best friend, Valerie, and I lived together on the Ann Arbor campus, where she was a nurse at the C.S. Mott Children's Hospital and I was a graduate student at the University of Michigan. But for me, far more was happening outside the classroom than in.

That fall, Valerie and I had taken an overnight bus to Washington, D.C., to protest the Vietnam War. Ours was among hundreds of buses crowding the highways into the capital, depositing half a million of us eager, if groggy, protesters. Once there, we were tear-gassed and entertained by rock bands, and lost even more sleep. It was exhilarating to be surrounded by so many of "us," even though we were ignored by the White House.

While "marching" in a crowd so dense that smokers held their cigarettes vertically, I rarely knew where we were, or where we were going. It did not matter. We had acted instead of just watching others do so on TV. We slept on a church basement floor, where our valuables were stolen, and we left town the next day tired and hungry. On the return trip to Ann Arbor, Valerie stood next to the bus driver to keep him awake; he had not slept the previous night. This kindness was typical of her, and we returned safely to Ann Arbor, feeling empowered and ready for more. Lots more.

Protests wracked the campus. An activist burst into my art history class, flashed the lights off and on, and shouted for the class to disperse. Then the Black Action Movement (BAM) shut the campus down for a week. Students took over the administration building, and the ROTC building was burned. There were even mini-sidewalk protests to "Free John Sinclair," a local hero jailed for using recreational, but still illegal, drugs. I never knew graduate school could be so much fun.

Mary surprised me that March with a short visit to Ann Arbor, after flying home for a few days. Even though we had not always been that close at home, her impromptu visit now felt natural and good. She had become a California hippie, the ultimate cool at the time. And pot was so widespread on our campus by then, it seemed all I had to do was inhale while walking to class. It was our new, but naughty, normal.

In that atmosphere, when Mary commented that drugs enabled us to "walk through walls," I agreed, although I had not walked through any myself. I was too embarrassed to reveal my ignorance of her hip lifestyle. I was trying to shed my cloistered past while somehow still getting to my classes. Many of my fellow students seemed to be majoring in Ann Arbor's scene of drug-induced "enlightenment" and experimentation. And Mary, sophisticated and cool, felt way ahead of me on that score.

Some of her old friends were now students there, too, living just a few blocks from my apartment. After visiting me, she stopped to see them, but none of us, including Mary, knew at the time that Mary was pregnant. She had not experienced the normal symptoms of pregnancy, and it would take an X-ray to discover the reason for her swelling abdomen. She and Peter then married on April 19, 1970, shortly after I had seen her. Marriage, with a baby on the way, would seem to change everything for them, but not in ways we expected.

Despite the distance, Mary and our brother Steve remained close. Early that following summer, he flew to Santa Barbara to visit her. But she was not home; she was in the hospital recovering from a bad acid trip, during which she hallucinated that she was dying. After Peter brought her home, she appeared to be herself again, much to Steve's relief. He believed that this bad experience marked the end of the couple's interest in drugs. And by now, he knew Peter far better than the rest of us, describing him as "the nicest person you will ever meet." Steve also believed that Peter "worshipped the ground Mary walked on," and Steve loved both of them.

WHEN SHE WAS born on November 7, 1970, there were no relatives around to coo over baby Mary Margaret, named after her two grandmothers. A few months later, our sister, Marcia, her husband Frank, and their young family, visited Mary and Peter in Santa Barbara. The family had driven down from Ukiah, north of San Francisco, where Frank's relatives, the Cordell family, lived. The Cordells had relocated from the Midwest, along with their church in Indiana.

As a biology teacher and early environmentalist, Frank admired the organic farm gardens kept by the Cordells' church, which bore the strange name of Peoples Temple — without an apostrophe. Frank and Marcia also attended a church service with the Cordells. Marcia did not care for their minister's preaching, but Frank, an atheist, was impressed by the church's community outreach. To him, its care facilities for orphans, the aged, and even abandoned animals, seemed remarkable.

When Frank raved about this unusual church community while visiting Mary and Peter, it piqued Peter's interest. Back in Pennsylvania, he and his parents had been active in their Presbyterian church. Owing to that, and perhaps a lingering sense of uprootedness, Peter accompanied Frank back to Ukiah. He wanted to check out Peoples Temple for himself. Marcia stayed behind with Mary. As it happened, Peter's van broke down in Ukiah, so the two men stayed with the Cordells for a few days. Rick Cordell, a mechanic, kindly repaired the van. By then, Peter had seen enough of the Peoples Temple church community to convince him that this was the place for his own little family.

Mary may have been struggling with postpartum depression at the time. In a letter to Sue, she mentions that she had been "sick lately," and seemed to be quite miserable. Without support or treatment, mothers in that era suffered through postpartum depression on their own. Our family back home had no idea that Mary was unwell. The distance between her and us was measured not only by miles, but by three time zones. Without the internet, cell phones, or universal phone coverage, keeping in touch was difficult. Our phone calls were short, and often made during off hours, like late at night, when long-distance rates were lower.

After feeling marooned in a strange state with no family close by, Mary probably needed little convincing from Peter to move north. A caring church community sounded good. When her baby was just three months old, Mary wrote again to Sue, saying they were "half-way" moved already. Then, a few weeks later, she mentioned that they were "very busy moving and searching."

Apparently, Mary was still struggling, questioning the meaning of life and her place in it.

In an undated letter, probably written soon after moving north to Redwood Valley, a rural community near Ukiah, Mary wrote:

There are so many rotten people in the world — I'm afraid they are making me rotten too.

I'm searching, desperately, for a concrete knowledge of God which I can hold on to, which will bring me above the bad things around me. I'm afraid that life will crack me up before I find what I am looking for. I want to be happy and make others happy. Just when I think I've [had] such bad luck, I see someone who is worse off than me. I wonder about my values of good and bad and why I am failure oriented. Why [do] I take good for granted and magnify the bad? Why do I create bad anyway. The things I worry about have no value. I'm in a rut. Gotta let off steam.

She also mentions a recent visit to San Francisco, where they stayed on Haight Street, the birthplace of the counterculture movement, but she describes it as "dead." She adds that she wishes she had the money to travel, and ends with: "Forgive my depressing letter, it's all I am right now."

IN JUNE OF that same year, 1971, I visited Mary again. My fiancé, David, and I stayed with Mary and Peter for about a week, never suspecting our visit would completely upend the rest of our travel plans. Mary seemed like herself again, but as a new mother with responsibilities, she was understandably a bit more serious. She and Peter were living in a quirky little cottage with a sloping front porch, and a front yard abutting the gravel parking lot of a small country store.

Baby Mary Margaret was now eight months old, and she was sitting in a playpen on their porch when we arrived. I immediately hopped out of the car and scooped her right into my arms before we even saw Mary, who was indoors, expecting us. That little girl filled our first few hours together. I fussed over her, with her big, bright eyes, shining in happy wonder as she studied me in turn.

Children rarely interested me back then, but "Baby New," as they called her, did. She was a sparkling little soul wrapped in diapers, and I could not help adoring her. With her spirited gaze, she seemed eager to see everything. And despite having numerous nieces and nephews, I had never encountered a baby quite like Baby New. Peter said that whenever they took her anywhere, they had to leave early due to all the fuss she received, even from strangers. She was that cute.

Peter was working once again for the Post Office, and was not home when we arrived, but Mary had skipped work, anticipating our arrival. Normally, she would be cleaning motel rooms, which troubled me, but she seemed fine with it. She could take the baby along while working on her own, and Mary Margaret was an easy little armful.

Clearly in the way, David and I camped out on the floor of their little house, yet we were warmly welcomed. Taking yet another day off from work, Mary then treated us to a day trip to Mendocino, a coastal village on the Pacific coast west of Redwood Valley. It was slow going, winding our way through the hilly terrain of redwood forests. We became increasingly awed by the soaring green canopy overhead; it felt more like a cathedral. Then, when the trees gave way to a panoramic vista of the Pacific Ocean, we were hit by another wave of awe.

Once a fishing community, historic Mendocino was now home to artists, hippies, and salty locals. Whales that were once hunted here were now protected during their coastal migrations. And what a coast! Its jagged headlands loomed over roaring surf, nothing like the soft sand dunes of our Lake Michigan shoreline. The white clapboard houses gracing this small village featuring a weathered, wooden water tower and storefronts were an enchantment. My Frisian "water genes" were now fully awakened, as no doubt Mary's were too. We were both drawn to water, and the waters here were magnificent.

David and I were gobsmacked by this stunning landscape, and we would have missed it completely without Mary. California, for me, had been mostly palm trees and Disneyland. Now, here was my younger sister, so grown up in her astonishingly beautiful new "neighborhood." The last time she and I had been in a car together, she was a college student, and I was dropping her off at a friend's apartment. This new Mary was a mature, hardworking wife and mother with serious responsibilities; I felt like the younger sister now. And on top of that, she had another family, too — her "church" family.

Mary, age 1, 1950. Family photo

Mary, age 4. Family photo

The "leftover" kids, 1957. Family photo

Mary, elementary school. Family photo

Mary, high school, 1967. Family photo

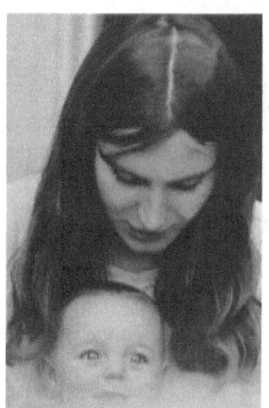

Mary, Mary Margaret, 1971. Family photo

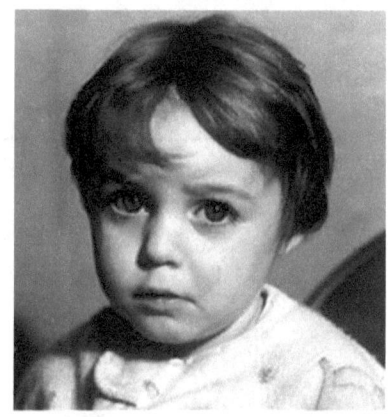

Mary Margaret, age 2. California Historical Society photo

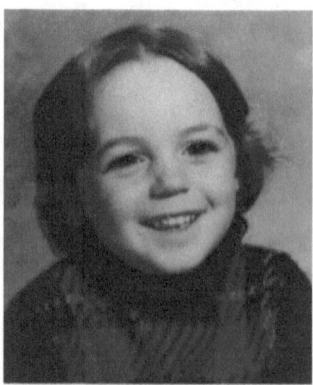

Mary Margaret. Family photo

Peter Wotherspoon, 1977. California Historical Society photo

PART II

TRANSPLANTED

CHAPTER 6

A TEMPLE IN THE VALLEY

REDWOOD VALLEY LOOKED LIKE A BACKROAD PARADISE, WITH ITS NEATLY COMBED ROWS OF GRAPEVINES FLOWING OVER GENTLE HILLS, CULTIVATING AN ORDERLY PEACE. But it wasn't the landscape that had captured Mary and Peter — it was their new church. Why would Mary join a church? This was hard for me to understand. I thought we had finally escaped churches, nasty ministers, and mean people.

As guests wanting to be good sports, however, David and I attended a fundraiser at Mary's new church. It was a pancake breakfast, and a surprise from beginning to end. There were no hippies like Mary and Peter in the mix. Instead, normal, everyday people and professionals — an attorney, an engineer, teachers, and others — welcomed us. Our repressive religious upbringing had cured me of any interest in traditional churches by then, but we would soon learn that Peoples Temple was anything but. They were flipping and serving their pancakes with obvious joy.

Staying in deferential guest mode, we also attended a Sunday morning church service. Mary suggested that we sit in the back of the church because services could last up to six hours. This alone was shocking, but we took her advice, sitting on folding chairs near the back. There were perhaps 500 other worshippers, and no wooden pews in sight. On our way into the sanctuary, I noticed a rather fetid-looking indoor swimming pool. In its former life, it was located in her minister's front yard, hand-built by his family. But now as part of the church, it stood enclosed and looking a bit forlorn. I wondered if it was used for baptisms — had Mary somehow become a Baptist? What kind of church was this, anyway? The sanctuary itself was rather unusual, too, resembling an auditorium or former gymnasium, with a low vaulted ceiling and high windows.

The singing and music that opened the service was lively but familiar; what followed was not. After singing, we remained standing. A palpable air of expectancy climaxed as her minister made a dramatic entrance like a celebrity or mafia don. Wearing a robe and dark, aviator-style sunglasses, Reverend Jim Jones then took his place on the dais. He was not alone. An entourage of what appeared to be church elders, or bodyguards, accompanied him. They wore dark suits, and stood behind him at a careful distance, impressive but creepy.

After we sat down, Jones began the service with "inspirational healings." We watched as he called out one member by name, asking him to stand up. He then gently shamed the man for smoking, and named the cigarette brand in the hapless man's chest pocket. The audience gasped at Jones's seeming clairvoyance, and then clapped after Jones announced that he was now curing the man of any cancer that might be harming him. Next, he called an older woman up to the stage and ran his hands over her, producing what looked like guts for the audience to see. Another cancer healed! The congregation remained spellbound in their uncomfortable folding chairs. David and I were uncomfortable, too, but it was not just our seats. In deference to Mary and Peter, however, we stayed put after the ridiculous show.

Next, another member stood up to ask Jones if it was OK to take the Silva Mind Control Method, a popular, if pricey, self-help program at the time. Hearing a member ask Jones's permission for something like that shocked us, even more so when Jones came down on him hard. He scolded the bewildered man, saying he had no business taking the course, and that it was a selfish waste of money. Afterward, Jones launched into an object lesson on reincarnation, which apparently was part of the church's belief system.

Jones warned that it was safest to be ignorant of past incarnations. To illustrate his point, he claimed that he had once healed someone from a past life; the wretched man had recited whole pages from

Hitler's book *Mein Kampf* from memory. Jones's inference was that the unfortunate man had been Hitler in a former life. Now thoroughly rebuked, the member asking for permission sat down. Unbeknownst to us at the time, Jones must have seen Silva Mind Control as a competitor to his own special brand of "Infinite Mind" for dealing with the supernatural. Even without knowing this, we found the whole interaction troubling.

Finally, it was time for Jones to preach. And preach he did, although he seemed to ramble. David and I were used to being sedated by neat, three-point sermons that lasted perhaps twenty minutes but felt like an hour. In view of that, Jones's ultimate message of social justice and caring for the poor was refreshing, especially when compared to our familiar doctrinal themes of original sin and total depravity.

Reverend Jones apparently aligned himself with Jesus's ministry to the forgotten; his church's laudable outreach to the aged, the discarded, and the poor, seemed to confirm that. But this activist Christian ministry seemed to collide with Jones's weird, and even grandiose behavior and claims. His theology felt like fair game for criticism, but we were put off by his showy "miracles." As recent graduates of a strictly Calvinist college, we had been marinated in Christian theology for years.

When the sermon ended, Reverend Jones invited the audience to participate in a question-and-answer period. This unusual preacher's willingness to be challenged in this manner was completely unexpected, and despite the fact that we were only visitors, David stood up to do just that. For perhaps thirty minutes, he proceeded to question Jim Jones while I remained seated next to him, transfixed.

At one point when the congregation grew restless, Jones roundly rebuked them. He scolded his flock by saying that David was asking important questions, and they needed to pay attention. After that, the floor belonged to the two of them. I do not remember Jones's responses to David's questions, or even the questions themselves. It was the interchange itself that riveted me. After David finally sat down, we were both exhausted, and quietly slipped out, confused, yet strangely excited. Jones had skillfully parried every one of David's challenges.

This unorthodox church's appeal only intensified as we learned more about its outreach in the area. Who would not admire a church that kept a barnyard for abandoned animals, provided bus trips for seniors, and funded dormitories for college students, sometimes even paying their tuition? Their ministries also included a youth center, food assistance, and support for recovering drug addicts. As Jones reminded his followers, his church was doing everything that the New Testament asked of believers, but what the churches that we knew conveniently ignored.

During our visit, it was obvious that Mary no longer used recreational drugs. No shared joints were passed around, as was still common at the time. This clear-headed Mary was fully present. So perhaps this new church was good for her. Yet at the same time, we were unaware that her church required 25% of members' incomes, and that it had to approve any vacations members might take—that is, if they could afford them after parting with so much of their income.

Later, when Mary and I were in her kitchen, she cooked while I held Baby New. Mary talked about their church, casually describing one of its practices which seemed odd, even for California's hardcore counterculture. She mentioned its White Night drills, when members pretended to drink poison and then die. As she spoke, I pictured people dressed like white knights, as in the KKK. Her church drills were also held during night, like the Klan. Drinking fake poison sounded like a weird fraternity initiation, or hazing ritual, to me. She talked as if the practice were no big deal, so I didn't think much of it at the time, either. It was her church's belief in reincarnation that floored me.

When I asked her about it, I tried to listen with an open mind. Eastern religions and reincarnation were popular at the time, and books by spiritualist Edgar Cayce, who espoused them, were even being sold in drugstores. Furthermore, our own Christian Bible exhorted, "Ye must be born again..." in John 3:7. Perhaps this held a hidden meaning. In addition, Christianity promised an afterlife of heaven or hell: I wondered if reincarnation could somehow be a variant of that. It all seemed somewhat fantastical, but perhaps only because it had not been taught in our traditional, conservative church.

Nevertheless, I had to wonder: had the psychedelic drugs from Mary's past been so "mind-bending" that they somehow made reincarnation make sense to her? After all, she once talked to me about walking through walls in Ann Arbor. Whatever the case, Mary was surprisingly sure of herself in her new church, so perhaps there was hidden value in it for her. I did not see the value, but I didn't challenge her, either.

Back at her church's breakfast fundraiser, an elegant elderly woman had invited David and me to visit her. She wanted to tell us more about Peoples Temple. We were not interested at the time, but after hearing Jones preach, we decided to pay her a visit. As we sat among her polished furnishings and expensive adornments, we soon realized there was no room for any questions. Totally enamored with the Temple, and Jim Jones himself, she declared her theology to be, "Beauty is truth, truth is beauty." She proudly volunteered that her house was now owned by the church because she had donated it to them.

It was obvious that by inviting us, she just wanted an audience, yet it would have been churlish for us to challenge her beliefs outright. Our questions about Jones's "miracle healings," six-hour services, and the rest of his quasi-religious trappings, were left hanging. We left her still feeling unsettled and confused.

It would have been far better to talk with Peter, but he was either at work, or staying in the background with the baby, allowing Mary and me time together. Peter was my age, disarmingly handsome, and obviously intelligent, but for now, I wanted to spend more time with my busy sister. To that end, she and I went to a laundromat together, doing laundry, and hanging out, just chatting, catching up on news from home — nothing heavy.

It was difficult to depart from this little family, but there would be plenty of time later to get to know Peter better and, of course, to enjoy more of Baby New. They might even move back to Michigan after their California adventure. I felt a little better about departing after leaving money for a proper crib for Mary Margaret. She had been sleeping in her playpen, and I wanted her to be safe.

By now, both of us were so disoriented by our experience with Peoples Temple that the rest of our travel plans felt frivolous. We forgot all about Mexico and cut our trip short. I, for one, needed to sort out the theological mind-bending we had just endured. Once home again, I asked a friend in seminary for his recommendation for the best, most current Bible translation. Then I bought the Jerusalem Bible, marking every passage possibly pertaining to reincarnation, searching for clues. I also picked up some paperbacks by Edgar Cayce.

Even so, when David and I tried to explain our experience with Jim Jones to our friends, we couldn't. We did not fully understand it ourselves. For the remainder of the summer, I taught art in a city park and worked on a presidential campaign, and then it was back to work in the fall. I taught art to 492 inner-city middle schoolers. Our school building had its own cop, and locked its doors after the final bell in the morning. I was busy. I left Jim Jones and reincarnation behind. For now.

IN THE FOLLOWING year, 1973, Mary and Peter moved ten miles south to the city of Ukiah, closer to San Francisco. Writing from Ukiah, Mary confessed to her friend Sue that she was "searching desperately for a concrete knowledge of God which I can hold on to, which will bring me above the bad things around me." And this: "I want to be happy and make others happy." Then, "Use your tongue for those who cannot talk," which she scribbled on pastel stationery above the main body of the following letter. In it, she continued:

> I struggle to bring us together again. You — someplace else, in another time. I have started many times — but this time I will finish. Something inside wants to come out. When a fight begins within himself, a man is worth something. I can no longer see the beauty in a flower for the tears of pain in my brothers' eyes. Dream? Yes of peace. And passive has turned to active. Have been blind too long. Someone, something has opened my eyes — my brain…. I saw a Vietnamese woman crying…carrying the bloody, crushed body of her baby and I [cried] because I am was white-middle class America. They killed Jesus for being a savior. (I probably threw the first stone.) They have killed every fighter for freedom…while we remained ignorant.
>
> GOD DAM[N] IGNORANT!!

There is too much pain Sue I'm crying while I'm writing this. Does your heart still speak Sue? As long as there is any form of slavery — I consider myself a slave. As long as people are kept poor — I myself will be poor. As long as there is the racist title Black I will be Black until....

I am the "lowest" as long as the degrees exist.

From there, I begin.

These were shocking sentiments. Who was speaking? Certainly not the gentle Mary I knew. Nor was this the quietly determined teenager who changed high schools, or the brave young woman protesting in Chicago. It did not sound like the responsible new mother I visited in Redwood Valley, either. I believe she was channeling Jim Jones, who for Mary, would soon embody the "concrete" knowledge of the God she was searching for.

As children, she and I learned from the Bible that our best works were but "filthy rags" in the sight of God. Plus, our shame-based Calvinist doctrines declared us to be "totally depraved." Obviously, Jim Jones was yet another master driving this bad news home, and Mary had gotten the message: "People are no damn good." Even so, her horrifying letter to Sue suggests an alarming change, one our family never heard about. We had no idea she believed that "I am the 'lowest' as long as the degrees exist."

My little sister was now carrying the world's suffering on her shoulders, while my only burden that summer was my backpack as I roamed across Europe. The postcards I sent her must have felt completely frivolous compared to the load of guilt and anguish she had assumed.

It MAY BE that Mary recovered from her hidden torment by putting her beliefs into action. In Ukiah, she took charge of one of the church's care homes for the elderly, who, in exchange for all their assets, were promised lifelong care from the church. The church owned several of these eldercare homes. Income garnered from the residents' Social

Security checks would become a major source of revenue for Peoples Temple as it "ministered" to the needy.

While Jones's church was growing financially, he was evolving theologically. His theological shift from orthodoxy to complete atheism can be documented in his sermons, as well as private conversations with other preachers. Starting out as a minister affiliated with The Disciples of Christ denomination, he later began to strike out on his own. His espousal of socialism marked the beginning of these changes. He used the book of Acts, verse 4:32, from the Christian New Testament as a foundation. "The multitude of believers was one in heart and soul. No one claimed that any of his possessions was his own, but they shared everything they owned."

His biblically based form of socialism remained a theological underpinning for some years, followed by far greater changes later. In time, he would claim to be a religious prophet, and then, in an alarming break from reality, the second incarnation of God. He would even claim to be God — a complete apostasy. It may also have signaled long-hidden, but "normalized," mental health issues.

Nevertheless, Jones strategically used biblical references to bolster his prophet-savior-God status. As a brilliant orator, he also employed the same religious trope that Mary and I had grown up with: We were to "be in the world, but not of the world." In keeping with Jesus's message of social justice and caring for the poor, Jones regularly excoriated the evils of capitalism, too. At the same time, he demonstrated a good head for business. Apparently, Mary's new minister played it both ways.

On one hand, he increased church revenues by setting up local businesses, like the laundromat and printing press, and also by investing in property. On the other, he encouraged socialism by having some members live together in church-owned housing, thereby reducing expenses. In fact, as a church employee running an eldercare home, Mary would have no personal income at all: just $2 a week for spending money. Her food and shelter were provided by the church, while Mary Margaret was looked after in the church's childcare center.

Communal sharing within the church became the new norm; private property was considered selfish, including home ownership. After Peter's mother bought Peter and Mary a house in Ukiah, they turned around and donated it to the church. Eventually, some thirty individual properties in Mendocino County would be donated to the Peoples Church.

Meanwhile, Jones used his oratorical prowess to tout self-denial to achieve the church's socialist ideals, claiming that he only owned one pair of shoes. New clothes and jewelry were regarded as self-indulgent; consequently, many members began wearing and trading used clothes. This may explain why Mary would later show up during a visit home looking surprisingly shabby. Her old friend, Sue, who saw her then, noted, "The beautiful girl who loved clothes and makeup was dowdy and looked like a missionary."

PRACTICING A HARDCORE socialist lifestyle was difficult enough, but the hardships for church members did not end there. Numerous bus trips to church services and revival meetings were made throughout California and across the country. They were often grueling.

Every other weekend, Mary rode the church buses to Temple services in Los Angeles, a 1,000-mile, round-trip ordeal from Ukiah and back. Jones acquired a fleet of eleven former Greyhound buses. Built to seat passengers in rows of four, these were now packed with six, or more passengers squeezed across. The weekend trips took eight hours each way, and Mary often made them with Mary Margaret sitting on her lap, which was better than having her strapped overhead in the luggage rack. Some passengers sat in the aisles, while still others reportedly rode underneath the bus in the luggage compartments. It was exhausting. After these trips, children starting school again on Monday mornings would sometimes fall asleep at their desks.

The church's cross-country trips could be even worse, and we know that Mary had endured them at least twice. The first one in 1972 was labeled as a vacation, and its riders were charged $200 for it. But it was not a vacation. Passengers were hungry much of the time. One Temple member described the food en route as abysmal: lunches made from large cans of tuna and dry bread. Mary was not on that trip, but she was on another one when the hungry travelers consumed yogurt spilled from a Dannon truck accident.

Adding to the misery, the overflowing bus toilets were disgusting; standing in long lines at public rest stops was equally uncomfortable. And how did Mary Margaret endure being strapped into the luggage racks with other children on long trips? How did Mary tolerate having her up there? My sister's obvious grit and determination must have seen her through. Meanwhile, my life on Lake Michigan must have looked like a vacation next to hers. And it was.

Still, she must have known that Jim Jones's private quarters in the bus caravans were similar to Air Force One. His bus had curtains, a bed, bathroom, air conditioning, and other creature comforts. Fearing bombs or harmful airwaves that could attack him while on the road, Jones had special steel reinforcements installed on his personal rolling fortress. It reportedly carried weapons, including a rifle, shotgun, and pistol. Those who rode with him there had special status — family, staff, security, and mistresses.

These rolling Temple revivals were not vacations. They were work. During stopovers, passengers worked at staffing the meetings, handling the crowds, distributing brochures, taking names at the door, and, of course, passing the collection plates. And Jones often chose impoverished Black neighborhoods for these events. People in need were more likely to be attracted to his promise of a better life. As a result, local accommodations for the bus riders were often spartan. Jones was notoriously cheap; instead of using hotels, he often exploited local hospitality for sleeping arrangements in private homes. Some members slept on a bus, others on church or gymnasium floors, and their occasional showers were a rare luxury.

They covered a lot of ground: the Deep South, New York, Philadelphia, and the Midwest, including Chicago and Detroit. It must have taken a lot of self-denial and humility to travel as they did, but saving money was paramount in penny-pinching Jones's tightly managed world.

RETURNING TO HER farmgirl roots, our mother bought an old farm and remodeled the farmhouse herself. Living close to Marcia's rural homestead made it easier to help Marcia as the sequelae from her brain tumor continued to dog her. In fact, everything about Marcia's life was now more difficult, and with two growing children, she struggled. There was turbulence elsewhere in the family as well.

Our brother Steve was now bouncing between jobs and hospitalizations, afflicted with worsening bouts of a mental illness. Our other brothers were busy supporting their growing families, and I would change addresses three times in early 1973. Busy living our separate lives, we were unaware of the worrisome changes in Mary, or her deepening involvement with the Temple. Then I went to see her again in July.

After a long engagement to be married ended, my life felt like that compost pile with its dead kittens at my grandfathers' farm. But at least I was free. I thought moving to California myself now sounded like a good idea. That state still represented the ultimate getaway, easy living, and, if nothing else, another chance. I could start out at Mary's new place in Ukiah, and then find work in beautiful Mendocino: surely, they needed unemployed art teachers there. So, with wishful thinking overriding common sense, I ditched my miserable teaching job, and bought an old travel van for the move.

But as it turned out, by the time I finally left for the West Coast, my plans had changed once again. I had not expected it, but there it was: I was in love. Some might have said "crazy" in love, but a former acquaintance had knocked me off my feet. We planned to marry. In spite of this new turn, I was still committed to visit Mary in Ukiah. After that, I would simply fly back to Michigan.

The road west to her felt liberating, and the route, surprisingly easy: first Chicago, then head west. I drove Interstate 80 all the way with the miles just slipping by: apparently marijuana could be good for travel, too. I had three riders paying for the gas, and we got along well, camping along the way. The first night we simply pulled off the road somewhere in Iowa and slept in an open field. The next day in Cheyenne, Wyoming, I bought cowboy boots at a sidewalk sale, but I seemed to be the only one who thought they were a bargain. Nevertheless, I enjoyed feeling like a cowgirl as we slept on the banks of the Green River that night.

Our next stop at Lake Tahoe convinced us to stick around for an extra day, soaking up its alpine beauty. The campground there was sublime, although jarringly juxtaposed to casinos a short distance away. After I lost 50 cents at one of them, even its famously cheap eats could not keep me there. All that neon bling could not compete with the fragrant pines at the campground. From there, it was only a short day's ride to the end of the trail: California.

After a brief stay in Mill Valley where I dropped off my riders, I headed 80 miles north to Ukiah. Feeling rather forlorn now on my own, I was comforted to know that Mary was at the end of the road. She felt like home.

Pulling into her driveway on that Monday morning, I noticed that her house in Ukiah was far better than the one in Redwood Valley. It stood on the scenic, but dry, Russian River. Mary had slept in, only waking up for my arrival. Realizing this, I regretted my intrusion, but I was so glad to see her that I did not ask why she was so tired. In hindsight, she was probably exhausted after her church's weekend commute to Los Angeles. She never said. She looked as if she needed more rest, but insisted that she was OK.

Little Mary Margaret, now almost three and still amazingly adorable, shied away when she first saw me. I was a stranger, so I held back, not wanting to scare her. But a bit later as Mary and I chatted, that bright-eyed little imp kept sidling closer to us with a mischievous look. We were sitting near an ornate desk, which was forbidden territory for her; she wanted to open its drawers. A quiet power struggle ensued between her and Mary, and I was surprised by how strict a parent my easygoing sister had become. Mary Margaret may have been named after both of her grandmothers, but she had inherited her own mother's stubborn streak. Adoring this little child once again, I was secretly rooting for her to win. Looking back, I wished I had just snuggled her onto my lap and made her laugh. But this visit felt different, and somehow, I felt like an outsider, unsure of my boundaries.

I was hoping that Mary and I could spend some time together as before, never suspecting how unrealistic and perhaps even selfish that hope had become. She and Peter worked full-time, but doing exactly what was unclear. Peoples Temple seemed to fill their lives, and I did not feel comfortable even asking about it. A strange new tension seemed to have taken root between us. During my last visit, they had been a warm, easygoing little family, but no longer. And the change was evident right from the start. Their lives felt mysteriously walled off, and though Mary was kind enough to tolerate my visit, I felt more like a houseguest than a sister.

Their new house was quite elegant, a surprise given how down-to-earth Mary was. It was also immaculate in an unlived-in way. There was no clutter. Its dated décor was from a different era, looking nothing like Mary and Peter, or at least my idea of them. At the time, I never suspected that it had probably been donated to the church. The expensive furniture looked more like that of a wealthy and perhaps elderly member. Some of Mary and Peter's artwork was visible, lending it a more personal touch. Peter's intricate macramé sculpture hanging in an enclosed porch was quite stunning. And there were musical instruments on the porch, too — did Peter still play and sing? He and Mary were both so talented, it was comforting to think they still had time to create. Or did they?

As Mary and I visited, I seemed to generate most of the conversation. But at one point, I felt comfortable enough to ask Mary what she used for birth control. I was having a hard time tolerating the pill, and due to our shared genes, I wondered if she had the same problem. However, she evaded my question, instead volunteering that Jim Jones had "cured" her molestation trauma from when we were kids — back when we were told to forget about it. Now as she spoke, I pictured her counseling sessions: Reverend Jones would be sitting at his desk, speaking kindly with Mary. As I would later learn, her predator-pastor's counseling sessions were probably quite different. He might have "healed" Mary just as he had other young, white, attractive church members by having sex with them. Repeatedly.

After telling me about Jones's "healing," Mary went on to say that he had also saved her family from certain death. A particular semi-truck, he warned, would be barreling down a mountain highway, and they needed to watch out for it while on the road. And sure enough, they had seen that particular semi-truck, but because of Jones's "intervention," it had not killed them. This story was bizarre in every way, yet questions felt off-limits. Did I challenge her trust in him? Point out the absurdities? I did not risk it. She was too guarded.

In addition, she and I were still running from our shared childhood, just now learning who we were as adults. Considering that, was it so terrible to have unshakable faith in your pastor? Still, I never imagined it would be the Reverend Jim Jones, and not a semi-truck, that would deliver her and her family to their deaths.

Later that day, Peter arrived from whatever work he did. Chatting amiably as he folded laundry, he talked about JFK's assassination. It was a safe topic, one that Jones, himself, reportedly fixated on. Peter seemed more at ease than Mary, but I was even less inclined to ask my new brother-in-law questions about himself — about his family, his past, his work, their church. Where did he grow up, did he have siblings? Natural questions like these felt oddly out of bounds now. Yet when he played his guitar and sang the John Lennon anthem, "Imagine," for me, I thought the lyrics described what little I did know of Peter: gentleness and kindness.

Even later, I was taken aback when Mary said they needed permission from Jim Jones to go out for dinner with me. I had wanted to treat them, thanking them for their hospitality. Jones allowed the dinner with the stipulation that it was at a restaurant he approved. Who would have thought eating at a restaurant was "elitist" or non-socialist behavior? Apparently, Jim Jones. And why did they need his permission? I did not ask, just grateful instead for their time, as I was feeling more and more like an intruder into their busy lives.

We went to a small Italian restaurant with red-checkered tablecloths, a cozy spot for relaxing conversation. There was much we could have shared over dinner: news about family back home, and their lives, their work, their interests. But we didn't. There was no give-and-take, and neither of them seemed at ease. I felt more comfortable focusing on little Mary Margaret in her high chair. With her playful brightness, she added some relief to the disappointingly awkward evening.

At one time, our family was told that Peter would be attending medical school in Mexico. Fluent in Spanish from his Chilean background, he would be sponsored by the church. Considering the Temple's humanitarian outreach, it made sense. A doctor would add value to its mission. It also meshed with Jones's claim to work "hand in hand" with medical science. It would have been a good time to ask about medical school over dinner now, but they didn't mention it, so I didn't either.

Nor did I ever suspect that Jim Jones split up some families. Sex between married couples was discouraged, as was even living together in the same house. Too much family involvement could undermine the church's unity and greater cause. If so, was having dinner together risky for Mary and Peter that night? And was spending time with family members like me, whom Jones considered "misinformed bigots," a further transgression? The only thing I felt at the time was that it was not my place to push, to question, to challenge. I felt strangely distanced from these dear people, without understanding why. It was a good thing I would be leaving the next day.

I left Mary my old van, which she accepted as a donation to the church, not her. It would be risky for me to make another cross-country drive with it, especially alone. So, I drove it one last time to the airport for my flight home, but once in San Francisco, Mary wisely offered to take the wheel. The tired old van and I were struggling to negotiate the city's traffic and steep hills, but Mary surprised me by expertly shifting gears up and down them like a pro. She obviously knew her way around San Francisco, but I never wondered why and she never explained.

I kept seeing my grown-up sister in new ways, and finally, through tears. While parting at the airport, she quietly handed me Peter's exquisite macramé sculpture, the one I had admired on their porch. Also, a necklace from India and a lovely dried-flower arrangement from their yard as parting gifts. This generosity, despite my inconvenient intrusion into their busy lives, was typical for Mary and Peter. They were both unselfconsciously kind and gentle people. And in some small but precious way, my sister at that moment was still my sister.

DESPITE THE RISK, Mary surreptitiously visited home during two of her church's cross-country bus tours. As usual, they were fundraising, recruiting, and bringing Jones's touted prophecies and healing to "thousands" along the way. When the tour stopped in Chicago for a few days, Mary used the proximity for quick visits home: once in February, and another in June of 1976.

After she called home, our mother made the two-hour dash to pick her up from the south side of Chicago, accompanied by Marcia and Steve. On a rainy February day, Mary waited for them inside their local host church. Upon arriving, Steve recognized the Temple's mechanic and bus driver, Rick Cordell, standing outside guarding the empty buses. Steve knew Rick from former family ties, and Rick offered to fetch Mary.

When Mary and Mary Margaret emerged from the building, they carried no luggage, but had a little boy with them, Tyrone Cartmell. We did not know who he was, or why he was with Mary. She had only two nights free, and once she was safely away from the tour, she asked our mother to buy Mary Margaret some Oshkosh overalls as she had no money herself. Temple members had to rely on the church for everything, including clothes donated by or shared with other members.

Mary also needed to return with cash for the church's fundraising campaign, perhaps a contingency compensation for visiting our family. Owing to that, she asked for donations wherever she went, including on a country road when our mother gave directions to a lost truck driver. She hit him up with no qualms, but he offered them a few dairy products instead of cash. Mary also showed up unannounced at the law office where her old friend Sue was working.

Sue reported:

> One day she showed up at my place of employment, and what a change I saw in her. The beautiful girl who loved clothes and makeup was dowdy and looked like a missionary. She had her young daughter with her. She talked in an emotionless, robotic manner, and said she was on a cross-country trip and had been given permission to visit me. I was indignant that she needed permission to visit me and thought she acted like she was brainwashed. She wanted me to join her group, but I wasn't at all interested. That was the last time I saw or heard from her.

Mary also hit up Sue for donations, which Sue declined, and then cut the visit short to return to work. Hustling for money did not fit the unassuming Mary I used to know. Perhaps her experience of panhandling for food during the Democratic convention in Chicago had changed that. Temple members, including their children, were known to panhandle in San Francisco.

During their stay at our mother's house, five-year-old Mary Margaret chatted easily with her Uncle Steve, and that is when she innocently mentioned that children at her church were beaten. Suddenly realizing that she had just broken a church rule by revealing this secret, she hung her little head, and mumbled, "Now I have to be whipped." Hearing this broke Steve's heart. No longer the precocious little imp that we knew her to be, she cowered now, a frightened little girl. We later learned that along with adults, children were regularly beaten during Temple services while guards stood watch at the doors. Jim Jones's evil reach had followed this little child clear across the country.

When Mary and the two children returned to Chicago with only a few donations, she was probably somehow punished for having so little to show for her risky absence. But of course, we never heard. At least they had been well-fed, and slept in real beds for two days. Owing to poor family communications, I never heard about this visit, or Mary Margaret's heartbreaking revelation, until years later.

Later that same year, Mary returned home one last time. She was in Chicago on another revival tour, this time even more subdued, her usual humor and easy manner completely absent. As before, she was collecting donations for the Temple while being chauffeured about by our mother and Marcia. She made the rounds, seeing as much of the family as possible, and on a warm spring day in early June, she came to see me, too.

My husband and I had just moved to a different county on Lake Michigan. We bought a rambling, old, turn-of-the-century summer cottage there, complete with a hand pump for water in the kitchen. We were effectively roughing it, camping indoors. And now, here was Mary sitting at our round oak kitchen table. With the shore breezes tickling the trees outside the windows, and the sun sparkling on the distant water, it felt surreal. But as we sat together there, it also felt completely natural to have my younger sister in our house. We were family. I do not remember the general conversation around the table, except for a story that Mary told, and how she told it.

Her humor, grace, and humility had somehow all disappeared. Instead, she sounded angry as she bitterly related a recent experience on her road trip to Chicago. She had been tasked with feeding the passengers on this particular tour, but apparently without the adequate funds to do so. Familiar with Jones's tactics for deploying busloads to protest or demonstrate in California, Mary had employed them now on the road. When the caravan of Temple buses stopped in Wisconsin at a Howard Johnson restaurant, she demanded that the restaurant feed all of them. For free. When the manager refused, Mary threatened a Temple-style protest in front of the restaurant. The manager relented, but only as far as giving everyone free coffee.

Mary related this bizarre incident as though she and her passengers had been greatly wronged. She added that later, when the caravan encountered a highway accident involving a Dannon yogurt truck, Mary had the passengers retrieve the spilled yogurt containers from the roadside to eat. They did so.

She related these incidents as if her passengers were entitled to free food. What had happened to her? For someone born without an arrogant or selfish bone in her body, she was talking like a stranger. As she left my house, I slipped her a $20 bill to make sure that, at least, she could eat or just use it for herself. But I suspected she would not take it, so I told her it was for her church. She took it. It was probably our grocery money, but she needed it more. It was painful to see her like this, and I was completely shaken by the whole encounter.

She seemed angry and strangely detached, and because of that, I did not feel comfortable hugging her goodbye before she climbed into the back seat of Marcia's two-door sedan. Instead, I just stood there waving goodbye as they drove away down our gravel road, never suspecting how vulnerable and needy she must have been during that last stolen visit back home.

And I will always, and forever, regret not hugging her one last time.

MARY WAS STRONG; she endured. In addition to her eldercare job, she had reportedly taken night classes toward a nursing degree. On top of that, her church's mandatory weeknight meetings were difficult to escape, consuming what little free time members might have. Their "catharsis" meetings, as they were called, drew hundreds in attendance, and dozens might line up at them to be acknowledged — or punished. Some invented "sins" or misbehavior to gain Jones's forgiveness, thereby proving their devotion to him. After their punishments were delivered, they were required to say, "Thank you, Father" to him.

As many as 100 whacks with a large, flat paddle could be administered for even slight infractions, such as not paying attention during one of Jones's endless sermons. The paddle, known as the "board of education," was said to have turned one victim's butt into "hamburger." She reported that she could not sit down for a week afterward. Over time, catharsis beatings could be so severe that nurses stood by to help with the wounded. This happened with Peter. He was once beaten so badly that he had to be hospitalized, and it became part of Temple lore, as well as a cautionary lesson for others. It wound up saving the life of one member, who later said that had he not witnessed that brutality, he would have gone to Jonestown, too.

Incredibly, many church members tolerated this kind of treatment. Mary may have been a member of the Planning Commission, a leadership group within the church. If so, this was not good news. Jones demanded absolute loyalty from this select group, and enforced it by frequent, iron-fisted testing. Their meetings could last late into the night, during which members were severely humiliated and beaten — sometimes by each other. Some were even knocked out. During one of these sessions, one member was reportedly urinated and vomited on. Dead-tired members were also forced to confess behaviors, both real and imagined, that were unbecoming of "true" socialism, their new theology. Jones would sometimes include himself in these confessions, but straddling the line between judge and the judged, he was often spared the worst.

Despite her demanding lifestyle, Mary stayed in touch with us. On Sunday nights when the long-distance telephone rates were low, Steve often made it a point to call her. They had always been close, and they chatted easily. Even so, some of their conversations troubled our mother. She feared that Jim Jones was using mind control, or "brainwashing," on his church members, including Mary. She wanted somehow to get Mary committed to our local psychiatric hospital to escape Jones's power over her. She even offered to give Mary her house if she left Peoples Temple. That small house represented decades of hard work at minimum pay, but by this time, our mother was desperately trying to snatch Mary from Jones's grip.

During his conversations with Mary, our brother Steve repeatedly tried to convince her that Jim Jones was not God. But Mary sidestepped him, preferring to talk instead about a television documentary series they were following together — anything but her strange, forbidden life. There was one isolated occasion, however, when Mary did let loose. Steve reported that she was "down on" Jim Jones, saying he was "no good," and that she was fed up with his "stupid religion" and "drug use." She wanted to leave the church. This was brave talk from her, but she said that Peter was committed to staying, and she could not leave.

During one of those calls, Mary reported that Peter was now back in college, taking courses at UC Berkeley, a two-hour drive from Ukiah. As a pre-med student for two years there, he worked part-time as a lab assistant for his chemistry professor. This might explain Peter's absence during Mary's phone calls home. I knew little about these calls, perhaps because they seemed routine at the time. Living in another town, I felt separated from the family by distance, and also by circumstances.

CHAPTER 7

CROSSING THE GOLDEN GATE

WHEN MARY AND I WERE TEENAGERS, CALIFORNIA MEANT THE BEACH BOYS, SURFING, THE DAZZLE OF HOLLYWOOD, AND DISNEYLAND. But that was not the California where the Jones family and about 85 church members first landed. The church that later became Peoples Temple had begun in Indianapolis as a racially integrated church, a daring undertaking in the mid-1950s. Jim Crow segregation was still an acceptable norm at the time; consequently, the church had an uneasy tenure there.

After later reading an *Esquire* magazine article describing Redwood Valley, California, as one of the few places safe from radioactive fallout, Reverend Jim Jones decided to move his ministry there. He was convinced that nuclear war was inevitable, so he relocated his church to Redwood Valley in 1965. It was an isolated rural community, with only a fire station, small store, restaurant, and gas station. Located 110 miles north of San Francisco, it was safe in the event of nuclear war — or so Jones wanted to believe.

The new arrivals had a hard landing. Getting to work right away, they took whatever jobs were available while depending on each other and their leader now more than ever. Jim Jones substitute-taught school and then took a full-time position at a middle school. Others in the church worked on local farms and ranches. Without its own sanctuary, the Midwestern transplants joined with a local church, sharing worship services in their church. It worked for a few years, but unfortunately racism bedeviled the newcomers here, just as it had in

Indiana. Their all-white host church was uncomfortable worshipping while sitting with "other" races, and the two congregations eventually parted.

As it was, the Redwood Valley area reminded some church members of the South, and with good reason: It had only one black family before Jones's outsiders arrived. Plus, Jones's "Rainbow Family" included two adopted Korean orphans, and the first and only black child to be adopted by a white family back in Indiana. The only white child in their "rainbow" was their biological son, Stephan Gandhi Jones. When six-year-old Stephan started school in Redwood Valley, he later described its endemic racism as "…unbelievable. They acted like they had never seen a black person before. They acted like they were inhuman. You'd hear the chants every day. Finally you got immune to it."

After making do in other locations, including the Jones family garage, the Peoples Temple built their own sanctuary in 1969 by combining all their resources. The church also invested in local business ventures: three senior care homes, a children's daycare, a laundry service, and a print shop. Then, over time, they purchased more land and buildings. Jones was not only an adept preacher; he was good at building equity, too. The senior care homes provided a steady income from the residents' Social Security benefits. Many of them were also persuaded to donate all of their assets to the church, in exchange for the church's promise of perpetual care. Mary became part of that plan by managing one of the care homes.

Jones also encouraged members to adopt children, thus causing the adoption rate in Mendocino County to shoot up. Public funds provided for them, in addition to income from the seniors' benefits, enlarged the church's coffers. Squeezing his members further, Jones ruled that if members were unable to make financial contributions to the church, they were allowed to volunteer their time working for it. Thus, communal living and sharing in common took hold.

Over time, the Temple's influence and power spread, with members sitting on the local school board, and Jones serving as the foreman of the Mendocino County Grand Jury. Police and sheriff departments included Temple members, as did almost all local businesses in Ukiah, ten miles south of Redwood Valley. The area's only answering service employed two Temple members, availing the church of private information including ambulance calls and medical issues. Information like this could be useful to Jones as he burrowed his way into the area's power structures. He also ingratiated himself with the local newspaper, the *Ukiah Daily Journal*, which published his articles touting Peoples Temple. He further promoted his church by giving frequent interviews on an area radio station.

Through Jones's skillful maneuvering, the Temple gradually became a local force to be reckoned with. Spreading its tentacles and benevolence further afield, church members assisted the county's neglected poor white community with their public-assistance benefits. And in doing so, the Temple attracted the attention of a new cohort of believers: white, middle-class professionals, attracted by its robust community outreach. These new members provided the growing church with valuable organizational, legal, and financial expertise. So for now, Peoples Temple inadvertently grew whiter.

Nevertheless, Jones continued to champion civil rights, frequently inveighing against racism. From his base in Redwood Valley, he also took his message on the road up and down the West Coast. In addition, people traveled to hear him in Redwood Valley. Hundreds of visitors, mostly black, were bused there aboard the church's growing fleet of buses. During services, Jones raged and roared about racism and inequality, naming their pain. What white man had ever talked to black people like that?

In time, he started to promise his listeners deliverance from that racism and inequality, a deliverance based upon biblically flavored socialism. For someone like Mary, who had joined racial protests instead of running from them, as I had, Jones's message must have been electrifying. Furthermore, he contended that people did not need some distant deity like the one in heaven she and I were used to: their savior now stood right in front of them, the second son of God, Jim Jones. Surprisingly, many bought it, and even our brother Steve could not convince Mary otherwise.

Bused-in Temple visitors were also treated to free lunches during the day-long services in Redwood Valley. Collection plates were passed, and then passed again, so as the visitors ate their "free" lunches,

Jones was raking in the dough. But trouble inevitably followed. Even if Redwood Valley could supposedly withstand nuclear fallout, its white community was unable, or unwilling, to withstand the "fallout" from Jones's active racial integration. Their opposition, coupled with a burgeoning membership, signaled the need for change.

In 1976, the year we last saw Mary in Michigan, Jones finally transferred his base of operations to San Francisco. It promised to be a more welcoming locale; the small-town preacher with the big voice would soon have an even louder one in the big city. And as it was, the church had already been active there for several years, owning property since 1972. I suspect that was why Mary had driven my old van and me through San Francisco's hills as expertly as she had. She already knew the city, but of course, never said why. Now, her church was rapidly expanding there, working out of its large facility on Geary Boulevard, a main thoroughfare in the iconic city.

After moving his base of operations to San Francisco, Jones began selling off properties back in Mendocino County, now cramming some of his members into group living situations, or communes, in the new city. At the time, both rural and urban hippie communes were still common, so the church's solution for housing the newcomers in San Francisco would not have raised any eyebrows.

The problem then became liquidating business holdings, houses, and even pets, back in Mendocino County. Houses were sold, valuables marketed in the church's antique store in San Francisco, and the rest dispensed of in local flea markets. However, former pets were a problem. Some found new homes, but others did not. Jones reportedly ordered dozens of dogs shot, and then buried in a pit on land still owned in Redwood Valley. How did Mary, an animal lover who once collected stray cats and dogs, react to this horror? Perhaps the church's operating mode of "all for the cause" had hardened her. Or maybe she had been silenced by Jones's total control over her life. It could also be that she was too busy to notice.

Now active in San Francisco, too, she was probably commuting between the care home she managed back in Ukiah, and Planning Commission meetings in San Francisco. In addition, there was work to do setting up facilities there for a large influx of new seniors — mostly elderly black widows. They needed housing and care, an enormous challenge that Mary could assist with due to her experience working with seniors.

With its large underclass of poor and homeless, San Francisco welcomed Peoples Temple — and no wonder. Their three-story headquarters at 1859 Geary Boulevard was in the heart of the Fillmore area, a beleaguered neighborhood bordering the seedy Tenderloin district, known for its rampant crime and drug abuse. The church's new headquarters was also near what had been the "hippie capital" of the country, Haight-Ashbury, which was in steep decline by then.

Accordingly, Peoples Temple soon became a cost-free mega-establishment for doing good in the neighborhood. Carrying on with admirable focus and dedication, church members now living in town worked hard. The Temple's brochures advertised a dizzying array of free community services, ranging from adjustment assistance for recently released prisoners, to free blood-pressure checks on site. They offered drug rehabilitation, childcare, legal help, and welfare benefits guidance, plus eviction rescue. On top of that, free meals provided by their "Community Kitchen" fed thousands.

In many ways, Peoples Temple was living its beliefs out loud, and in public. Mary and Peter must have been proud of their new family, now a vital, if unofficial, adjunct to San Francisco's social welfare programs. And there was more. The church's brochures advertised healings, miracles, and resuscitations, as well as prophecies and revelations, all available in their church services. Despite these questionable claims, what mayor would not welcome the church's help in caring for the city's needy — especially when the same church's "get out the vote" campaign may have helped to put him in office?

IN DECEMBER 1975, Mayor Moscone had won his office in part due to Jones's fast-growing influence in town. Gifted at reading and managing people, Jones had lunged full-bore into the politics there, finding time to host political fundraisers and receptions in town. The preacher was also on the spot to greet Jimmy and Rosalynn Carter during their 1976 campaign swing. He wrangled a seat at their head table during a Democratic dinner in town, after which Rosalynn briefly stopped at the Temple. Photos of these occasions were widely touted, adding to Jones's political prestige, and local and state politicians apparently took note.

By then, Jones claimed to have 20,000 church members state-wide, but even if it was just 2,000, as others reported, he arguably controlled a significant number of votes. Hence, leaders appreciating his endorsement included Governor Jerry Brown, State Assemblyman Willie Brown, and Los Angeles Mayor Tom Bradley. Jones and Mayor Moscone met privately with Walter Mondale on one occasion. Jones lent considerable local support to San Francisco's chief prosecuting attorney and sheriff, both of whom would later come to regret it.

Jones was now at the peak of his influence, a political powerhouse both in the "City by the Bay" and statewide. With his fashionable sunglasses and jet-black hair (which he made sure stayed black), he presented a photogenic and commanding presence wherever he went. And he seemed to be everywhere, seeking leadership and clout by any means necessary. With clever maneuvering and relentless pressure, this relative newcomer managed to get himself appointed to the San Francisco Housing Commission, and then named head of it. He also had plenty of money to spread around to fund popular causes: keeping neighborhood centers open, rescuing a struggling pet clinic, providing a senior citizen escort service, and supporting widows of slain policemen. Donations also went to local newspapers fighting for freedom of the press, farm workers' unions, and the NAACP and ACLU.

Just as he had in Ukiah, Jones strategically used the news media, and upped his game by shrewdly glomming on to a former television newscaster, Mike Prokes. How many preachers had their own media director and advisor back then? If there was a hot issue in town now, and Jones could somehow wedge himself into it, media-savvy Prokes was there to advise him on how best to play it. Ever the showman, Jones also knew how to generate the news. He sent hundreds of his dutiful members to protest, support, or just make noise whenever and wherever their leader pointed them. Some members also became precinct workers and held rallies.

Promoting his deep, heart-felt commitment to racial justice, Jones reached across the Bay to align with Huey Newton, a leader in the new Black Panther movement. Jones also made friends with Angela Davis, the well-known black activist whose large Afro hairstyle served as her trademark, inspiring others across the country to follow suit. In addition, Jones championed the "Free Mandela" campaign in South Africa, while also throwing his weight into local movements for racial and economic equality, including fair housing in San Francisco.

As a white minister with a large black congregation, he was a local sensation, steadily building his brand, excoriating racism. By now, anti-racism formed the bedrock of his expanding ministry; at one point, the Nation of Islam even shared a service with the Temple. Jones also showed public support for Dennis Banks, the leader of the American Indian Movement (AIM), while scores of lesser-known community organizers and political figures also earned his attention.

Jones's liberal theology-cum-ideology meshed well with San Francisco's equally progressive norms. He drew hundreds to his church services, where armed guards patrolled the aisles. By now, his congregation was almost 80–90% black, and as a result, some local black ministers resented this renegade newcomer for "stealing" their church members. For all that, those who knew Jim Jones well believed that his virulent antiracism came from his heart, a legacy from his quirky, but fiercely anti-racist mother, Lynetta. Her brave voice back in Jim Crow Indiana now carried far. From a Temple tape transcript, we hear her son proclaim:

[You] Say, "I'm not a nigger." Settin' back there, you're light. Oh, yes, you're a nigger. I'm a nigger. I'm a nigger until everybody is free, till everybody that's treated niggardly is free, I am a nigger. I don't care if you're an Italian nigger, or you're Jewish or an Indian, the only people that're getting anything in this country are the people that got the money, baby. That's the only one. They're the only ones not niggers in this country.

A highly skilled orator, Jones covered all his bases by directing his religious grandiloquence to other audiences, too. Atheists in the crowd might be inspired by his overarching message of social, racial, and economic justice. Biblical references might help to keep Christians in their seats by mentioning Christians living communally, as many Temple members did. He might also bandy about the idea of "apostolic justice" when addressing racial and economic inequality. To attract New Agers with their countercultural beliefs of reincarnation, astrology, psychics, and spiritualism, he could easily season his message with reincarnation, a fundamental part of the Temple's liberal canon.

To further enhance his reach, Jones somehow found the time to write a 24-page pamphlet outlining the errors in the Christian bible. Considering his claims to be God incarnate, some might say he was editing his own autobiography. Yet over time he changed again, this time by freeing himself from all religious underpinnings. He focused his prodigious energy instead on socialism, soon to be followed by an anti-government campaign. His metamorphosis took him from being God incarnate to agnosticism, and then finally to atheism. In a retrieved Temple transcript, we hear, "I'm an agnostic. Off the record, I don't believe in any loving God. Our people are 90 percent atheist."

The Temple's robust outreach also included its choir, which performed not only in the San Francisco area, but also statewide. According to former church member Mike Cartmell:

> The choir was the creation of more than any single individual; it reflected the talent and genius of all its participants. Many Temple members of all races came out of musically expressive spiritual traditions and displayed astonishing talent. We were invited to perform all over California. Of course, Jim Jones conditioned each acceptance on his being given an opportunity to speak. The Peoples Temple Choir was in itself extraordinary, and in its appeal, a wonderful introduction to the Temple and a symbol of all the greater organization wished to be.

IN JULY 1976, as our nation celebrated its bicentennial, and Mary worked hard in both San Francisco and Ukiah, our family celebrated our mother's 63rd birthday. We gathered at my big old house on the shore, expansive enough for a large family get-together. While I was showing one brother through it, he advised me to "just burn it." As a former building contractor, he was probably right, yet it would take me a few winters to realize this, after frozen food on the kitchen counter stayed frozen, and tracked-in snow never melted.

But after the birthday cake was cut on that warm summer day, we surprised our mother with train tickets to California — tickets to see Mary. She would be traveling with her sister Helen, who once declared that she would fly only if someone "ran under the plane with a large pillow beneath it." So that September, the two sisters — still best friends — would have another adventure together, now to see Mary, and with no need for a pillow.

They stayed with Mary at her eldercare home in Ukiah, and no doubt helped out, too. At one time, both sisters had cared for geriatric patients themselves as nurse's aides. Perhaps Mary's volunteer work with elderly patients back in high school foreshadowed her present calling. Our mother returned from the trip proud of Mary, impressed by the way she ran the facility, even calling her a "natural." And from our mother, this was high praise.

It is unclear if this visit occurred before, or after, Mary took nurse's training. At one time, she apparently attended evening classes in Ukiah. As was their custom, her church mixed business with worship, so when her care home was being discussed, Jim Jones praised her hard work and intelligence from the pulpit. He said of Mary that "she is college material," and that she had "high work achievement levels." After Mary's embarrassing middle school placement in the slow learners' group, his praise must have felt like redemption for her. Mary's friend and former Temple member, Laura Johnston Kohl, would later write:

> One of my [dearest] friends in California and in Jonestown was Mary [Wotherspoon]. In California, I sometimes spent the night at her care home so that she could get a break. She

was a Light — in every setting, her cheer and calmness were like a sweet balm. She handled great responsibility with ease, and was a caring and utterly dependable friend. We had many riotous times in our outings with her patients from her care home. She was always thoughtful and I [miss] her. Her parenting of her darling daughter Mary was wonderful to see. Mary worked so hard to make a better world for her daughter Mary. She would have had a great impact on the world had she survived.

Although our mother was delighted by Mary's excellent work at her care home, she returned worried. Mary was alarmingly thin, nothing like the child who used to be teased for being chubby. And "too thin" rarely happened in our Dutch family. Even so, had our mother witnessed Jim Jones's ranting sermons, or seen his members being beaten, or forced to beat each other, she would have had far more to worry about than Mary's weight. We all would have.

Only months before our mother visited Mary, we think Peter had endured that brutal beating at Jim Jones's command. His penis had dripped blood: his crime — pedophilia. He was accused of molesting a teenage boy, a church member. And supposedly this incident had not been the first. Mary may have witnessed Peter's beating, or if not, she certainly soon knew about it. When our mother visited her a while later, Mary's worrisome weight loss may have been due to the trauma, causing her to shut down and lose her appetite. But how could she have explained any of that to family visiting from home?

Trouble was brewing elsewhere as well. Jim Jones's "romance" with San Francisco and beyond would soon encounter turbulence, all of his own making. His political ties would be strained, his religious orientation turned upside down, and his relationship with the press completely reversed. Some members who had left Peoples Temple would become outspoken defectors. And if that was not enough, another group would formally coalesce to have Jones investigated.

CHAPTER 8

EXODUS

FOUR YEARS EARLIER, IN 1972, JONES HAD TASKED THE EDITOR OF THE CHURCH'S NEWSLETTER TO INCLUDE THE PHRASE "LAW OF KARMA," IN SUPPORT OF HIS REINCARNATION THEOLOGY. Then, as he gained more power in California, he began privately flirting with communism. Yet publicly, he latched on to its prettier little sister, socialism, as the way forward; only in private would Jones's inner circle hear him use terms like "anarchists," "comrade," and "fascist." Some believe that what would become his unrequited love affair with the USSR was already blossoming by then.

As he turned sharply to the political left, he strategically dubbed socialism as "divine," or "revolutionary," to soften and legitimize it. He lightly espoused it in public by mentioning to the press that he "favored it," which perhaps landed more easily in liberal San Francisco than in the rest of the country. At the time, anticommunism was still rife, with socialism considered its gateway.

Remaining cautious, he also avoided talking publicly about Vladimir Lenin, whom he privately claimed to have been in a past life, after Jesus. Only his inner circle was privy to these astounding assertions. In his expanding public ministry, he hammered on religious, social, and political issues by mirroring Martin Luther King Jr., Bobby Kennedy, and others. But behind closed church doors, with armed guards standing by, he portrayed capitalism as a selfish economic system, responsible for greed and consumerism, along with its underbelly of poverty and injustice.

Jones also employed guilt, a powerful tool, with great success. Guilt over racism, inequality, and capitalist-induced poverty became familiar themes inside Peoples Temple. Infusing his congregation with it helped to maintain a steady hold on them. Mary was no stranger to guilt. As children, we had to sing, "Not what my hands have done can save my guilty soul; not what my toiling flesh has borne can make my spirit whole." Yet roiling throughout his preaching, Jones managed to say it even better.

In his constantly evolving theology, he also caricatured a childhood image of God up in heaven by thundering the phrase, "Sky God!" He considered it a useless — and inconvenient for him — version of God. During a Temple service in Los Angeles, he is said to have slammed a Christian bible down on the floor, proclaiming that it, too, harmed foolish believers. This startling stagecraft managed to attract even more followers, with many believing they had a new savior now.

Jones was adept at telling people what they wanted to hear, or more often, what he wanted them to hear. And if necessary, he could pivot halfway through a sentence to lead the unsuspecting wherever he wanted them to land with complete disregard for the truth. But now as a public figure in San Francisco, he also had more to hide. In sharp contrast to his cozy public relations with elected officials, both local and national, his church's internal newsletters became highly politicized. Governmental wrongdoing, CIA schemes, and anything else to convince his people of the government's evil ways, were included with church news.

For some followers, their savior's "feet of clay" would undermine their trust in him. In 1973, Jones was arrested in Los Angeles for indecent exposure in a public men's restroom. His attorneys eventually wrangled him out of the scandal. This time. Thereafter, Jones defensively, if irrationally, decreed that all men were homosexual except for him. Apparently, he believed he could manage reality by fiat, and incredibly, his muddled rationales seemed to work for members who believed him to be God. His disordered thinking continued unabated.

An experienced charlatan, he could switch justifications for his erratic behaviors whenever challenged. Jones maintained that his exposure incident was only an attempt to understand homosexuality. Accordingly, Jones is said to have forced a number of his male followers into sex with him, to "allow them" to discover their latent homosexuality.

At one time, he held that as a divine being, he was the only person who should have sex. He kept moving the line between what was allowed for him and what was forbidden for others. Meanwhile, his abuse of his followers as a steady source of sex partners, including his female secretaries and Temple men, would become normalized within the church, his sex life woven right into his ministry.

Even early on while teaching adult education history classes in Ukiah, Jones allegedly had better ideas than following the class syllabus. Instead, he talked about masturbation, advocating it as a substitute for sex, and favoring his students with his own techniques, perhaps to the amusement of some, but not all. According to an unpublished report by Lester Kinsolving from the *San Francisco Examiner* in 1972, Jones is quoted as saying, "I masturbated five times a day before I got married." The same report mentioned complaints to the local school board, which included Temple members, as going unheeded.

All the while, the Temple's mounting riches were used to protect Jones from embarrassment. By employing a cadre of expensive attorneys, he largely squelched news of his indecent exposure arrest in Los Angeles. Jones also made strategic contributions to political campaigns that could prove useful, sometimes giving to the opposing candidates as well. Causes like freedom of the press and fair labor movements also benefited from his deep pockets. Money was used to soothe disgruntled church members, too. He sent them on vacations if the cheaper options of promoting them in the church hierarchy, or allowing them special privileges, failed to work. If bribery or flattery failed, he could always have them beaten, humiliated, and then ostracized.

In San Francisco, prospective members now encountered Jones solely in public appearances, the news, or at political rallies. The Temple's services were closed to the public, with security guards screening out prospective visitors at the doors. Jones's brutal catharsis sessions continued, including beatings and scorching abuse, while his guards kept prying eyes away. Hence, the divide between the private and public church and its leader continued to sharpen. Jones's tenure in San Francisco was packed with dirty laundry, destined soon to be unpacked.

His radical shifts may have enhanced his sense of omnipotence, but if so, they also made him more vulnerable. And inevitably, when his outlandish behaviors began to leak out, some of the press began to notice. Previously, his attorneys could cover his mistakes, but his missteps now would become too large for even San Francisco to absorb. Certain members of its press there started to track them. When a reporter at the city's Housing Commission meetings noticed that Jones arrived for the meetings with armed guards, he sensed a story.

And unlike Ukiah's press, San Francisco's was not in Jones's back pocket.

BACK IN 1972, a reporter from Indianapolis had contacted Bay area newspapers, tracking down rumors of the Temple's questionable practices already evident in Indiana. As a result, Lester Kinsolving, the religion reporter from the *San Francisco Examiner*, had published four stories revealing Jones's purported ability to raise people from the dead, his questionable financial practices, and his placement of church members on local governing boards and agencies. The articles exposed his use of armed security guards, which had made some residents in Ukiah uneasy.

But Kinsolving's stories were not well-substantiated, nor was any of Jones's behavior actually illegal. Yet Jones reacted to the publications by having his members buy up all the newspapers they could find in the Ukiah area. He also deployed a large group of members to protest outside the *Examiner* offices in San Francisco. After that, his attorneys successfully stifled any further publications—at least for five years.

Now, in early 1977, reporter Marshall Kilduff from the *San Francisco Chronicle* picked up the scent again by returning to the Kinsolving articles. For him, there was something strange about Jones and his church. Kilduff's beat covered the city's Housing Authority meetings, which Jones chaired. The reporter noticed Jones's armed guards waiting in the hallway during these meetings. Why the guards, and why the guns?

Kilduff thought he might do a story on this eccentric preacher, so he kept an eye on him. Jones returned the favor by having his spies search the reporter's trash and follow him everywhere. Undeterred,

Kilduff, a San Francisco native and Stanford alumnus, continued his investigation. Jones then reacted by barring any further Temple visits from reporters. He was spooked.

Whereas before Jones had used the media to his advantage, now it was becoming a potential adversary. Adding to his growing panic, Jones would soon be publicly confronted by a newly formed group, Concerned Relatives, started by two former Temple members and other critics. In time, this group — and not the feared U.S. government — would become his fiercest enemies. But for the moment, a powerful press that he could not control was coming at him. It terrified him.

He made a momentous decision. He had once relocated his church from Indiana to California; he could move it again now. This time it would be to Guyana.

And he would do so before Kilduff's investigations were published.

HAUNTED BY HIS nagging fear of nuclear war, Jones had already searched for an offshore location for his church long before choosing Redwood Valley. A search in Brazil had not panned out, nor had a visit to Cuba and several other Caribbean locations. Continuing his search for a place that was also safe from outside interference, Jones had visited Guyana several times. Ultimately, he signed a lease there in December 1973, for 3,000 acres of its jungle. After he assured Guyana's prime minister of an investment worth at least $1-2 million U.S. in his cash-poor country, Jones's proposal for an "agricultural project" there was welcomed.

This lease then functioned as an insurance plan, providing a future sanctuary where Jones would be free from the U.S. government and other "enemies." He would be in complete control there. Soon after signing, he visited Guyana once again, but now with some of his staff and family. While there, they made a short promotional movie of their new "paradise." They staged their amateur production in the jungle with colorful tropical fruits and attractive backdrops, none of which could be found in the future Jonestown. It was propaganda. Now, that future in Guyana reserved for "someday" had suddenly landed like a meteor for the Peoples Temple in San Francisco.

Operating in fast-forward, its rattled leader quickly convened a meeting with Jones's church administrators in Georgetown, Guyana. They gathered there at Lamaha House, purchased to serve as a future headquarters. Now, it served as one from April 27 through May 1, as the hurriedly assembled group hashed out some kind of a future for Peoples Temple, Guyana.

After he returned to San Francisco for the last time, Jones's decision to remove his church from the U.S. triggered a frenzy of activity. He himself left the country on June 17, never to return. On June 18, more trouble threatened when San Francisco's Prosecuting Attorney's office opened a six-week investigation into Peoples Temple. Ultimately, their investigation found only what the press had already uncovered.

But at that moment, both the press and authorities were all playing catch-up with a man hell-bent on not being caught. An editorial cartoon — had there been one — of Jones jousting with reporters with one hand, while shooing his members onto planes with the other, might have alerted readers. But Jones was way ahead of them, and already gone.

A geyser erupted within the Temple leadership. Tim Stoen, its top attorney, financial advisor, and most powerful member, defected on June 12. It was a mighty shock and a tremendous blow. Only weeks before, Stoen had been an important member of the planning session in Georgetown, but now he disappeared. Stoen's stunning defection signaled a profound reproach of Jones, who considered separation from the Temple not only a threat, but a personal betrayal. And by now, Jones was the church. Another trusted staff member, Stoen's wife, Grace, had already defected, leaving their biological son, John Victor Stoen, behind with the church. By the time Tim Stoen defected, the boy was already in Guyana with Jones. What kind of parents would leave their child like that? Conceivably, ones who were blinded by devotion to Jim Jones. Or feared him. Or both.

As it was, Temple children often lived in cost-effective group settings, allowing their parents to get more work done. But more importantly, Jones frequently behaved as if he not only owned people but owned their children, too. By his own outlandish logic, he had decided early on that the Stoen's baby was his child. It belonged to him.

To secure his ludicrous claim, he even took legal measures to prove it, and by pressuring the Stoen parents, he had actually succeeded. This, despite the fact that Tim Stoen was a highly trained attorney. Now with mounting troubles for Peoples Temple, three-year-old John Victor Stoen had been proactively spirited out of U.S. jurisdiction to Guyana, out of his parents' reach.

How DID MARY and her family fare in all this turmoil? During her Sunday night phone visits with Steve, there was no mention of any trouble within the church or for her. Had Mary regained a healthy weight again? How about her relationship with Peter? Knowing their gentle, easygoing natures, the couple may have worked that out. But how about Mary's state of mind? Was she frightened by all the Temple turmoil? None of this was ever mentioned, but as it turned out, Mary and Mary Margaret would be among the first Temple members to leave the country.

They were allowed only one suitcase each, but were otherwise prepared. With an eye to the nebulous future, Jones insisted that members ready their passports, receive inoculations, and tie up loose ends if and when possible. Some had done so. But now the Immigration and Naturalization Service in San Francisco was swamped, processing hundreds of Temple members. Mary's passport photo shows a sister I hardly recognize, with her glance turned aside, and her thick, beautiful hair completely covered. Peter looks confident in his photo, even a bit cocky — while Mary Margaret looks like the unsuspecting, innocent little first-grader that she was at the time.

Temple buses began exiting San Francisco during the dead of night so as not to disturb or frighten those members left behind. Reportedly, far more wanted to go than were able, that is if Jones's estimate of 3,000 members was accurate. At the time, many residents in the church's communes were unhappy, complaining of overcrowding and inadequate money for food. And now, the Temple's overloaded buses were transporting some members across the country to New York and Florida, leaving many others behind. Some leaving never bothered to notify relatives of their departures. But Mary did.

On July 17, she called home to say that she was leaving the country. She was in New York at JFK Airport's international terminal, about to board a plane for South America. In a great hurry, she had very little time to talk. She asked Steve to pray for her safety — their safety: Mary Margaret was with her. A long flight loomed, and Mary was uncharacteristically scared and nervous. There is little doubt that her call was also made in secret. Jim Jones severely disapproved of family ties, and now was the time to sever, not honor, them.

Our two Marys were leaving for Guyana, a country completely unfamiliar to both Steve and our mother at the time of the call. Mary confided that they were escaping "persecution from our government." She said it was "against" her church, which seemed somewhat plausible at the time. Given the country's current FBI surveillance of the Black Panthers, anti-war activists, and even environmentalists, why not Peoples Temple, too? Apparently, the Temple's growing rebellion against the government was no longer a secret by then. Yet Michigan was too far from California for news of the church's troubles there to have reached us until this moment. Mary's imminent exile was absolutely dumbfounding, and a worrisome surprise.

Before she ended the short call, Mary quickly asked our mother to send her two sets of matching gold post earrings to Guyana; one for her, one for Mary Margaret, now almost six years old. It was a bizarre request given the momentous transition they were about to undertake. Or was it? Due to the hurried nature of the call, Mary was not questioned about the earrings or why Guyana. She had to hang up, and it was the last time our mother and Steve would ever hear her voice.

The earrings were sent, but never acknowledged.

MEANWHILE, BACK IN San Francisco, investigative reporter Kilduff was struggling to find support for his work, finally succeeding when joined by another reporter, Phil Tracy of *New West* magazine. The two journalists worked together under the magazine's new editor. Their first published article highlighted the Temple's armed guards and its paranoia and secrecy. But for all that, it failed to blow a hole in Jones's defenses. It raised more questions than it answered. Nevertheless, this narrow focus would prove to be just the opening volley. All hell would soon be loosed upon Jones and his Temple.

Even though he was safely in Guyana by now, Jones was still brawling with the press, calling in favors from far and wide. And they were considerable. Notable professionals from many walks pummeled local media with support for Jones. They included the Lieutenant Governor of California, a California State Assemblyman, the Executive Director of San Francisco Council of Churches, the California Legislature Majority Whip, the President of the San Francisco NAACP Branch, and the Supervisor of San Francisco Public Schools.

Jones's connections encompassed Rupert Murdoch, who was paradoxically also the owner of the *New West* magazine. Murdoch and other heavyweights weighed in against possible future adverse publications by the *San Francisco Chronicle*. That paper's editors were flabbergasted by all the noise, especially since they had already denied Kilduff publication. What was going on? Ironically, Jones's ferocious campaign against press coverage boomeranged. He would be hit hard after inadvertently calling attention to everything he was trying to hide. The astonishing level of opposition to publication had alerted local editors. There had to be a story lurking somewhere behind this powerful minister with his dark glasses and armed guards.

The story exploded in all directions. Temple defectors in the area realized they might now finally be heard. Their stories mattered; the press was listening. Anonymous phone calls rained down on San Francisco's news media. It was open season. Consequently, editors unleashed their firepower, despite respected figures like physician-publisher Carlton Goodlett, MD, Mayor Moscone, and State Assemblyman Willie Brown all standing with Jones. Up until then, the preacher had been a valuable political asset for them with his money, votes, and flash-crowds dispersed on command. But now Jones's private sadism and savage abuses would become blockbuster material.

Leading the way, the editors at *New West* insisted that Kilduff and Tracy interview the defectors in person. Up until now, suspicion and innuendo had ruled the Temple story, and they wanted hard, verifiable facts. Consequently, Tracy and Kilduff met with over a dozen defectors, including two that had risked their lives by leaving the church, changed their names, and moved to a different city. Many were risking their safety now once again by speaking out. Even so, the two reporters managed to convince several of the defectors to be photographed, arguing it would strengthen their stories, as well as protect them. If they were harmed in any way, the Temple would be suspected.

Their stories were published in *New West* magazine, appearing on newsstands that July. Its "Inside Peoples Temple" exposé recounted a brief history of Peoples Temple and described its support among California's rich and powerful. Then, after outlining the church's widespread philanthropy for a variety of causes and charitable services, it drew back the curtain, exposing what Jones, his armed guards, and silenced members had been hiding.

Tracy and Kilduff reported that members had given up all of their assets, left their jobs, and lived communally. As a result, many were dead broke, while the church was raking in millions. Most members owned nothing, and if they left the church, they had nowhere to go, having signed over everything to the church. Many defectors had also severed family ties back home, and were now completely isolated.

Jones's greed was fully exposed. Some defectors had witnessed Los Angeles Temple services that brought in between $15–20,000 every other weekend, while the audiences were told that only $5–700 had been given. Collection plates were passed repeatedly as a result.

The church's care homes for 130 boys with emotional disturbance and behavioral disorders were another good example of Jones's avarice. As wards of the state, these children were provided for by the government, but Jones looked to this "Youth Mission" as another source of income. The church skimped on the boys' care, with poor food and used clothing. When the care homes were later returned to the state, some of the boys reportedly had scabies due to their filthy living conditions.

The senior homes had also been vulnerable to skimming. With six to fourteen residents in each, their Social Security checks provided a lucrative revenue stream for the church. In addition, Jones is said to have warned elderly black people in Los Angeles that the federal government planned to place them in concentration camps, where they would be gassed, citing Nazi history. He then promised them safety and lifelong care if they signed over their Social Security checks to the church. Many did.

The report also illustrated how the Temple continually extended its reach, looking for donations, and seeking to influence elections and causes. The magazine's readers learned that church members conducted regular letter-writing campaigns for various causes, using form letters and aliases taken from phone books. I had received at least one from Mary, and several more written by other Temple members. In addition, Jones's faithful followers were forced to write real or fictional self-incriminating letters to be kept on file to be weaponized later, if needed. Others signed blank papers for the same purpose.

According to the defectors, Temple members were pushed hard. Every other weekend, many worked the services at their Los Angeles location. It was exhausting: they would board buses on Friday afternoons, drive through the night, then return at dawn the following Monday after driving through the night again. They confirmed allegations of Jones packing in 70–80 riders in the 43–seat buses.

On Sundays, after enduring the six-hour Temple services in L.A., followed by the overnight drive north again, Mary, Mary Margaret, and the rest faced another demanding week of work. As if that were not enough, they were expected to attend Temple meetings two to four nights a week, some of which lasted all night. Jones wrenched every last ounce of strength out of his followers.

Furthermore, since they were ordered to report on each other, even mentioning leaving the church could be dangerous. When defectors were caught, reprisals were swift and inhumane. Jones's ruthless threats, armed guards, and locked doors all served as prison walls. After defections, relatives remaining in the church could be scapegoated, with Jones holding them responsible. Also, several unsolved murders occurred among members who had escaped his tyranny. As a result, most of those who got away had done so only after meticulous planning, and at great personal risk. Even when successful, many feared that no one would believe the conditions they had escaped: they were still outsiders.

In their marathon interview with the defectors, reporters Kilduff and Tracy witnessed the defectors' scorn for California's public and political figures, including local authorities. While armed guards hid many of Jones's abuses behind Temple walls, the defectors contended that public authorities routinely ignored his locked doors, bodyguards, and controlled votes, all of which were in plain sight.

Shortly after this interview, investigative reporters Tim Reiterman and Nancy Dooley from the *San Francisco Examiner* were invited to meet with more defectors. They spent an afternoon with eighteen of them. Reporters Kilduff and Tracy joined with this second group-interview, as everyone seemed eager to move the story forward. This meeting produced two blockbuster articles: August 1, 1977: "Rev. Jones: The Power Broker; Political Maneuverings of A Preacher Man"; and two weeks later, "The Temple, a Nightmare World." This front-page coverage revealed even wider abuse under Jones.

This second gathering of escapees detailed Jim Jones's draconian code of silence, describing it as almost a mafia-like gag of omertà on everyone. But these brave defectors now talked. They told of members being drugged to appear dead so Jones could miraculously raise them from the dead, wowing his audiences. (Mary had reportedly done this for Jones at a Harlem revival.) They told of a boy having to eat his own vomit as punishment for disobeying Jones. One woman had been stripped naked and beaten for confessing an unauthorized sexual attraction. A twelve-year-old may have died after being "treated" for an illness by members placing a photo of Jones on him, instead of seeking medical aid.

The former members stated that Temple children were sent out on the streets to beg. They were given electric shocks for misbehaving, and Jones sadistically amplified the effects of these shocks by having the children's screams electronically broadcast, thereby traumatizing other children who were listening. It is heartbreaking to realize that Mary Margaret may have been abused like this.

Adults were regularly humiliated. Those who worked for the church, or had turned over all of their assets and income to the Temple, were allotted only $2 a week for personal use. They also endured frequent loyalty tests, including the White Night poison rituals that Mary had described to me. But back then, I thought the practice resembled a Klan-like, odd behavior. Jones needed constant reassurance of their loyalty, thus his punishments for "betrayals" could be severe. Even after escaping the Temple, some defectors continued to fear his reach.

After being thus exposed, Jim Jones could only sputter his fury and exasperation from 4,500 miles away. Using a short-wave radio to address members back home, he painted a ludicrously positive picture of Jonestown as a paradise with entertainment, dances, and weekend hikes. Yet at the same time, millions of readers back in the U.S. would continue to learn more about the private Peoples Temple, the one behind closed doors. A series of news articles would follow, and even *Newsweek* magazine picked up the story, although no one in our family ever saw it. We were still in the dark.

But by then, almost 1,000 Temple members had made it to Guyana, with Mary, Peter, and Mary Margaret among them. And that little family would never get to experience Jones's deluded version of Jonestown's "paradise." They were now completely trapped there. As one defector at the Kilduff and Tracy interview had remarked, "Whether the church will permit those who moved to Guyana the option of ever leaving is questionable."

Investigative reporter Tim Reiterman would travel to Jonestown the following year to find out.

Jim Jones, children, Redwood Valley. Jonestown Institute photo

Jim Jones, San Francisco, 1976. California
Historical Society photo

Peoples Temple bus tour. California Historical Society photo

PART III

SOWING LIES

CHAPTER 9

AN UNPROMISING LAND

THE MASS EXODUS FROM THE U.S. began during the dead of night, and ended several days later in the "Promised Land" of Guyana. These exiles landed in a country with no effective press, a hands-off government, little infrastructure, and mighty jungles. Inside one of them, Jim Jones's utopian plans would be undisturbed by outsiders. It was a disaster. Nevertheless, some members would still say it was the best time of their lives.

When she set foot in Guyana, Mary became the third successive generation in our family to emigrate from their native land, and Mary Margaret the fourth. The two of them arrived in Guyana's capital of Georgetown on July 19, 1977. Arriving in a group of 40–50 members, they were among the first to forge a new home in this impoverished country. Fleeing from alleged persecution by the U.S. government and press, they were hopeful. But as it was, this new country would challenge them on a completely different level: their own survival.

Why Guyana, a small country that few had even heard of? After ruling out countries too cold for the Temple's elderly, Jones considered several Caribbean countries, including Trinidad, Barbados, and Granada. But it was Guyana, a former British colony on the northeast coast of South America, where English was the national language, that won his final approval. Even so, it was a hard landing for his people. His enormous tract of isolated, leased land in this distant country guaranteed that his authority there would be almost absolute. In addition, his predominately black congregation would no longer be a minority. Most of Guyana's population were of East Indian and African descent. The Guyanese jungle, however, was color blind, and it would prove to be their greatest challenge.

Guyana had seen many outsiders before. The Dutch were the first to colonize it for trade, and they left their mark in this small South American frontier. Employing hydrological engineering expertise gained in their native land, the Dutch dug canals to dry out what would become Guyana's capital city. Later known as Georgetown, it was eight feet below sea level. They also laid out a grid pattern for the nascent city. After that, British colonizers brought enslaved Africans and, after the African slave trade was abolished, contract laborers from Britain's colony in India, to work on Guyana's sugar and rice plantations. Yet Guyana was still a young country, having gained its independence from Britain in 1966, and becoming a republic in 1970. Only seven years later, Peoples Temple would arrive.

In many ways, Guyana served Jones's aspirations nicely. Black descendants of plantation slaves now governed much of the country, which bode well for Jones's mostly black congregation. In addition, its government was fashioned by a quasi-socialist-communist system, which accorded with Jones's brand of socialism. And by now, he had completely turned away from all religion; there would be no religious services in Jonestown. He had ditched his clerical collar, and Bibles were prohibited as he attempted to align with the USSR — a perfectly "godless" country.

Although he had long been planning an offshore commune, it did not work out as as planned. Instead, he was reacting to the negative press with a sudden decision to evacuate. So members slipped away by ship and plane in small groups of 50 - 100 at a time. Thus ,the first arrivals in Guyana, which included Mary and Mary Margaret, had traveled light, taking only what they could carry. And their faith in their latter day Moses would soon be tested in his unlikely promised land.

Processing large groups of arrivals through the poky Guyanese customs bureau, and then feeding and lodging them in its capital, was a logistical nightmare. But Jones was a master organizer, using his considerable pull with the local government to make things happen. Georgetown itself, as an attractive Caribbean port city, proved to be a tropical sensation. Fragrant flowers and aromatic food stalls among colorful buildings greeted the new arrivals. An elegant array of minarets, domes, and cathedrals dotted the skyline in this culturally diverse city, where streets were named after Dutch settlers and English nobility. Moreover, the locals were friendly. I like to think that Mary was enchanted by it, but perhaps she was too scared to enjoy any of it. We never heard.

Located near the equator, Guyana was always hot, but with prevailing sea breezes often cooling its coastal inhabitants. With two rainy seasons, it was often wet, too. Its steamy capital city was located on the Demerara River estuary, which empties into the Atlantic Ocean. Life in Georgetown, surrounded by marsh, swamp, and flat farm lands, was lived out in the open, or on shady verandas. Many of its more upscale houses also had open-air second stories.

During her stayover in Georgetown, did Mary have time to poke around this fascinating city, or perhaps take Mary Margaret to its zoo and botanical gardens? Its mesmerizing street life and open-air markets alone were enough to captivate any child. Either way, Mary Margaret would soon be living in a zoo and tropical garden of her very own: the jungle.

THE COUNTRY'S NATIONAL airlines, Guyana Airways, reflected the country's general poverty at the time; there were very few planes, and its unpaved runways could be unreliable. The weather often created further drawbacks to air travel. In addition, the country's poor road system served only a small number of towns and villages. Most Guyanese lived beside the country's plentiful waters, and they traveled by them, too. Transporting large numbers of people and goods to the country's interior often required both sea and river voyages.

To reach their new jungle home, Temple members had to sail for up to three days. Their itinerary included the Demerara River to the ocean, then north over the Atlantic Ocean, then west through the Caribbean, and then finally south on an inland river system. Jim Jones's son, Stephan, made the trip repeatedly, and described the ocean crossing as "hellish." At that time, oceangoing vessels were not equipped with stabilizers, so passengers were at the mercy of the wind and the waves. And unlike our father's comfortable ocean voyage to America, first class travel on these Guyanese boats was in name only. These passengers traveled much like cargo. Furthermore, the shallow waters created by river silt deposited along the Atlantic shoreline threatened boat traffic with grounding. As a result, navigation was tedious, and the passengers' pitch-and-roll miseries on the ocean included danger, too. Boats traversing Guyana's coastline had to stay fourteen miles offshore, often disappearing from sight.

It was a great relief, then, for seagoing passengers to turn at last toward land once again. Disembarking at the Caribbean port of Mabaruma near the Venezuelan border, they could stretch their legs on solid, level ground and rest for a bit. Children like Mary Margaret could run around the primitive but bustling little seaport. From there, she and Mary would have boarded shallow-draft river boats for the final leg of their journey. Their group was probably split up between the Temple's repurposed shrimp boat, the Cudjoe, and other available vessels, including government mail boats.

Rural inhabitants living along Guyana's inland rivers were accustomed to frequent water traffic. Temple passengers here, however, would become new neighbors, not just tourists or missionaries. And fortunately, from Mabaruma on, the travel-weary Temple groups could enjoy smooth sailing. Stephan Jones described this leg of the journey, with its gentle waters and riveting scenery, as "heavenly."

It began with the Barima-Mora Passage, a magical and almost other-worldly ecosystem of 1,000 square kilometers of mangrove forests, swamps, savannahs, and rivers. Unlike ocean travel, the world here no longer pitched and heaved. It was utterly flat, with the horizon evenly splitting sky and earth. From on high, hundreds of migratory birds traced their route by flying above the ribbons of orange-brown waterways that meandered through the Passage below. This shining "map" of watery bends and sharp curves led to the Barima River, and then to the narrowing Kaituma River. The complete river voyage would be 50 river miles and take 12 hours. Mary would soon learn that life in Guyana was no vacation, nor cruising through its jungles a theme park adventure.

They were arriving during summer's rainy season, when blinding sheets of rain were a daily occurrence. But even so, there was still much for them to see. They encountered indigenous tribes of Waraos and Arawaks living in simple wooden houses. Built on stilts, with roofs fashioned from troolie palm leaves, these basic structures lined the river's edge.

Due to the many marshes, streams, and rivers that formed their world, native children often learned to swim before they could walk. The water served as their road, fish market, and front yard for these amphibious folks. Little boys speared fish from dugout canoes, and women washed their laundry on the riverbanks. Then as the Kaituma River narrowed, boats passed closer to shore, and Mary and her daughter must have gaped in wonder at their new neighborhood. But it was probably nature that would demand all of their attention.

Congregations of scarlet ibises flew in formation, festooning the sky overhead like windblown confetti. Clinging to bushes and trees, brilliant bougainvillea flowers bedazzled from the riverbanks. Among Guyana's 800 species of birds, its brilliantly colored red and green macaws sometimes resembled tropical flowers. In turn, the feathery petals of flowers could be mistaken for birds. Nature's splendor was on full display. Alerted by the familiar hum of passing boat engines, friendly locals waved, and giant river otters peeped shyly above the water line. It is easy to imagine Mary Margaret peering back at them over the boat railing.

Without the ambient din of a mechanized world, the hinterland stillness here magnified each call, cry, and screech of the jungle. The distant roar of howler monkeys could be heard for miles. The water-borne laughter of women selling their produce on the shoreline rang out. The putt-putt motors of small skiffs and the thwacking blades of the rare helicopter all carried with pristine clarity.

River boats, even if not pretty, needed to be dependable here, for a swim in the rivers could be deadly. The opaque waters were hazardous. Foreigners had to be warned about the green anaconda, one of the longest, and largest, lethal snakes in the world, glided unseen below. Danger also lurked in the form of schools of red-bellied piranhas, and electric eels with their stunning jolts. These slithery creatures also go by the equally disconcerting name of "knife fish."

Heading upriver, the jungle itself marched right up to the Kaituma's riverbanks, where the loudmouth howler monkeys lived among treetops thick as broccoli. These jungle comedians liked to observe humans from up above, hurling excrement down at them if they felt threatened. The trees here averaged 115 to 137 feet high, with the tallest reaching up to 275 feet. From above, these giants filtered both the light and heavy downpours of rain. A midlevel of palm and rubber trees, plus the lower brush below, provided a more familiar neighborhood for humans on the ground.

MARY'S RIVER JOURNEY finally ended at Port Kaituma, a remote outpost initially established to serve a manganese mining operation. At one time, the narrow silty river this far inland had been dredged to accommodate that industry's ore-boat traffic. But no more. After the mines shut down in 1954, Port Kaituma's shanty town, street market, and police outpost maintained a slower pace. Here, poverty ruled. The local cop's uniform might have been a badge worn on a T-shirt, while a single dirt landing strip served as its airport, but only when free of mud. Port Kaituma was considered a make-do backwater, a "slum on stilts."

What must it have been like for this isolated port's residents to see hundreds of Americans, Black and white, arriving in their village? For its thirty families, this sudden influx of strangers would soon quicken their pace, from languid to lively. River traffic and shipping would increase dramatically. Meanwhile, their primitive airstrip, a 20-minute walk from town, would prove an even more important link to Georgetown. Yet no one expected that it would someday be featured on the front pages of newspapers around the world.

MARY'S GROUP WERE not the first outsiders here. Others had attempted establishing a jungle settlement in the area, but had failed, and most of the land they once cleared had been reclaimed by the rainforest. Only a network of footpaths forged by the indigenous Amerindians remained. Nevertheless, several crude structures had survived. In

1974, and again in 1976, a small group of Temple members, known as the Jonestown "pioneers," arrived in Port Kaituma. Aided by local villagers, this group of mostly young men had cleared roughly 100 acres, started crops, and erected rudimentary housing structures. It had been slow going.

Fueled by idealism, these pioneers were determined to succeed, despite the fact that most of their lumber had to be imported. Local wood was too hard to work. Hardcore themselves, many worked up to fifteen hours a day with no days off. They worked through the pale light of dawn and the fading dusk of night. At first, they slept in Port Kaituma and "commuted" the six miles to their work site, the first three miles on the unpaved Port Kaituma-Matthews Ridge Road. It was manageable compared to their last three miles. Originally a footpath, this muddy last passage had to be hacked from the jungle, and would eventually serve as the only road in and out of what would become Jonestown.

Clearing the virgin jungle was brutally hard work, but they did not do it alone. Local Amerindians, descendants of the first people to inhabit this part of South America, came to their aid. In addition to providing extra hands, their wilderness survival skills proved vital for the North Americans. They showed them how to live both in, and with, the jungle. And perhaps their best student was 16-year-old Stephan Jones, who later said that despite its perils, the jungle felt like his true home.

Even so, venomous snakes and spiders, poison dart frogs, and malaria-bearing mosquitos could make life difficult, or even end it. Tiger-teeth plants tore at bare legs. Open cuts became infected. Foreigners needed sunscreen, mosquito repellent, hats, boots, long sleeves, and pants. But not these "pioneers." With minimal protection, they gutted it out, getting bitten and scratched, and for the most part, they loved it. The jungle had apparently met its match.

THAT SAME JUNGLE, with all its hardship and wonders, was waiting for Mary's group, too. But when they disembarked at Port Kaituma, they did not have to walk the last six miles to their new home. Instead, they climbed aboard a flatbed trailer pulled by the settlement's farm tractor, or into the bed of its large dump truck. What must that have been like for Mary, traveling like that with a six-year-old and two suitcases?

According to Stephan Jones, this last leg of the journey was another "hell." They jostled and bumped along for 45 minutes on the Temple's rutted road, darkened by the jungle's thick canopy overhead. Its mid-level of trees formed yet another light-filtering umbrella. As their vehicle tunneled through the dense undergrowth at ground level, Mary's world was shifting gears, too. Life moved slowly in this hinterland where the roads were crude and the tropical heat ruled.

From their first step down into the light and clearing that was to be their new home, they had to hit the ground running: Jonestown was not ready for them. By nature, Mary was tough and undemanding, but even she must have been sobered by what she and Mary Margaret first encountered. Due to the Temple's hasty exodus and premature arrival, there was not enough room to house everyone. Disoriented and unsettled, they had to rely now more than ever on Jim Jones's leadership. And their hardships would only worsen over time. How did they manage to get the machinery, mattresses, linens, chairs, appliances, food, staples, and building supplies needed for their survival?

It was a massive operation resourced from long distances, and often in debilitating heat, or heavy rains, or both. Supplies were imported via the ports of Mabaruma on the Caribbean, or Georgetown on the Atlantic, the same slow route Mary had just completed. A generator was purchased for electricity, but as was the case even in Georgetown, they still had frequent power outages. Not much was fast or easy in this part of the world, except for growth and rot in the cycle of life.

Seeking to boost its own economy, the Guyanese government prohibited buying food from other countries. Goods could be imported from Miami and elsewhere, but not food. This was good news for the area's smugglers, who filled the gap. Caribbean ports were legendary havens for their trade, where grains and other durable food stuffs could be shipped illegally. Accordingly, numerous food containers labeled "concrete" led some Port Kaituma villagers to wonder what their new neighbors were building out there. Like the smugglers, Jim Jones knew how to bend the rules, too.

The new arrivals faced the brutal challenge of continuing the pioneers' early work, mindful of many others back in the U.S. pressing to join them. As it was, about 900 souls eventually crowded into the compound originally meant to house only 700. The settlers had to improvise by adding to the simple structures they found, but there would never be enough room. And to make matters worse, Guyana's poor infrastructure created frequent delays for deliveries.

There was no letup. Tackling the vital and endless task of clearing more land to grow their food, the arrivals had to work long, hard hours in the open fields. Mary went from managing a senior care facility in the U.S. to being a farm laborer here. At first there was no Peter to commiserate with. He would join the family two months later, in September. Yet, almost miraculously, these tough new immigrants somehow managed to create a working community within a short time, 150 air miles from Georgetown, and six miles from Port Kaituma. And soon, what Jones had officially named "The Peoples Temple Agricultural Project in Guyana" became known colloquially as "Jonestown." The name stuck.

From the air, Jonestown's compound of brightly painted cottages resembled a family campground. But it was no campground, nor was it family-oriented. Instead, it was attempting a "revolutionary socialist utopia" despite the armed guards patrolling its perimeter. Families were not a priority, either. Just as he had in the U.S., Jones continued to split up families here, claiming they inhibited the Temple's goal of true communal life. He had never experienced a functioning, intact family himself, so perhaps he had no idea how wrong he was. But others did.

Several families did manage to live together in small cottages, but unfortunately, not the Wotherspoon family. Mary Margaret lived in cottage number 29, Mary in 46, and Peter in 11. What must it have been like for Mary to experience her spouse as just another Temple member? Or had he already become that back in the U.S.? And how did she feel about having her cherished little girl living among 300 other children there? Did the little family ever get to talk, hug, or spend time alone together? I wanted to believe that, and I hoped that at the very least, Mary was comforted by knowing Peter was somewhere in that jungle with her.

As a "banana republic" that actually grew bananas, Guyana also produced sugarcane and rice on its large plantations. Its rain forests and precious mineral deposits further supported the struggling country. But in 1977, its main economic resource was bauxite, used to make aluminum. Now the country had scored a 99-year lease for a chunk of its remote, uninhabited jungle, with a promise from Jones for a large influx of American money. As an added bonus, his new settlement was located 30 miles from the Venezuelan border, in a disputed region claimed by both Guyana and Venezuela. For the Guyanese government, having a large number of Americans living there could possibly deter Venezuela from attempting a land grab. So, in addition to its much needed "rent," Jonestown might serve as a human shield against losing territory.

Establishing a home for hundreds of people here proved a tremendous undertaking, but somehow the newcomers created a remarkable working community, despite supplies and equipment having to be shipped from Georgetown and even further afield. Driven by necessity — and for many, dedication, and faith in their mission — they also did so without reliable electricity, plumbing, or running water. They had to make do at the most basic levels. Considering all of that, they had a lot to show for the sixteen months that Mary and her family spent there.

According to Stephan Jones, they ran the place like a small government, with different departments such as Agriculture, Construction, Education, and Medical Care. Department heads reported to the Jonestown leadership. A map compiled from Temple documents and survivor recollections indicates a sprawling compound that included many facilities: an animal shelter, bakery, brick factory, laundry, and medical facilities. Its kitchens prepared nearly a thousand meals, three times a day. They had a dental clinic, pharmacy, generator, nursery, office, and radio room, plus crude showers, and a playground. But the generator was unreliable, and some of the listed facilities were more aspirational than functional, according to other survivors.

With perhaps 300 children and 300–400 seniors in the community, more than half of the Jonestown population were either too young or too old to perform the really hard work. Nonetheless, in order for their socialist experiment to work, they all had to pitch in. Seniors were not required to do heavy field work, but many had small vegetable and herb gardens to produce food. Other seniors made hand-crafted goods, like dolls, to sell. Teenagers contributed what they could, but it fell to the able-bodied to create a fully functioning operation. Despite being far removed from adequate roads, reliable power sources, and communications, they included electricians, carpenters, mechanics, engineers, nurses, teachers, and skilled laborers among their ranks. They worked hard, and they had to be flexible: some who had previously been white-collar professionals found new pleasure in driving a tractor or building a cottage.

Handwritten lists from recovered Jonestown records include a partial listing of skills that Mary and Peter contributed to the cause. At age 29, Mary was listed as a teacher, residential care home operator, secretarial work, bookkeeper, buyer, and salesperson. We know from other reports that she also worked in nursing, the cassava crops, and farm and business management, as well as the warehouse in Port Kaituma. At age 31, Peter was listed as a bilingual (Spanish) teacher, translator, musician, artist, weaver, and food preserver. His other roles encompassed weapons and safety. Yet for all the expertise and talent in Jonestown, it would become just a forced-labor camp for many of its members.

Housing varied. Five dormitories, six huts, 48 cottages, and several guest cottages served as sleeping quarters, most with precious little privacy. Meanwhile, Jim Jones lived with his mistress, Carolyn Layton, and two children in his private cottage, known as West House. His personal food supply was stored there in a refrigerator run by a generator. In this way, his medical needs for extra protein and level blood sugar could be readily met, and his abiding fear of being poisoned, ameliorated. His trusty bottle of Jack Daniels may have helped with that, too.

For decades, I had unknowingly pictured Mary and Peter miserably camping in a tent or hut, never imagining that Mary Margaret might have had a simple playground, much less a creative elementary school in Jonestown. Or that the family had access to medical facilities on site, as well as hospitals in Georgetown. I was also glad to learn that the compound's rustic laundry, radio room, and bakery helped to lessen the settlers' numerous deprivations. When their generator functioned, lighting and electricity provided them with a certain amount of security and communications, too. During the rainy seasons, their wooden walkways would ease passages over the abundant mud.

This radical lifestyle was experienced differently among the exiles: some felt it as freedom, others as bondage. For many of them, the experience would change over time. Even so, I never imagined that anyone in Jonestown enjoyed their time there. Had Mary? And what about Peter, and Mary Margaret? What had Jonestown meant for them?

In accord with its socialist mission, the Temple continued its practice of social welfare and community outreach, even in the jungle. During the week, locals would line up outside Jonestown's medical clinic to see its doctor. It is easy to imagine Mary appreciating this kind of service, never losing her heart for others' well-being, even at the cost of her own.

DESPITE THE LOFTY goals, farming in the jungle had been a cockamamie idea from the beginning. Jones attempted what native Guyanese knew to be impossible. They farmed along coastlines, and their successful banana plantations spread out across open lands. They harvested fish from the abundant waters, and rice grown in their wetlands. Their sugarcane plantations thrived, right along with their cassava fields. But in Jonestown, the torrential seasonal rains leached the soil at an alarming rate on the land so laboriously cleared from the jungle. Without tree roots to anchor the soil, vital nutrients were eventually washed away, right along with Jim Jones's ill-considered plans. This was not California, and he was no farmer.

Although staples such as wheat and rice were purchased, growing the residents' own food remained critical. Members worked hard, but with mixed results. Their bananas did well, as did peppers and cassava root. Sweet potato, papaya, and cabbage, plus okra, pineapple and bean crops were also successful. They managed to raise livestock, including chickens, cows, pigs, and boars, as well as two horses. Local streams provided them with fresh fish. Even so, farming here took enormous amounts of labor, much of it back-bending, and all of it in the intense jungle heat. No wonder, then, that security guards patrolled the farm fields as members worked; there could be no escape.

Despite Jones's poor decisions, Guyanese agriculture officials did their best to help out. They advised on soil drainage, crops, and animal breeding. But the Guyanese climate had other plans. During its rainy season, pumps were needed to drain water-logged fields, while work crews bailed others out by hand. At other times, seasonal droughts triggered bucket brigades to water thirsty crops. Either way, it was a losing battle.

From church records, we know that Mary initially worked with the large cassava crops as a field manager. Grown along their one interior road, this crop's spikey, umbrella-shaped leaves were large enough to provide a bit of shade. Its huge edible roots were a staple throughout the Caribbean. During one "Ag" meeting, Mary is recorded as fretting over pests possibly destroying this crucial crop. She also suggests that milling dried cassava could be a possible source of income. Another report describes how Mary helped to carry someone who had fainted from the heat in her cassava field to safety. Her natural kindness was apparently not diminished despite their wretched conditions, and would have been familiar to anyone who knew her.

But how did she keep up with that kind of workload? How did anyone? Without shade, their long workdays must have been almost unbearable. There were no siestas during the worst of the heat, and lunch breaks for many field hands were spent just getting to the food line and then returning to the fields. After work, they did not return to air conditioning, refreshing cool showers, or even adequate rest. Outhouse latrines and solar-heated showers, followed by a short break sitting down for dinner, had to suffice. And without modern laundry facilities, dry, clean clothes were a luxury in the humid jungle. Some would dry their clothes by using the heat generated from the kitchen, making do as best they could.

There was no place for slackers to hide, either. Using his far-reaching and oppressive public address system, Jones awakened everyone at 6:00 a.m. Breakfast was at 7:00. Their work days lasted until 6:00 p.m., six days a week. These punishing hours often included older children and some of the able-bodied older adults. On Sundays, they were allowed to work shorter days, but for all their hard work, Jones's "agricultural project" ultimately produced more misery than food. Toward the end, food shortages would lead to rationing.

WHILE STUDYING FOR a graduate degree in education in Ann Arbor, I had been more interested in life outside the classroom than in. Yet one radical theory of learning stuck with me. At that time, rote memorization was still the norm; as a result, educational theorist John Dewey's theory of "learning by doing" sounded both revolutionary and practical. But I never thought that my own niece would be learning by this method herself, in a remote jungle. Or that her classroom would actually be a tent. Perhaps by choice, but surely by necessity, her education in Jonestown was far more progressive than traditional education back in the States.

Mary Margaret learned by doing, and also by working with other students. She and her classmates helped to build their own playground, an effort that took teamwork and dedication. She could also advance in school according to her ability, instead of age. This, too, was innovative at the time. The school's hands-on learning may have also benefited children who otherwise did not fit in a traditional classroom.

A virtual Eden of exotic animals to learn and write about enhanced Mary Margaret's unusual education. With bird calls, monkey howls, and disembodied critter voices both near and far, her extraordinary habitat became part of her education. Her skies held rainbows of colorful birds, and at ground level wondrous flowers bloomed as large as her precious little head. Guyana also had ten-foot-wide water lilies strong enough to seat a little child. Perhaps Mary Margaret could even cuddle the settlement's baby sloth in her arms, or visit its chimpanzee, Mr. Muggs. Originally bought as a pet back in the U.S., he had been flown to Guyana during Jonestown's pioneer days, and was now Jonestown's community mascot, literally hanging out in his cage.

Jonestown's schools were fashioned in accordance with their "revolutionary" mission of living in common, and sharing equally. Due to a scarcity of school supplies, including pens, pencils, and even paper, the schools had to augment supplies by ordering from Georgetown, or importing them from the U.S., all expensive and slow undertakings. They appealed for help from families back home, and I received requests for art supplies. Teachers also used whatever they had on hand, including palm leaves, wood, clay, natural dyes, and more, just as their indigenous neighbors did every day. Older students in the industrial arts classes also produced candles, soap, and other saleable items, thereby helping to support Jonestown. In doing so, its children shared a sense of responsibility and importance in their community. Their work counted. They counted.

The older children attended school in the pavilion, a roofed, open-air structure with wooden benches. Many attended afternoon classes after field work in the morning, while others studied in the evening, after having dinner with adults. Guyanese history, art, music, crafts, and language arts were taught to different age groups. This is where Peter's extraordinary intelligence and versatility must have shone. He taught math, science, poetry, art, and Spanish, at different age levels. He often collaborated with Edith Roller, the Temple's ad hoc diarist, sharing teaching assignments in poetry and English with her. With her Ph.D. in English, she served as head of Jonestown's education, and while collecting teacher resumés for accreditation by the Guyanese government, she once noted that "Peter has an astonishing number of skills."

Jonestown had evening adult education, too. Classes included the Russian language, ostensibly preparing them for a future exodus to the Soviet Union with its perfected communalism. For a time, learning Russian was even mandatory, impressing — or perhaps puzzling — Russian dignitaries visiting from the USSR's Georgetown Embassy. Regular socialism classes were also held, including specialized ones for women, oddly enough. Classes were augmented by discussion groups, and even tests.

BY DESIGN, JONESTOWN residents received no news from the outside world other than what Jim Jones allowed. He curated it, often editing it on the fly while broadcasting at all hours of the day and night. He thus controlled their understanding of life beyond Jonestown. According to him, their unique socialist community surpassed all others, except, of course, the Soviet Union. Moreover, in depicting the outside world as the enemy, he discouraged members from leaving Jonestown — their "real family." But perhaps he needed his people more than they needed him. It has been said that he used others to confirm his worth, to validate him as a person. And of course, Jones also wanted his people to believe it was dangerous outside of Jonestown; he may also have believed that himself, as his paranoia continued unabated.

A master at creating alternate realities, Jones continually fed his followers a steady diet of lies. Even though there were no more religious sermons in the settlement, he reminded them that they were now living in the world, but no longer of the world. By now, most of them may have believed that racism was the cardinal sin, topping all others. For his increasingly beleaguered flock, this continued drumbeat of bad news from on high helped to keep them in place.

AT LEAST MEALTIMES in the compound could be sociable. While waiting in lines to be served by the kitchen crew, and then sitting together in the dining tent, residents could enjoy each other's company for a short while. Still, even then they had to be careful. Trusting another person could be dangerous. Jones had ordered them to spy on each other: children on their parents, parents on their children — and even partners and best friends on each other. They were to trust only in him, their "father." Selfish behavior was also considered a punishable infraction.

While Jonestown adults lived highly regimented lives, their children lived in special cottages grouped by age. They could see their parents each evening, just as many children with working parents do everywhere. But these were just visits; they did not live together as a family. Parents could visit their children after dinner for a short time, but then, the evening's scheduled events kicked in, and off they went.

Tuesday and Saturday evenings were devoted to meetings, beginning at 7:30 p.m. In these, committee chairs reported on agriculture, livestock, construction, and more. Everyone was expected to attend, and if you dozed off, security guards would poke you awake for the infraction. Jones also meted out discipline and praise during the meetings. Considering their hard work and long days, if any people ever needed rest and rejuvenation, Jones's "family" in Jonestown did. Thankfully, they also had entertainment.

Jones presided over these evenings ensconced in his personal chair, which functioned as a throne, its large size and blue color denoting his power. Sunday night movies included *Three Days of the Condor, Airport, The Grapes of Wrath, One Flew Over the Cuckoo's Nest*, documentaries, and more. Jonestown's children had their own entertainment, watching tapes of *Sesame Street* in their nursery, or at school. I like to picture Mary Margaret laughing at Cookie Monster along with millions of other children across the world.

The adults also had live entertainment, although producing shows in a jungle took both imagination and improvisation. But they had the talent for it. Shanda James was in charge, often singing solos herself, as did many others with fine voices. The community band, "The Jonestown Express," might play, but instead of hymns, R&B, funk, and Motown covers were now popular. Peter sang in duets and played his guitar, just as he had in California. And improbably for a crowd that wore and traded used clothes, they even had a fashion show.

The Soul Steppers, a comedic dance group, plus humorous skits, had everyone laughing. There were also karate exhibitions and drill team performances. The more polished acts that included The Jonestown Express band were occasionally sent to Georgetown to promote good public relations. Back in the U.S., the Temple's famous choir had drawn crowds throughout California, and Jones liked to boast to white pastors that nothing could surpass his Black choir's voices lifted in song. They were "the best." Although they no longer sang hymns, their voices were still raising the roof, but now under the sky.

Improbable as it was, Jonestown even had a basketball team. It had come together spontaneously. While several of the compound's young men were working on a construction project one day, they realized that a hardwood floor in an unfinished building might make a good basketball court. They began shooting hoops, and discovered they were right. At first, Jones reportedly opposed the idea of basketball, viewing it as a diversion from work, but he eventually came around.

He figured that having a team might even be good public relations, so he gave them the green light to form one.

The guys found a coach, had tryouts, and were allowed to quit work early to practice. Using moves gleaned from inner-city basketball courts back in San Francisco, the new team rapidly improved. Equally implausibly, when a sportscaster from Georgetown happened to visit Jonestown, he noticed them practicing, and arrangements were soon made for a tournament with the Guyanese national team.

Basketball would prove to be more than just P.R.; it would ultimately save lives.

DESPITE SEVERE HARDSHIPS, many in Jonestown were proud of the socialist community they were building, sometimes literally from the ground up. They were making it work, and there were small pleasures, too. People planted flowers, took pride in their crops. Some even managed to live with spouses, or partners. They had good times, hopeful times, joined together by hard work and shared adversity. Realizing this, I desperately hoped that Mary and her family lived with occasional joy, too.

According to one former church member, Mary worked "with the river boat captains." It is unclear if he meant that she sailed with the captains on Jonestown business, or that she supervised their deliveries to their Port Kaituma warehouse. If she indeed sailed with them, experiencing the rivers' languid peace would have been a rare freedom and pleasure. She would have been entrusted with this kind of freedom only because Jim Jones counted on her loyalty. He could "read" his people. But even if she ever considered escaping on one of the boats, leaving Mary Margaret behind would have stopped her. By all accounts, Mary remained a devoted mother in Jonestown.

It may also be that Mary marketed Jonestown's handmade goods to surrounding villages on the river. Wooden toys and dolls made by Jonestown seniors, plus candles, soap, and other goods crafted by the high school students, all brought in revenue. If Mary sold these products in Georgetown's lively street markets, she would have stayed with other members at their "Lamaha Gardens" headquarters there.

Lamaha was critical to Jonestown's survival, keeping it connected with the rest of the world. Situated on a gravel road across from a canal, it had two stories built in traditional, wooden Caribbean style, with wraparound porches on the upper level. The living quarters up there stayed dry during the tropical downpours, and caught sea breezes year-round. A large house on the outskirts of Georgetown, Lamaha functioned not only as Jonestown's headquarters, but also office, storehouse, and lodging for staff and visiting members. It also served as a reception venue for meeting with Guyanese officials, and although surrounded by a fence, Lamaha was thus Jonestown's public face to the world.

The ground level housed storage and office space, plus a radio and electronics room, where the staff ordered crucial supplies. Some claim they also processed contraband from there; if so, then guns, drugs, and American currency could all have been used or sold at a large profit. The staff was on duty around the clock, but unlike the rest of their Temple family in the jungle, they had indoor plumbing, and readily available water. They had a rental car to buy groceries, and a kitchen in which to prepare them. They also had access to hospitals, street markets, and the greater world. They could even take in a movie at the city's lone movie theater. Consequently, only the most dedicated of Jones's followers were allowed to work at Lamaha.

Meanwhile, Jones was a savvy operator within Georgetown, expertly "assisting" the Guyanese authorities there at keeping a blind eye in his direction. With his blessing, one of the Lamaha staff, Paula Adams, conducted an affair with a high Guyanese official, enabling her to spy on his government through the connection. As a result, Jones could run his private fiefdom from the jungle using inside information with little interference. Compared to California, the loosely regulated country of Guyana made things easy. Jones managed to rule there with almost complete autonomy from government oversight and demands.

CHAPTER 10

THE JUNGLE WINS

PAVING THE WAY FOR JONES'S RELENTLESS CRUELTY AND ARBITRARY RULES, HE JUSTIFIED HIS EXTREME MEANS IN JONESTOWN WITH HIS IDEALISTIC ENDS, JUST AS HE HAD IN THE U.S. He claimed they were necessary to achieve a perfect socialist community, where everyone was equal, all resources were shared, and there were no elites. Yet, his rhetoric collided head-on with reality. Jones did not live by his own rules, and he lived in his own private cottage. His inner circle in the predominantly Black community was all white, save for one, and they, too, enjoyed special privileges. On the other hand, they all had to deal with the same jungle.

Everyone shared the ground with deadly, six-foot-long bushmaster snakes. Green anacondas hung from their branches above, hungry piranhas patrolled their rivers, and their night sky pulsed with vampire bats. Jonestown folks, all of them, had to be careful. Black flies, chiggers, mosquitoes, ticks, and tarantulas did not respect privilege, either. It was a dangerous neighborhood. Meanwhile, Jones maintained that only his goodness and supernatural power kept everyone safe there. But they had to obey him to keep it that way.

Offering an outrageous example of his protective powers, Jones once horrified his people by announcing that they had eaten the body of an intruder. He bragged that he had personally killed the man to protect them, and that his dead body had been chopped up and mixed into their evening soup. Some of the more gullible believed him, and vomited up their dinners. Too many others kept swallowing all the other lies he was regularly feeding them.

And just as in the U.S., harsh punishments continued in the jungle, but now with inventive variations. There were more categories of wrongdoing, too. Behaviors associated with "capitalist elitism," such as talking back, having a bad attitude, or talking down, were often punished by time in the Learning Crew. Its glorified title was a euphemism for latrine cleaning, field work, and ditch draining. Minor offenders placed in the Crew could work off their punishments; the chores got done, and victims learned to monitor their speech. Other punishments ranged from the merely inconvenient to the sadistic. Some were even more unique; "Big Foot" was a good example.

Debbie Layton, a former Temple leader entrusted with inside information, had defected from Jonestown in May 1978. Once free, she revealed some of its darker aspects. It must be noted that some Jonestown survivors disputed her stories as "evil lies," but her take on Jonestown remains valuable. During an interview with British journalist Gordon Lindsay, she reported that in Jonestown, children aged five to twelve were punished with "Big Foot." Described as a deep well, it was a hole into which they were thrown, then caught by an adult at the bottom. When tossed back up, the children had to shout, "Thank you, Dad!" to Jim Jones standing above. Mary Margaret herself had reportedly endured this horror. Like her mother, she was stubborn, and it's not hard to imagine her acting out, but horrifying to think of her being abused in this way.

Layton also reported that Jonestown's littlest children often just played in the dirt, while the babies were corralled inside a small enclosure. Other survivors reported that Jones frightened parents by claiming that "fascists" from the outside wanted to kill their children. Yet paradoxically, as their "protector," he punished these same children sometimes by sending them into the jungle where they might be eaten by tigers. And the helpless children knew it. These innocents also witnessed adults being mistreated, demonstrating Jones's absolute power over not only them, but their parents, too.

Before, back in the U.S., Jones had once reportedly had a snake crawl all over the body of a woman who was terrified of snakes. Here in the jungle, other forms of terror could be invoked by tying wrongdoers to a wooden stake, making them vulnerable to jungle predators. Still other punishments consisted of fellow members slapping or punching one another, just as in California. When punishments like these had failed for one particular transgressor, diarist Edith Roller recorded that, "Jim wants her worked to death tonight...keep her up all night and at work."

His punishments for adults included a narrow, coffin-like structure known as the "box." Buried four feet underground, it caused sensory deprivation and claustrophobia for anyone trapped inside, sometimes for days. Other members were then tasked to stand overhead, berating the wrongdoer below for their crime. This particular punishment was invoked for serious offenses. Reportedly, Peter had been buried in it after being caught trying to escape. He may also have attempted escape once again, triggering constant supervision. Diarist Edith Roller recorded:

I talked in the pavilion for some time with Peter. We discussed teaching methods, specifically. He told me how he teaches poetry. He seemed not to want to let me go. [So] I had to escort [him] home to the library and turn him over to another responsible adult as he is not allowed to be alone.

Back in California, Peter had been the one who wanted to stay in the Temple when Mary wanted out. Now, he wanted out, but he was obviously too valuable for the Temple to lose. Retrieved FBI documents later listed Peter as biologist, teacher, musician, artist, construction worker, and security guard. He also translated documents sent from their Spanish-speaking neighbor, Venezuela, for Jones. But despite his apparent misery, Peter still had the moxie to make his own hot sauce from peppers grown on the farm, as Roller had also reported. This is the resilient Peter I like to remember.

Apparently, there were no murders in Jonestown up until its demise, although there were a few deaths from natural causes. Jim Jones's own mother, Lynetta, died there in 1977, at age 75. Several other elderly residents, and a newborn infant, also died — all lawfully documented by Guyanese authorities. Nonetheless, human life appeared to be cheap in Jones's imaginary utopia, and he continued to brutalize it with ease.

AFTER MARY LEFT the country in July 1977, I foolishly bragged about my radical sister living in political exile; to me, she was still the anti-war protester. In those post-Watergate, post-Vietnam days of popular distrust in our government, I had no reason to question her church's political reaction to the U.S. government — yet. I also naively assumed that the Temple's move to Guyana was a way of "getting back to the land," a popular counterculture movement renouncing the "plastic-fantastic" American lifestyle. At that time, rural hippie communes were sprouting across the country from Kentucky to California. Places where nature was embraced, and handmade goods, organic gardens, and meditation replaced shopping malls and mindless consumerism. Even so, I had to look up Guyana on a map.

At summer's end in 1978, I moved into a small cabin on Lake Michigan by myself, grieving my way through a sad but necessary divorce. I was feeling unmoored and lost; my husband of five years had been my soulmate. Flat-out crazy about each other, he had proposed on the third date. He was older than me, and an experienced gambler, while I had nothing to lose. Plus, marriage felt like a mere formality. I was wrong. Now all we seemed to share were our broken hearts. We parted as good friends.

Beside losing my partner, I also lost the first and only real home I could call my own. Now using a wood stove for warmth, and with my black lab for company, I felt relatively safe in my cozy two-room cabin. Its off-season, deserted beach was all mine, and as an introvert, I was thankful for long stretches when I saw no one.

Around that time, I got a surprise letter from Mary, from whom I had not heard since she emigrated. When I opened it, however, I immediately knew it was not Mary's handwriting. The undated letter read as follows:

> *Greetings from Guyana*
>
> *So. I guess it has been a long time. I hope all is well with you and your nice house in [deleted]. You wouldn't believe how beautiful this land is. Everything is green and the plants that grow here are the same ones you see in stores being sold in*

stores for $25 dollars or more. We chop them down because here they are weeds which interfere with the growth of our banana trees & and other crops. (alot of wandering jew & rubber tree plants, colius [sic] etc etc) I work with nursing and agriculture. I have been studying about cassava (a potato type crop) and have been using it to make corn bread, grainola [sic], & hot cereal. We grow 4 different kinds of bananas, pineapples, papaya, oranges, watermelon, okra, sweet potatoes, eddoes, cassava, greens, corn you name it- we grow it. The water we drink flows fresh cold and sweet from the jungle streams. The skys are a blue you have never seen before. The clouds look like huge cotton puffs & the sunsets are never the same. We have double rainbows frequently after our rain showers. I could go on and on about the beauty and peace we have here but I could never describe the feeling of unity one gets when they see people working together. Simple basics of life – something we had long forgotten. Something very important gets lost in a highly technical civilization. Well that's all for now. If you ever make any donations to any missionary programs, send one here to me. We are helping the Amerindians; they are very appreciative of any help they get. It gives a person a good feeling of being of help. Lots of love,

c. Mary Wotherspoon

I felt cheated reading this, as if Mary did not care enough to write herself, and I felt no obligation to send any money. I wanted to hear how she was, what she was doing, and if she was content with her move. And there was no return address, other than Jonestown. At the same time, I was busy with all the changes in my life that needed attention, and soon forgot about the strange letter.

Then I received another one, but once again, I knew it had been written by someone other than Mary. Yet the writer was aware that I was an artist and asked me to send art supplies to Jonestown. However, the request was so preposterous that I threw the letter out. Who were these people, anyway? And why was Mary not writing to me herself?

One of our brothers received a letter, too, absurdly asking him to buy the church an airplane. He also declined.

MEANWHILE, OUR BROTHER Steve's life was fraught with a worsening illness, and he was struggling mightily. As the last of the "loose change" kids in our family, he often had only the television for company as a boy. Now, as an adult, he was frequently too ill to function by himself. I acted as the family liaison with his doctors, who ultimately made the dreaded diagnosis of paranoid schizophrenia. There was no broadly effective treatment for it at the time, and it was mercilessly flattening our youngest brother. If ever he needed Mary's support, it was then, but she never knew. We had no way of contacting her, no return address — nothing. She was AWOL in Jonestown.

BACK IN JONESTOWN, residents existed in an increasingly solitary manner, despite being crowded together in their sleeping huts, and working side by side. Aware of Jones's command to report on each other for "disloyalty," they found it safest not to talk or complain. Even their own children were not to be trusted; "Father" Jones had instructed them to keep an eye on their parents. Residents' letters, both written and received, were monitored — radio communications, too. They were deprived of their most basic freedoms, including speech.

Their trusted leader still hammered on about what he called their freedom there in the jungle. They were now free from the government, poverty, crime, and injustice. Yet he governed them; they owned nothing; he brutalized them. He determined when they woke up, what they ate, and where they worked. He decided how long they worked, who they lived with, and where. He owned them. No wonder petty theft of food and clothing was common.

Jones also had them write letters to him confessing their faults, including private sexual attractions and practices. He broke up some marriages and rearranged others; as already mentioned, Mary and Peter no longer lived together. He determined who could have sex, and with whom. At the same time, he used younger, attractive women for sex himself, having shunted his faithful wife aside for his regular mistresses. In this remote jungle, his control now was absolute.

Mary Margaret went to sleep without being tucked in by her parents, nor could she be comforted by them when she was sick, or had a bad dream. Ordered to spy on Mary and Peter, would she even trust them? And why would she? Hatred of nuclear families was encouraged. The Jonestown family was to be their only family, and Jim Jones their father. Yet this father punished them with Big Foot. He had them beaten. In the U.S., Jones would have been jailed for child abuse, but in Jonestown, it was normal.

Jones's fierce vigilance aimed at preventing insurrection, and criticism of Jonestown was treason. Furthermore, there was no escape from his voice; his broadcasted rants on their P.A. system could be heard even in the farm fields. At any time, he could order everyone to the pavilion for an emergency meeting, and he sometimes did so in the middle of the night. When self-medicated with drugs, he could be incoherent, using his loudspeaker to steal their sleep with rambling lectures and tirades. For prisoners of war, this kind of sleep deprivation would be labeled torture by the International Court of Justice in the Hague. But in Jonestown, this, too, was normal.

In spite of everything, some of Jones's followers continued to worship him with canine devotion. But others were fed up. At one point after a punishingly long day of construction work, Jones's son Stephan could no longer stand it. During another middle-of-the-night broadcast, Stephan picked up an axe to chop down the pole holding the loudspeaker. Once there, he noticed a small group of other sleep-deprived members groggily gathering on Jones's outrageous command. In spite of his intense frustration, Stephan could not bear to undo his own hard work — he had planted that very pole himself. He put the axe down. He noticed the weary group there was smiling, looking his way. They understood his anger, but also his unwillingness to undo his work.

Stephan lived a fractured life of privilege as Jones's son. While Jonestown had become hell for many inhabitants, he managed to escape some of that hell. For him, the jungle was a paradise. It was his sanctuary, and he spent as much time in it as he could. As his heart's true home, he felt safe there despite its dangerous animals. Sensing a connection and sympathy for them, he actually delighted in their company. He was never bitten, not even by a snake. In fact, whenever a snake was sighted inside the compound, he was the one called to handle it. "I was the guy who everyone called when they needed a snake killed." But when on his own, he allowed the numerous snakes frequenting his sleeping hut their freedom.

As one of Jonestown's early pioneers, Stephan had learned the ways of the jungle from his indigenous coworkers. When encountering a potentially dangerous jungle cat, he knew how to react safely: stand tall to thwart a jaguar. As he embraced the jungle, it seemed to return the favor. He was bitten only once — by a rat. To protect himself from the rainforest's dangerous insects, he wisely wore long pants tucked into high boots.

But the jungle that Stephan so loved, over time felt increasingly punishing to many of the city transplants back inside the compound.

FROM ABOVE, THE land cleared for Jonestown resembled a peculiar bald spot on a thick, green carpet. Without trees to protect them there, people had to make their own shade under hats, tents, metal roofs, and dried palm leaves. But over time, heat exhaustion eventually wore the settlers down. Field workers baked under the merciless equatorial sun, and there were no sea breezes or beaches to cool them. A downpour while working in the fields might help, but the community's makeshift showers could only wash mud away, not heat. And how long did it take for laundry to dry in the humid jungle? Rot and fungus were common, and comforts few.

Troubles intensified as their ailing leader grew increasingly delusional. Jones still believed they lived under constant threat of siege, while most residents were working hard just to get through the day, and others, through the night. Restful sleep eluded many due to the heat and Jones's nocturnal broadcasts. Meanwhile Jones himself enjoyed air conditioning and a special bed with a mosquito net in his private cabin.

The hardships were mounting. Jonestown's farm was struggling to produce food, resulting in rationing. Most meals now consisted of rice soup, or rice and beans, with meat perhaps once a week. A weekly cookie was a treat. In fact, the settlers should not have needed to go hungry. Later reports of Jones's offshore accounts, from Switzerland to Romania and Panama, were reportedly worth about $8.5 million USD. So while his people were losing weight and sleep, Jones's hidden offshore bank accounts were gaining interest.

As if hunger were not cruel enough, with no immunity to tropical diseases or pests, the struggling inhabitants were weakened by overwork and ill health. Children were sick, many with ringworm or other parasites. Open wounds were common, often with only cassava root powder to treat them. Despite the onsite pharmacy, many proper medications were unavailable. If toddlers played in the dirt, and babies were fenced inside a small enclosure — as was reported — they were sure to pick up parasites. As it was, children had to be regularly dewormed and given anti-malarial pills.

When visitors were on site, everyone ate better, rules were relaxed, and work hours were shortened, to keep up appearances. Members were instructed to address Jones as "Jim." He became "Father" and "Dad" once again as soon as the outsiders left. But by now, his "children" were suffering from hunger and exhaustion.

ACCORDING TO STEPHAN Jones, his father had once been a loving, sensitive parent, and only over time did he become a totally different person: one who believed his own lies. Stephan also believed that Jones initially used drugs to numb himself while tormented by the cruelty and sadistic punishments he inflicted upon his followers. He believed his father had a conscience.

Back in the U.S., Mary had been disgusted by Jim Jones's blatant drug use. Now in Jonestown, drugs eventually disabled him. He stumbled while speaking; his voice was often weak or inaudible even when broadcasting. And no wonder. Injectable Valium, Quaaludes, barbiturates, and stimulants were all available to him on demand, according to investigative journalist Tim Reiterman. While on stimulants Jones would broadcast for hours, tripping on words as his addled brain raced ahead of his tongue. Jones also lost weight — some estimated 30 pounds—and his handshake became noticeably weak. Due to his increasing deterioration, by the fall of 1978 the leadership in Jonestown was fast becoming a house of cards.

In addition to poor crops, failing health, and supposedly dwindling revenues, Jones's backup plan for escape to Russia had also fizzled. Perhaps a Soviet official's refusal to accept money from him during a recent visit to Jonestown felt insulting. Whatever the case, Jones tried to save face by claiming that Russia was not living up to his socialist standards after all. This was another reality check, one that backed Jones into yet another corner of his own making. Inconsistent and increasingly muddled, he was losing direction with nowhere to turn, first flirting with the Soviet Union, then denouncing it.

He was riding the proverbial tiger: it was becoming too dangerous to continue, yet also too risky to hop off. Either way, he could not escape. He was cornered, and the master manipulator would soon face a hard reckoning with almost nothing left but his delusions. And even those were about to be challenged.

Drugs no longer soothed him; they incapacitated him. He was more paranoid, declaring that anyone leaving Jonestown was a "traitor" and would be killed. But by then, many were too weak or otherwise unable to leave; Jonestown's 300 children and 400 seniors had no choice at all. They were all stuck. Dissatisfaction was mounting, with some feeling more loyalty to each other than to their increasingly impaired leader. Yet escape was almost impossible.

It was six miles on foot to Port Kaituma's river boats, airstrip, and the promise of freedom. There was only one road out, and navigating under the jungle's dense canopy without the sun or a horizon to gauge direction was hopeless. The dense understory harbored insects, jungle cats, and snakes, further discouraging escape. Members' passports had been confiscated, and they had no money. Armed security guards at the gate could stop them if they even got that far. If that was not enough, Jones threatened that anyone making it to Port Kaituma would be easily found and returned to Jonestown. This was another lie.

While still in California, when met with opposition from certain authorities, Jones had reportedly employed the threat of mass suicide of his members. Now in Jonestown, he rehearsed this practice again in his White Night drills, the latest one occurring as late as October of '78. To his people, he now portrayed mass suicide as a type of noble martyrdom, much like Buddhist monks' protests of self-immolation. Or Native Americans refusing surrender to the white man. He claimed that Jonestown's socialist-communist ideals were worth dying for, too. He called it "revolutionary suicide," a dramatic denunciation of the greed and injustice of American capitalist imperialism. However, his rationale ignored the fact that this shocking protest method would effectively destroy its so-called message. Their means would obliterate — not justify — their ends.

During Jonestown's final months, Jim Jones increased his control over defiant and unruly members by drugging them. It was easier than beatings or complicated punishments. Hence, his formerly bright head of entertainment, Shanda James, was seen staggering around, dysfunctional and incoherent. She and other "difficult" members were drugged, sometimes kept in Jones's cynically named "Extended Care Unit." Select others were drugged to ensure proper behavior when outsiders would visit. Now in his final descent into madness, Jones's health rapidly deteriorated, with alcohol and other drugs paving the way.

As conditions worsened, the flailing patriarch ordered drugs for all. Soon, almost every member wound up ingesting a mild sedative in their mealtime drinks. Lightly sedated members would be easier to manage, while still able to do their work. So Jonestown's unsuspecting settlers were now ingesting Valium and Quaaludes mixed into their beverages. Stimulants could then be strategically used to maximize work output when needed.

How could so many drugs be procured deep inside a remote jungle, in a distant third-world country, where food was scarce? This was the work of Larry Schacht, M.D., Jonestown member and physician. According to Guyana's chief medical officer, George Baird, M.D., Schacht's incomplete medical training made him unfit to practice. Yet Baird had done nothing to rectify this serious violation of medical ethics. His concerns conveniently faded along with other lax Guyanese government oversight of Jonestown, and Dr. Schacht was left to do Jim Jones's bidding undisturbed.

CHAPTER 11

IT WAS MURDER

A SMALL GROUP OF JONES'S TRUSTED STAFF MEMBERS HAD STAYED BEHIND IN SAN FRANCISCO TO MANAGE THE TEMPLE'S AFFAIRS THERE. They also kept Jones updated on current issues via a shortwave radio powerful enough to reach Jonestown's Lamaha headquarters. One concern in particular was a source of worry.

A local California group, Concerned Relatives, had formed a few months before the Temple's exodus, seeking to expose the Temple's abuse of its members. The group included former members and relatives of current members. They had contacted local, state, and federal authorities, as well as the media, but with little success. At the same time, others unaffiliated with the Concerned Relatives group had reported the church's purported abuses to various authorities, also with little or no success.

When the Concerned Relatives learned that members in Jonestown were being kept there against their will, their fears intensified. Their efforts to alert authorities finally succeeded when U.S. Representative Leo Ryan of California agreed to investigate their claims. Ryan himself was no stranger to controversial issues, or to using unorthodox tactics to investigate them. He once got himself incarcerated in order to examine California prison conditions firsthand. Many believed that he carried out such risky ventures with good intentions, while others would say with a thick head. He could be clumsy.

Impediments to Ryan's proposed trip to Guyana did not stop him now, either. Several other congressmen had initially agreed to accompany him, but one by one they opted out. In addition, both the U.S. State Department and its embassy in Georgetown advised Ryan and the Concerned Relatives that Jonestown was private property and they had no authority to enter it without permission. Despite these headwinds, Ryan decided to continue, although his visit would have to be unofficial.

During a briefing before his trip, the State Department informed Ryan that rumors of mass suicide drills and members being held against their will in Jonestown were "nonsense." Other reports suggest that Ryan was warned about the dangers of visiting, or interfering in Jonestown. Whatever he was told, the congressman forged ahead. And he did not go alone.

What eventually became known as the "Ryan group" included two of his congressional aides, nine from the media, and 14 from the Concerned Relatives group. What Ryan failed to include was security for himself. Due to the unofficial status of his trip, the federal government could not offer him any, either. But Ryan felt safe having a news crew with him. The news crew, in turn, felt safe by having a U.S. congressman with them.

When Jones learned that Ryan's visit would include the press and the Relatives group, his opposition to the visit intensified. The unwelcomed included the NBC crew of Bob Flick, Don Harris, Bob Brown, Greg Robinson, and Steve Sung. Print reporters included Ron Javers of the *San Francisco Chronicle*, and Tim Reiterman and photographer Greg Robinson from the *San Francisco Examiner*. Charles Krause of the *Washington Post*, and independent British reporter, Gordon Lindsay, also joined the group. Fourteen Concerned Relatives then rounded out the travel roster.

Many in the group departed for Guyana either foolishly misinformed, or dangerously ignorant of the threat that Jones might pose. Only the Concerned Relatives appreciated their mission's danger. They knew firsthand the ruthless leader they faced, and they hoped to extract their loved ones from his terrible grip. But in turn, with their inside knowledge of Jones's behavior, they presented the gravest threat to him. And he knew it.

When Ryan had initially contacted Jones for permission to visit in October, Jones turned him down, and he remained defiant. However, his advisors inside Jonestown convinced him that a visit from Ryan could highlight Jones's wonderful socialist utopia, and thereby silence his critics. Somewhat reassured, Jones then attempted to control the unwanted intrusion by forbidding the press and the Concerned Relatives entry inside Jonestown. For him, allowing the hated U.S. government, personified by the congressman, into his private domain was risky enough.

Adding to the potentially perilous situation, Jones was seriously ill by then. After purportedly suffering a heart attack, he was visibly so weak that at times he needed help walking, and had trouble speaking. One visitor in Ryan's group would later describe him as 30 pounds lighter than when she had last seen him back in California. At age 47, Jones had turned into a frail, old man. In fact, his personal physician, Carlton Goodlett, MD, had recently, but unsuccessfully, pleaded with him to get proper medical attention in Georgetown. According to Goodlett, Jones refused critical treatment by claiming that he, Jones, was the real healer.

This precarious state of affairs in Jonestown was now advancing at a deadly pace. Unable to thwart the feared intrusion, Jones ordered his members not to speak with Ryan, or the press whom he labeled as "fascists." But even this attempt to control the visit would fail.

Jim Jones actively feared the congressman's visit, but what about his followers? Were they fearful, too? Or were some hoping that Ryan's visit might somehow liberate them? As far as we know, both reactions were rippling through the compound.

Two among the hopeful group had met up by accident. Vernon Gosney, a slightly built 25-year-old and longtime Temple member, had been in Jonestown for over seven months by then. He was desperately unhappy there, but he doubted himself for wanting to leave, wondering if he was just a bad socialist. Yet he was not a self-centered person. He was known for his generous heart, and was troubled by what it was telling him now. He wanted to escape, but kept his misery to himself, except for one of his trusted bunkmates. Together, they commiserated over poor food, sleep deprivation, endless meetings, and Jones's haranguing broadcasts. Life had become torture.

Then, one day while walking along a secluded path, Monica Bagby, a brash 18-year-old and friend of Gosney's bunkmate, approached Gosney. She astonished him by saying, "Let's get the fuck out of this place!" Absolutely no one spoke like that — spies were everywhere. But she was a young and insufficiently fearful newcomer in Jonestown. Fortunately, Gosney did not turn away from this desperate young woman. The two bonded. She was black, he was white, and both were gay.

Gosney was a humble man who did not quite trust himself, while Monica was a headstrong, rebellious teenager placed in Jonestown by her mother to beat a drug addiction. Monica's strong desire to leave encouraged Gosney, and together they made plans to leave with Congressman Ryan.

THE PRESENCE OF so many journalists in Ryan's encourage was bound to make Jones feel threatened. NBC reporter Don Harris, a physically imposing presence, was known for an often aggressive investigative style. The *Washington Post's* Charles Krause added the potential for unprecedented national coverage. Taken together, all these reporters caused Jones to see the visit as an ambush. Yet it was the Concerned Relatives who had been flooding the American Embassy in Georgetown with requests to investigate Jonestown that presented the greatest peril for Jones himself.

At about midnight on November 15, 1978, the "Ryan group" landed in Georgetown, Guyana, only to discover that their hotel reservations had fallen through. As the only decent lodging in the rustic capital, the Pegasus Hotel was fully booked. Had Jones pulled strings with local officials to orchestrate this inconvenience? A number of the weary arrivals chose to sleep in the hotel's lobby. Others found alternative lodging. Ryan and his two aides—Jackie Speier, who was a raven-haired beauty, and James Schollaert, stayed at the home of the American Ambassador, John Burke.

While poking around the capital city the next day, several of the Ryan group encountered members of the Jonestown basketball team in town for a tournament. Perhaps this encounter was happenstance, but then again, perhaps not. Jim Jones could play puppet master from afar; he had instructed the team to make a good impression if they met up with the visitors. With a bit of money and some precious freedom now, the young team members were having a good time, and were in no hurry to return to leave. The players were friendly toward the visitors, and dutifully enthusiastic about Jonestown. Jim Jones had been right: a basketball team was good public relations.

After casually chatting about Jonestown around town, Ryan decided to begin his investigation in earnest. Accompanied by the *Washington Post's* Charles Krause, he headed straight for the Temple's headquarters at Lamaha House. Once there, Ryan reportedly climbed over its perimeter fence while Krause stayed back. If Ryan was counting on his charm to facilitate his visit to Jonestown through the Lamaha staff, he was greatly mistaken. On the contrary: his sudden appearance frightened the dozen or so members on duty at the time. They were angry, and outright rejected Ryan's rude assumption that they were being held against their will by Jones. The brief encounter did not go well. Nor did the following one by the Concerned Relatives, who approached the staff later that day. Lamaha's staff held fast, obeying Jones's order to ignore the Ryan group.

As it turned out, Ryan's presumptuous manner inadvertently validated Jones's rants about U.S. governmental spying and interference. Jones's paranoia was widely known and called for extreme caution: Ryan may have shown too little caution in these dangerous circumstances. Or, if the congressman had been adequately briefed by the State Department regarding possible danger in Jonestown, would he have been more careful? Perhaps State had held back warnings. As it was, Ryan had not bothered to find a replacement after the initial psychologist decided not to go. Would lives have been spared it he had not simply plowed ahead without a full team?

Other factors contributed to the impending disaster by fueling Jones's fears of government interference. Jones was aware of the CIA presence in Georgetown, apparently an open secret in the small capital. But he failed to realize that they might have been there to keep an eye on nearby communist Cuba — not him. He was also bothered by rumors about U.S. Customs in Miami having checked Jonestown's imports for smuggled guns and cash. On top of that, the U.S. Social Security Administration had delivered a blow to the settlement's main source of income by halting payments to Jonestown's seniors. It had been only a temporary move, but one that Jones would not forget.

These mounting threats, real and perceived, continued to feed Jones's paranoia. And now the "treacherous" outside world that he and his followers had fled was about to crash into their private sanctuary.

Still putting up a fight, Jones advised Georgetown's airport that Port Kaituma's landing strip was unserviceable due to muddy conditions. But his ploy failed. On Friday, November 17, the visitors' chartered plane left Georgetown at 2:00 p.m. for the 90-minute flight to Port Kaituma. Their small Twin Otter aircraft had a carrying capacity of only 18 passengers. These included Temple attorneys Mark Lane and Charles Garry, four Concerned Relatives, the Embassy's Deputy Chief of Mission (DCM) Richard Dwyer, and Neville Annibourne from the Guyanese Ministry of Information. Leo Ryan, Jackie Speier, and members of the press filled the rest of the seats. A disappointed band of Concerned Relatives had to be left behind in Georgetown.

As a country, Guyana was considered dangerous by much of the developed world. During the final leg of their journey to Jonestown, some of the airborne visitors now sensed that danger, too. Flying over the country's vast territory of thick, unrelenting jungle unnerved them. It did not help that when approaching Port Kaituma for the first time, the pilot performed a flyover of its landing strip to check conditions there. After that, he banked in a low flyover of Jonestown itself, allowing an aerial view of the whole compound.

The plane's loud engines must have torn like a buzzsaw through the afternoon below, where preparations for the Ryan visit were underway. Where were Mary and Peter at the time? Did they look up at the low-flying plane? Did Ryan's impending visit frighten them? For some on the ground, the visit may have spelled doom, while for others, perhaps hope. But for Jim Jones, the unwelcome flyover must have felt like his enemy's first shot across the bow.

As the Twin Otter approached the airstrip once again, the jungle seemed to race up to meet the visitors during their final, steep descent. After a fast landing on the hard, short runway, the relieved passengers applauded. Descending the plane's creaky gangway, they were immediately met by regional officials, including a local policeman wearing sandals and a badge; a visit from an American congressman was a big deal here. The officer announced right at the outset that Gordon Lindsay, the British journalist who had written unfavorably about Peoples Temple in the past, was denied entry to Jonestown. As a result, Lindsay reboarded the plane.

The officer then invited the rest to Port Kaituma, a 20-minute walk from the airstrip. But then word came from a different official that the visitors were not allowed to enter the village. Apparently, the visitors' long journey to Jonestown was not yet over, and they had no choice but to wait at the airstrip. Negotiations over just who would be allowed to enter Jonestown ensued, as Jim Jones continued to fight them, now from a perilously short distance.

Meanwhile, Jonestown's security guards, on hand for the arrival, did their best to project a sense of threat, looking tough from the sidelines while awaiting instructions from Jones. After a while, they left and then returned again to announce that the two Temple attorneys and DCM Dwyer would be allowed into Jonestown. Congressman Ryan and Speier could also come. This select, small group departed with the security guards, leaving the rest behind.

Friendly locals treated the remaining visitors to cold beer underneath Guyana's hot equatorial sun. After a while, they moved to the shade under the plane's wings, where they waited for three hours. During that time, a Port Kaituma police constable talked with Beverly Oliver from the Concerned Relatives group. As the young officer quietly related tales of terrible beatings inside Jonestown to her, Oliver motioned to reporter Reiterman to come and listen. The constable described mysterious night flights when wounded Jonestown members with broken limbs and severe wounds were picked up for transport to hospitals in Georgetown. As he spoke, it was clear that he despised Jim Jones.

Meanwhile, inside Jonestown, the first group of visitors negotiated with Jones, arguing that allowing the rest of the waiting group inside would be good publicity. He could show off the wonders of his agricultural project to them. Eventually, Jones relented. His dump-truck taxi then returned to the airstrip to collect the rest of Ryan's entourage, allowing the waiting Twin Otter to take off with its lone passenger, Gordon Lindsay.

But by now, it was late in the day as the rest of the visitors boarded the truck, standing in its open bed under a gentle rain. They passed by the village of Port Kaituma, and continued on for three miles to the entrance of Jonestown's property. Armed guards at its gatehouse allowed them to proceed for the last three miles of their journey, now through the jungle. They finally arrived at the compound itself in the early equatorial dusk.

The late arrivals were greeted not by Jim Jones, but by attorneys Garry and Lane. Reporter Tim Reiterman noticed that Ryan and Speier were already at work in a large, open-air pavilion, interviewing residents from a list provided by the Concerned Relatives. As they did so, small clusters of curious Temple members were hanging out nearby, but maintaining a polite distance. As the reporter followed the two attorneys, Reiterman also noticed a playground with swings and a wooden jungle gym, a surprisingly ordinary sight in this highly unusual setting.

Unwilling to wait for a formal introduction to Jonestown's leader, Reiterman, an imposing figure at six-feet-four and 200 pounds, respectfully introduced himself to Jim Jones. Having seen Jones earlier in San Francisco, the reporter was surprised to see how frail and shrunken he had become. His glazed eyes, hollow cheeks, and feeble handshake alone would make news back in California. But surprisingly, Jones was in a talkative mood, extoling the wonders of Jonestown to Reiterman as they stood near a large sign that read, "Those who do not remember the past are condemned to repeat it."

By now it was late, and time for the guests' dinner. In her practiced and gracious way, Marceline Jones, known as "Marci," served as host, formally welcoming the visitors as they gathered in the dining tent. The residents had already had their dinner, so they lingered about, wearing their best clothes, and stealing glances at the intruders. Jim Jones ate with some of the press at the head table, while the Concerned Relatives sat with their Jonestown family members elsewhere. Dinner, by all reports, was delicious. They were served pork, sourced from Jonestown's own piggery, and gravy; from their bakery, biscuits; and from their farm garden, fresh vegetables. Cool, sweet water from their wells completed their surprisingly good meal.

As they dined, Jim Jones answered questions, and expounded on the wonders of Jonestown. Reiterman took notes as the leader also complained about abuses by the U.S. government, citing arson, gunshots, threats, and assassination attempts on himself. The journalist noticed that Jones lost his train of thought at times. At other times, he mangled or slurred his words, which seemed to embarrass Jones's ever-present aides. None of that, however, deterred Jones's persistent, if awkward, performance. He kept talking until the evening's entertainment of live music drowned out all conversation. Elsewhere, as the print reporters lingered with Jones after dinner, the NBC crew were shooting film and nosing about, recording, and interviewing some of the residents.

After the musical entertainment finished, Jones started up again, letting loose an astonishing compendium of complaints and revelations, with the reporters around him paying close attention. Jones now seemed despondent, lapsing between despair and complaint. He repeated the glories of Jonestown, but then would pivot back to U.S. government evils, ricocheting between the two. At one point, he protested, "Power? … I hate power, just as I don't want money," and, "I wish I had never been born because I never would have made mistakes. I brought 1,200 people here." When asked why he favored Marxism, he simply replied, "It's a reflection of what I thought best." He then confessed, "I curse the day I was born."

This was an astounding revelation, and the reporters kept the interview moving with more questions. Perhaps sensing he was near the end of his life, Jones used the past tense as he talked. At another point, he moaned, "Sometimes I feel like a dying man … I don't know why these people hate me." He protested, claiming that "I don't want anything in life." Hearing all of this, Reiterman thought Jones talked like an "ill, trapped and despondent" prisoner.

Jones's dark mood at the table clashed dramatically with the entertainment starting up again on the nearby stage. Up there the Soul Steppers energized the crowd with their dance music, inspiring everyone to stand. Even toddlers and seniors bopped and boogeyed to the compelling beat. Then, after the stage show, Congressman Ryan was asked to address the crowd. He obliged, praising the entertainment and what he had seen thus far of Jonestown. The relieved and delighted residents gave him a standing ovation, easing some of the tension. Even so, the joyful mood failed to affect Jones—until a radio call from the Lamaha headquarters seemed to lift his spirits.

Stephan Jones called to report the results of their basketball tournament in Georgetown. The Guyanese national team had won by only ten points, which, for the Jonestown team, was considered a win considering their opponents' superior skill. However, Jones revised the score to a win by ten points when he announced it to everyone at the pavilion. He was still editing their reality.

After that, Jones returned to the press reporters at the table to continue his recitation of woe, complaining about false and unfair accusations aimed at Jonestown. He argued, "There's no barbed wire here. We don't have three, let alone 300, who want to leave." Since many of his listeners around that table had yet to hear complaints about life there, his declaration may have rung true for the moment. What Jones did not acknowledge was that he and his security guards functioned as Jonestown's "barbed wire." As did the jungle, itself. And soon enough, his delusions about members not wanting to leave would also be challenged for all the world to see. He was cornered.

Nevertheless, the weary leader continued to exhibit an astounding disconnect from reality. When asked about his reported ban on sex in Jonestown, he cited the birth of 33 babies there in rebuttal. His tight control over all relationships, sexual and otherwise, went unmentioned. He also maintained that seniors could keep their Social Security checks, which was patently untrue for most. He mentioned member beatings somewhat obliquely, quickly adding these were now all in the past — done. None of that mattered now. When asked about rumors of mass suicide, he dismissed them as yet another misunderstanding.

During their long interview, the reporters sitting with Jones may not have noticed NBC's Don Harris. During the stage performances, Harris had taken off on his own, quietly walking around the perimeter, just observing, and making himself available to anyone wanting to contact him privately. His intuition proved right: things were happening offstage.

One member privately asked DCM Dwyer for help getting out of Jonestown, and Dwyer quietly passed the request along to Ryan. Then another request came, this time from Vernon Gosney. Gosney would later report his experience to the FBI:

When one of the reporters was walking around the edge of the pavilion [Harris], I stuck the note in the fold of his arm and it fell to the ground, and so I picked up the note and gave it back to him and said, 'You dropped something' and this little boy about nine years old started saying, 'He passed a note! He passed a note!' ... I managed to pass a note ... asking Congressman Ryan to please help me and Monica get out of Jonestown ... He [Ryan] came to talk to me that night, and said that we had the first two seats on the plane leaving the next day. I tried to convey to him the extreme danger he was in, but he felt that he had the 'Congressional shield of protection' on him and wouldn't be harmed.

BOTH REQUESTS TO Dwyer and Harris were handled secretly. When they reached Congressman Ryan and Speier, the two of them finally realized that something was "very, very wrong." Up until then, their interactions with Jonestown residents had been pleasantly reassuring. Members had claimed to be content with their situation, including family members of the Concerned Relatives.

With nightfall now hard upon them, the NBC film crew said they needed to return the next day for better light. It had been a long, trying day, and it was time to put it to bed. But which beds, where, and for whom? After their welcoming dinner and pleasant entertainment, the crew was surprised that their request to spend the night due to the late hour was rejected. They thought they might simply camp out in the pavilion, but Jones would not allow it. He allowed only certain people to stay. Ryan and Speier were given a cabin, and the diplomats Dwyer and Annibourne took Marci Jones's private cottage. The two attorneys were also given shelter. But the news media and the four Concerned Relatives had to make the slow trek back to Port Kaituma in the dark.

While these "rejects" were making their way back to Port Kaituma, Jones radioed Lamaha. He talked with Stephan again, ordering the basketball team to immediately return to Jonestown: most of them were also his personal bodyguards. But Stephan resisted, saying they wanted to stay another day. Jones then recruited Marci to reinforce his order to return. Since Stephan and his mother were close, he knew by the tone of her voice that she did not mean it, so he stood his ground. Thoroughly defeated, Jones reportedly sputtered and raged against two of the only people who dared to disobey him.

ASSISTED BY JOHNNY Brown Jones, one of Jones's adopted sons, the ousted visitors found lodging in Port Kaituma. Offered the empty upstairs of a house there, some of them spread out their stuff on the floor. Their impromptu host, Mike, also owned one of the village's two pubs, "Mike and Sons' Weekend and Disco," right next door. For tonight, it would also serve as a gathering spot for the news crew.

Despite the late hour, the journalists filed into Mike's pub to relax and compare notes. However, its loud music and walls adorned with Day-Glo paintings of naked women, drove them outside to the patio where they could hear themselves talk. And laugh — they needed to decompress. When a local entered, cautiously seeking them out, Reiterman noticed him. The reporter was tired by now, but he was also a relentless newshound, so he approached the man. It was the same young constable from the airstrip, now out of "uniform," meaning without his shotgun. He was on a personal mission, and he wanted to talk to the visitors.

The constable quietly invited Reiterman to join him outside on the road, but asked to do so discreetly as he did not want to be seen. Apparently, Mike, the bar owner, and their temporary host, was "friendly with Jonestown," and the policeman did not want any trouble from that direction. Exiting separately to avoid attention, reporters Krause and Javers joined Reiterman and the officer outside. He led the three men away from the noisy bar, crossed railroad tracks, a footbridge, and then up a hill to a distant and windowless building. It was the police station for this humble hamlet.

Once inside, the four men sat together in a sparsely furnished room, lit only by a candle. The off-duty police officer believed he was risking his safety by talking about Jonestown; his revelations were chilling. In the dim light, the three newsmen were told of torture and secrecy inside Jonestown, related in hushed tones. But now safely out of sight, the constable took his time, elaborating on the sketchy information he had first related at the airstrip.

He reported that he had been inside Jonestown, and had actually seen the notorious "torture hole" where Peter and others had been punished. He had first heard about it from an escaped, injured Jonestown member. The frightened officer went on to describe mysterious night flights in and out of Port Kaituma, when wounded Jonestown residents with broken limbs and "terrible wounds" were evacuated. He explained that locals had noticed these strange activities because of all the flares being used to light their crude, dark airstrip.

The constable momentarily stopped talking, becoming guarded after hearing approaching footsteps. It turned out to be only the village's electrical plant engineer, on duty for the 2:00 a.m. power stoppage to conserve energy. The little group there was still safe. The three reporters then left after discussing a possible visit the next morning to the compound, accompanied by the officer who could show them the "torture hole."

Back at the disco-pub, the others were still drinking and relaxing. They had been comparing notes and impressions about the creepy, and even dangerous, signals they picked up on inside Jonestown. It dominated their conversation. After rejoining them now, Javers, Krause, and Reiterman said nothing about their clandestine encounter with the constable. At the same time, the NBC crew had discoveries of their own, which they also kept to themselves. News like theirs was a prized commodity in this competitive crowd.

When Reiterman and the others were absent, NBC's Don Harris revealed Gosney's note, tucked safely inside his boot, to his buddies at the pub. Its plea for help to escape Jonestown was headline news. Those at the table realized they now had the answer to the Ryan investigation right there in that note: members were being held against their will. It was a bombshell.

As it was, the two news groups did not exchange their "scoops" until the next morning, and even then, guardedly so. When NBC's Steve Sung inadvertently let slip something about their discovery, the others then shared theirs about the secret meeting at the police station.

Considering their revelations, both crews now regarded Jonestown as a powder keg, and one with a glowing fuse.

WITH RYAN STAYING inside Jonestown, normal routines were completely set aside. His presence supercharged the leadership's sense of danger; Jones's frazzled inner circle were arguing among themselves. To make matters worse, the media crews and Concerned Relatives would soon be returning to Jonestown. The visit was far from over.

Early the next morning, a group of nine Jonestown residents decided to execute a secret escape plan. The distraction of the Ryan visit had presented an unexpected opportunity to put it into action. These plotters arose at their normal time of 6 a.m. this Saturday, but nothing else about this day — November 18, 1978 — would be normal. Jim Jones had not awakened everyone on the loudspeaker as usual, and they did not have to go to work today, either. Nor were there any security guards on duty at breakfast.

Seizing this opportunity, the clandestine group of five adults and four children asked for permission from the security force to go on a phony picnic. The adults indicated the piggery, located far out on the compound's outer perimeter, as their given destination for their picnic. Perhaps distracted by Ryan's presence onsite, the guards gave them permission. The group then left immediately.

After reaching the piggery, they continued on toward the guard shack at the front gate, but carefully avoided the guards there. Instead of turning left onto the main road toward Port Kaituma three miles away where they could readily be found, they headed in the opposite direction. They were aiming for Matthews Ridge, more than 20 miles away. While using a jungle path in that direction, two men, also defectors, joined them as planned. They continued on together. The group hurried toward railroad tracks originally built for the area's former mining operation. These tracks would then lead them all the way to Matthews Ridge, a remote government outpost with a police station, and to safety.

BACK IN PORT Kaituma that morning, the news media and Relatives waited for a suspiciously tardy pickup from their Jonestown hosts. Ostensibly, the dump truck-taxi had steering trouble, which, by now, felt like outright deterrence. Consequently, the group arrived in Jonestown late, at about 11 a.m. They were offered breakfast by Marci, once again their host. Due to their late start, most of the news crew skipped breakfast. They had work to do.

While approaching the pavilion area, Reiterman noted two boys ineptly playing catch. Upon seeing a large group of children happily watching a *Willy Wonka & the Chocolate Factory* tape near the stage, the reporter sensed that both of these scenarios felt staged for the visitors. On the last morning of her life, little Mary Margaret was probably watching the movie with the other children. This diversion may have spared her and the other children from the intensity that was building all around, but it did not fool Reiterman. The odd juxtaposition of joy and misery seemed true for all of Jonestown, and the contrasts were often extreme. The Ryan group encountered members who seemed genuinely proud of their work there, and they appeared to be content. But on this particular morning, it was the discontented members who would change the course of history.

NBC's DON HARRIS had originally been warned against interviewing Jim Jones. Nevertheless, the media star plowed ahead despite Jim Jones's precarious condition. He conducted a private, one-on-one interview with the weakened leader that morning. In contrast with Jones, tall, robust Harris was an imposing figure, dressed safari-style, and he looked good on camera. But very few would ever see his interview.

According to an NBC producer, Patricia Lynch, who later watched the tape, he broke traditional interview rules. She claimed that Harris was poorly prepared, and therefore irresponsible. She described his interview manner with Jones as "take no prisoner," and "unorthodox." In fact, to avoid culpability and public blame, NBC would later conceal the tape, as well as three hours of additional tapes made during the visit. NBC and the FBI withdrew the Harris tape from circulation.

But on that ill-fated morning, there can be little doubt that media-savvy Jones feared that the world that he had fled would soon witness his humiliation by the visit and the interview. They would all be watching it on their televisions.

As the Harris-Jones interview was taking place inside Jones's cottage that morning, a sickly foreboding was permeating the compound outside of it. Rumors of mounting defections were spreading, and fear electrified even the most casual interactions. With Ryan right there, other so-called "traitors" were feeling safe enough to step forward. They could see the congressman interviewing members in the pavilion as he worked through his Concerned Relatives' list of members for "rescue." But as it turned out, those on the list were not the ones who actually wanted to leave.

Off to one side, members of the Parks and Bogue families, all longtime Temple members, gathered around Jackie Speier. The 28-year-old attorney was recording their information to legally process them back into the U.S. Upon seeing the entire Parks family deciding to leave, Jones, already feeling bruised and defeated after the Harris interview, tried desperately to convince them to stay.

Family groups formed the very core of Jonestown, and the Parks family were a large and important part of it. Now they wanted to leave with Ryan. After having branded all defectors as "traitors," Jones, by his own definition, would now be publicly shamed by their departure. So, he fought back, speaking quietly off to the side with them, desperately trying to change their minds. But for once, his legendary powers of persuasion failed him. Confused about what to do, the Parks then turned to attorney Mark Lane, who was standing nearby, seeking his advice: should they stay and leave later, as Jones suggested? Lane advised that it was more practical to leave now.

Jones overheard this exchange, but remained uncharacteristically silent. Lane believed that, at that moment, his advice to the Parks instantly transformed him from being Jones's legal counsel, to being his reviled, double-crossing enemy. He'd committed a serious and life-threatening betrayal.

The added strain of yet another anchor-family, the Bogues, asking for assistance to leave Jonestown, further inflamed the already volatile situation. Vernon Gosney would later testify that "hundreds" actually wanted to escape Jonestown at the time. Defector Debbie Layton, who had escaped earlier, claimed that all but ten members might have left, had they been able to.

Despite his poor health and lapses into incoherence, Jones tried to maintain a charade of benevolence toward the growing numbers of defectors. But it was too late. The gap between his twisted reality, and the actual one in front of him, was widening at an alarming speed.

WHILE THESE DRAMAS were taking place, some of the news media were working elsewhere inside the compound. Journalists Reiterman and Krause were taking a guided tour, aware they were seeing only what Jones had approved. They visited the nursery where babies born in Jonestown were cared for by staff under Marci's supervision. A nurse herself, these babies were her favorite charges, and on this day, the nursery was clean and cheery. But once again, Reiterman was uncomfortable with what felt like the staged aspects of it. He noticed one toddler being read to from a book for much older children.

The reporters seemed to encounter a lack of spontaneity wherever they went. When they asked to enter a shuttered, and eerily quiet, cottage on the outer edge of the settlement, their official guide denied them permission. But the two reporters persisted, and after a suspiciously long delay, they were granted entrance while accompanied by their unhappy guide. When the door to the cottage opened, Krause and Rieterman were shocked to discover 60–80 elderly, black women, packed together "like the hold of a slave ship." Densely stacked in bunk beds, the frail, old women blinked in the sudden daylight from the opened door. Reiterman described the interior being "as crowded and stifling as a prisoner of war camp."

Upon interviewing one of the women, Reiterman noted that she said "all the right things," but with a suspicious lack of expression. Her response seemed scripted, as if reciting rather than speaking naturally. Apparently, her tomb-like cottage named "The Jane Pittman Gardens," housed only a fraction of the purportedly 300–400 elders then living in Jonestown. Most of them were black and widows, many of whom had joined the Temple for its guarantee of lifelong care. Back in the U.S., they had indeed received good care, including medical checks, nursing care, housing, and other help. But now these seniors in Jonestown were on the losing end of the bargain. Their care had been reduced to being warehoused in the squalid conditions now witnessed by the two reporters.

Their guided tour disbanded early after Marci, who later joined them, received some whispered news. Judging from the look on her face, it was not good. At the same time, the two reporters noticed a general flow of foot traffic back toward the pavilion, and so they joined it.

At the central meeting area near the pavilion, a now-defeated Jones was feigning a farewell blessing for a group of 14 defectors. Until recently, he rarely left his private cottage, the "command center," relying, instead, on his public address system to communicate. Now he was compelled to perform publicly once again, while enduring what, for him, was a personal humiliation. He proclaimed to the group that they were free to leave. He declared that he was not angry with them, and that they would be welcomed back if they wished to return later. This speech marked Jones's last public charade as a magnanimous, forgiving leader. Every one of his followers listening knew he considered defectors to be traitors, and that under his orders, they could be shot if they left.

According to Stephan Jones, his father's self-worth depended almost solely upon what others thought of him. In light of that, a defection this large and this public for Jones, was apparently more than he could tolerate. He was "crushed." In effect, his self-image and dignity were collapsing right along with his utopian socialist dream. To make matters worse, this humiliation would be witnessed by a television crew and news reporters.

Jones allowed departing members to take their passports and $5,000 (Guyanese) to help with their transportation costs. Gathering belongings and saying goodbyes then continued for the defectors. Jackie Speier processed the latecomers, recording their information, while the NBC crew set up a final interview with Jones. Given the emotional intensity of the situation, another interview seemed ludicrous, but the media had come a long way for the opportunity. Reiterman, too, used this last chance to question Jones.

However, this time, Jones flatly denied beatings and corporal punishments. He also disavowed the presence of the underground box, or "torture hold." He refuted ownership of any automatic rifles, stating their guns were only for hunting. He labeled all information to the contrary as lies. He stated, "I've given my life for people, serving people."

Then Don Harris stepped into the conversation.

As if to deliver his knockout punch, Harris handed Jones the Gosney note asking for help to get out of Jonestown. It was an extremely foolish gambit, endangering Gosney who was still there. Showing Jones this damning evidence was unnecessary. As Reiterman observed, "His nose was being rubbed in his humiliation, his failure, his catastrophe."

Indeed, Jones acted numb after that, unable, or unwilling, to respond to further volleys from the press. Seemingly resigned, Jones tenderly bent to hug a parting child and others goodbye. When Reiterman then bid Jones farewell, thanking him for his time, Jones uttered one last sentiment: "I feel sorry that we are being destroyed from within. All we want is to be left in peace."

Like the rain that had returned, a heavy gloom descended over Jonestown: was it fear, or sorrow, or both? The Concerned Relatives were not leaving with the loved ones they had hoped to extract. Moreover, Jones's inner leadership circle seemed to be falling apart. The only hopeful people were the defectors, but even they were not completely free yet. And they knew it.

With all the tension and upheaval, Mary and Peter would have witnessed the unfolding crisis. Since Peter had once attempted escape himself, was he tempted to join the group leaving now? Would Mary have left with him? And what about their beloved Mary Margaret? Some Jonestown survivors later reported that many members were afraid to stay, but also that many were afraid to leave. They were trapped. And it was not like Jones to allow "traitors" to go unpunished; his previous "kill order" for them was still in effect.

Perhaps Mary and Peter were playing it safe. Perhaps they were aware of Jones's order for the departing planes, with the defectors and the Ryan group onboard, to be "shot down from the sky."

To accommodate the large number of defectors on what would now be two planes, Ryan had volunteered to stay behind for another day.

Yet troubles multiplied during the few short hours between the media's arrival late that morning, and their anticipated departure in mid-afternoon. The perilous situation was unravelling in all directions.

As the defectors crowded aboard the dump truck for their exit to the airstrip, there was violence back at the pavilion. A Jones devotee, Don Sly, had approached Ryan from behind, put Ryan in a headlock, and held a knife to his throat while loudly threatening to kill him. Jim Jones was right there, observing the attack without stopping it. At the same time, attorney Lane grabbed the attacker's knife hand, and Don Harris pulled the attacker off Ryan. This assault instantly changed everything for Ryan, who lay on the ground completely stunned. Blood from the attacker's wounded hand stained his shirt, leading the congressman to wonder for a moment if it was his.

After the attack, Dwyer vetoed Ryan's plan to stay behind, declaring it no longer safe. He had radioed the embassy back in Georgetown for the additional plane to accommodate the defecting members. But now, both he and Ryan would be leaving with them.

REITERMAN AND DEFECTOR Vernon Gosney shared the perilous ride out of Jonestown, describing it as a slow, tense journey. Rain had delayed their departure until about 3:00 p.m., after which 16 people crowded aboard the heavy-duty dump truck. Their crates, suitcases, and backpacks were stacked up near the cab. But the truck stalled in the mud even before leaving the compound. It was nerve-wracking. Then, at the last minute, Dwyer had climbed on board along with Ryan in his bloodied shirt. Following them, Joe Wilson, Jim Jones's personal bodyguard, also joined the crowd. It was an ominous sendoff.

The diverse group on board resembled a tightly packed box of colored crayons, with officials, defectors, media, and more, all mixed together. It was so crowded, some had to ride standing on the open tailgate. They lurched about, bumping into one another, or clinging to the side of the truck as it labored over the crude roadbed. Along the way, Wilson, the muscular bodyguard, asked Gosney why he was leaving Jonestown, complaining that leaving now made Jim Jones look bad in front of the press. Gosney simply replied that he was leaving because of the lack of freedom there.

As Deputy Chief of Mission for the U.S. State Department in Guyana, Dwyer's powerful position may have provided the fleeing defectors with a measure of reassurance. Even so, as an Army veteran previously posted in dangerous countries, Dwyer knew better. He sensed an imminent threat. As the overloaded truck plowed along, defector Jim Cobb quietly warned Dwyer that Larry Layton, Jim Jones's devoted aide, was among them there. Dwyer would not have recognized Layton, or known that he was Jones's blond, curly-haired "lapdog," and therefore, not be trusted. But other defectors on board knew Layton, and they also knew there was no way Layton would be defecting.

Their unusually slow passage felt deliberate, with the driver repeatedly getting stuck in the mud. At one point, the farm's bulldozer was radioed to get it unstuck, further impeding their exit. Gosney reported being on edge the whole time. Why the suspicious delays? And why were Larry Layton and Joe Wilson on board?

Using the sound of the truck's engine for cover, Ryan and Dwyer quietly conferred, deciding to give up their plane seats to the frightened defectors. The six-seater Cessna that Dwyer managed to secure had been the only spare plane available, and the two planes would not have enough room for everyone now. Dwyer also knew firsthand the difficulties of air travel in Guyana, with only a few planes and sketchy runways. Poor visibility, mud, and tropical downpours further encumbered air travel there. In spite of that, the two men decided to wait for a later flight out, putting the welfare of the defectors ahead of their own.

When their truck finally arrived at the end of Jonestown property, they were detained yet again, now by guards at the gate shack. According to Reiterman, a small group of armed men awaited them. Brandishing their weapons, they ordered everyone to stand aside so they could search the group, ostensibly for unauthorized members from Jonestown on board. One of them claimed to be searching for his wife onboard, but apparently, this kind of search was a common ploy to hassle visitors.

After being given the all clear, the truck was allowed to continue on, with Joe Wilson now holding on at the cab window in front. The menacing security guard was completely unaware that, at that very moment, his family was walking away from Jonestown on railroad tracks, seeking their freedom, too.

WILSON'S WIFE, LESLIE, and their three-year-old son were among the fleeing "picnic" escapees, who rarely stopped despite the intense heat out on the open tracks. Later in the afternoon, a slow, narrow-gage train approached them from the opposite direction. Upon seeing the haggard group coming his way, the startled train engineer stopped, and then assured them he would pick all of them up soon during his return trip. He kept his word. He boarded the exhausted escapees into one of his cargo cars, and they rode in it for the last 15 miles up to Matthews Ridge. As a substation for the Guyanese military, the fleeing group would be safe there. They were taken to its small police station, having arrived without money or passports — only the clothes they wore. But they had their lives and their freedom.

And for now, they were unaware of the unfolding catastrophe they had just escaped.

BACK IN JONESTOWN, after the defectors and visitors departed, Marceline instructed everyone to return to their cabins for a rest. As a nurse, and also known as Jonestown's "Mother," she sensed that everyone needed time to recuperate after the stressful Ryan visit. Since it was only midafternoon, this was a highly unusual opportunity for the hardworking members; but then, this was a highly unusual day.

After only 20 minutes, Jim Jones ordered everyone back to the pavilion again; he was reverting back to his usual form. Assemblies were regularly held to discourage members from leaving Jonestown. During these special rallies, Jones would damn defectors, threaten them with terrible punishments, and rage about the dangerous world out there. Ordering a rally after this day's events was, in many ways, standard procedure. However, this one would be their last.

BACK AT THE airstrip, the two chartered planes had not yet arrived when the overloaded dump truck-taxi arrived. It was about 4:30 p.m. After helping the others down off the truck, the news crew went to work again. In the metal shack that served as a makeshift air terminal there, they briefly met with Ryan, who filled them in on the knife attack he had just survived. Then he gave a private interview to Don Harris, recounting the attack once again, this time adding his impressions of Jonestown.

During the wait for the planes, the Jonestown truck driver pulled his empty truck off to the other end of the airstrip, and acted like he was working on its engine. Security guard Joe Wilson kept him company there, along with perhaps a dozen other guards hanging around Jonestown's red tractor-trailer. Don Harris carefully eyed them, wondering what they were waiting for. What were they up to? According to Reiterman, Harris stood there "like a field general," and quietly announced, "I think we've got trouble."

Wilson and some of his cocky buddies then wandered over to Ryan and Speier, where the two of them were making passenger manifests for each plane during the wait. The men wanted to know who was boarding which plane, but were not given that information. Rumors of a possible shootdown had the waiting crowd on high alert; some of the defectors had recognized the security guards loitering near the Jonestown vehicles. Because of that, Ryan decided that all defectors in line should be frisked; some might be plants, willing to take down the planes with themselves and everyone on board. At this point, anything seemed possible.

As the anxious passengers awaited the planes, several Guyanese soldiers could be seen idly guarding a disabled plane at the far end of the airstrip. It was quiet here, save for the nervous chatter among the waiting crowd. Then, the distant sound of planes grew louder, and suddenly the two chartered planes were landing in close succession with a welcome roar of their engines. The Twin Otter's engines remained running as a rush of activity quickly followed.

First in line to leave — just as Ryan had promised — Vernon Gosney hastily climbed aboard the small Cessna along with his friend, Monica Bagby. Waiting in that same line, Larry Layton, was hiding a gun. He had avoided detection by temporarily handing it off to others on his secret mission. Gosney sat in the second of the three rows in the narrow, six-seater plane, while Layton sat behind him. In the din of its running engines, the larger Twin Otter also began boarding passengers. Meanwhile, the NBC camera crew filmed the newsworthy event from the ground.

Working together, Reiterman and Speier awkwardly frisked the line for the Twin Otter. Tensions were skyrocketing, and the boarding quickened, slowed only by the hasty weapons search. Suddenly, a commotion erupted down the airstrip among the Jonestown gang there. They were busily mounting the tractor-trailer, and slowly heading toward the two planes. Along the way, they shooed away villagers who had come to watch the congressman's departure.

Then another truck suddenly arrived at the busy airstrip, but it was not from Jonestown. Out stepped Dwyer, bringing several armed police constables for protection. However, the constables quickly disappeared, presumably tipped off about the trouble that was about to ensue. As Reiterman processed another passenger with his back to the airstrip, he heard shots fired and someone shout, "Hit the dirt!"

Vernon Gosney later reported:

> *Then a farm tractor hauling a trailer filled with members of Jones's security team drove across the runway and stopped, blocking the planes. The security team, known as the Red Brigade, opened fire on the Twin Otter. "I looked out the window and said, 'They're killing everybody!' I turned around, and Larry Layton — someone I had known for many years — shot me three times. Twice in the leg."*

As the loaded Cessna was beginning its taxi, Larry Layton shot Gosney from behind, using the gun hidden in his shirt. Then he shot Monica twice in the back as she sat up front with the pilot. Layton then pointed the gun at another passenger, defector Dale Parks, aiming at his face, but the gun jammed and Parks wrestled it away from Layton. According to Gosney, the pilot then ordered everyone out of the plane. However, Monica was too wounded to move.

While Layton was shooting at close range inside the smaller plane, the Jonestown gunmen were shooting from a distance at the waiting crowd still on the ground. Then their tractor-trailer pulled right in front of the Cessna, blocking it from takeoff. From there, the shooters targeted the Twin Otter at close range, blowing out a tire and spraying its fuselage with bullets.

Reiterman, who had been standing next to the Twin Otter, dove behind one of its tires. People all around him were being hit, their bodies tumbling to the ground. After he hit the ground, he quickly decided to make a run for it. The reporter sprinted directly across the airstrip, heading for the bush on the far side. He plunged into the high grass there, and then crawled further into it. He was bleeding heavily, having been shot through the arm and wrist.

Back on the airstrip, some of Jones's hitmen dismounted from their trailer. One walked directly over to Ryan, who was already down, and shot him in his head, killing him. The congressman had been targeted, as were NBC's Don Harris, and cameraman Bob Brown — both murdered, as well. The photographer, Greg Robinson, was also killed. One of the defectors, Patricia Parks, was shot in the head, accidentally killed through one of the Twin Otter's windows during the chaos. After being wounded, and then playing dead while lying on the ground, Jackie Speier, NBC's Steve Sung, and Dwyer all survived the attack: Four dead, nine wounded.

The ambush had struck like lightning, lasting only a few minutes, after which the shooters sped away. Dwyer, shot in his flank, noted that during the bloody chaos, the calmest group were the defectors aboard the Twin Otter. Their fast-thinking children immediately slammed the plane's door shut to avoid further slaughter. Dwyer described them as a "remarkable group," acting while others were just stumbling about in shock.

Reportedly, a young villager was grazed in the leg by a stray bullet while standing at the edge of the airstrip. The Guyanese soldiers guarding the disabled plane at the far end of the airstrip, as well as others stationed at a small tent camp there, stood back during the surprise attack. Their information from Jonestown erroneously portrayed Ryan as CIA, and heavily armed. Because of that, the Guyanese army present had no orders to interfere, hesitant to intervene in the "American situation" with Americans shooting at other Americans.

After about 15 minutes, the Cessna pilot managed to take off while carrying the pilot, copilot, and steward from the Twin Otter, along with seriously injured Monica Bagby. One of the pilots aboard then radioed the tower at Georgetown to report the attack. Staff there immediately notified Guyanese Prime Minister Burnham, who summoned American Ambassador Burke to inform him of the situation. PM Burnham then ordered the Guyanese Defense Forces (GDF) to Matthews Ridge, some thirty miles from Jonestown, and Port Kaituma. Matthews Ridge had the only airstrip with landing lights for incoming night flights.

Pierced with bullet holes, and tilting over a flattened tire, the now disabled Twin Otter sat mutely on the airstrip. Discarded luggage and debris lay strewn about among the dead, silent witnesses to the deafening ambush. The deadly chaos had lasted only minutes; however, its consequences would echo for lifetimes.

THE EVENTS DURING Jonestown's last hours were reported by a handful of its survivors, gleaned from records retrieved by the FBI, or shared by the Guyanese government. But incredibly, the world has also been able to eavesdrop on the members' final agonies there. Along with his many sermons and speeches, Jim Jones also recorded his greatest atrocity during its final hours, as more than 900 people slowly perished.

BACK AT JONES's emergency rally in the pavilion, Odell Rhodes, a calm and sensitive man from Detroit, was among the gathering there. He observed the two Temple attorneys, Lane and Garry, being walked away by two armed security guards. At the same time, other Jonestown guards were checking all the cottages making sure everyone was at the meeting, except for those in the infirmary, or too weak to leave their housing.

While his visitors lay dead on the airstrip, hiding in the jungle, lying in army tents, or sheltering in Port Kaituma, Jones was very busy. After feeling demeaned and humiliated by the Harris interview and the many defections, this once charismatic mastermind and powerful leader was in charge again for one last time.

At the pavilion where most of his 900 followers faced him, he declared that everyone must "commit suicide." He announced that the plane with Congressman Ryan aboard would soon be shot out of the air and crash into the jungle. Because of this crime, everyone in Jonestown would be punished by the Guyanese Defense Forces (GDF). He warned that its soldiers would torture and kill their children, so their little ones needed immediate protection. The Jonestown community must act. To bring them together in this, their last endeavor, "Father" Jones asked for a response from his "children."

The shocking lack of dissent that followed his announcement may have been due to paralyzing fear among the members. Others may have thought this was just another White Night drill which Jones would order at odd times. Reportedly, now only one member directly objected to Jones's suicide command. Christine Miller, a 60-year-old from Los Angeles, was a solid, outspoken woman. She had picked cotton as a child, and had worked hard all her life. Miller had a strong presence and placid demeanor, and was one of the very few who ever spoke back to Jim Jones. She did so again now.

Miller objected to the idea of a mass suicide, arguing there might be another way out, or that the plane may not be shot down. Jones countered, stating the Ryan visitors could be shot while still on the ground. Miller then maintained that the relatively small group of defectors who had left that day did not mean that "twelve hundred people give their lives for those that left." She suggested that, instead, they could all fly to Russia, reasoning that their children did not deserve to die. She asked Jim Jones if he wanted to see his little "son," John Victor, die, too.

This brave woman was unique. She had publicly challenged Jim Jones before, successfully standing her ground even when he criticized her. Although some members voiced agreement with Miller now, other residents in the crowd shouted her down, their blind obedience to Jones bringing them ever closer to their own deaths. Tragically, this discussion between Jones and Miller lasted for only a few minutes before Miller relented, and she would soon be forced to her death, still resisting to the end.

Jones quelled any further dissension by pointing out that, "it's over, they'll parachute in here on us, and the children will be butchered." His delusional paranoia was now reaching its deadly zenith as he argued that they had no other choice: Forces beyond their control would soon destroy them. All of them.

At about this time, a vehicle came speeding into the compound. Its driver, Johnny, another one of Jones's adopted children and member of his security team, went straight to his father. He reported the successful attack at the airstrip to Jones there on his wooden "throne." Jones then announced to all that it was now too late, "everybody" is dead, meaning that his targeted tormentors had been killed. He ordered the cyanide poison brought forward. As recorded on the Temple's "death tape," Jones proclaimed,

> *Well, it's all over, all over. What a legacy, what a legacy. What the Red Brigade doin' one bit that made any sense anyway? They invaded our privacy. They came into our home. They followed us six thousand miles away. Red Brigade showed them justice. The congressman's dead.*

Jonestown's doctor, Larry Schacht, dutifully took charge, organizing the administration of the poison. Security guards, some fresh from the airstrip, stood guard during the process. Metal casks of cyanide were mixed with a powdered drink, Flavor Aid, and a table was set up in the pavilion. About a dozen people organized the staging area while Jones hurried them on, reminding them that babies should die first. This may have been a planned strategy: Once parents lost their children, they would lose their own will to live. They would want to "join" them right away, and the massive suicide would go more smoothly.

But it did not go smoothly.

The Temple's belief in reincarnation was critical now. Jones urged that death was just a "stepping over" to the next world. Also, by declaring themselves as martyrs, they would be making a powerful statement to the world they were leaving behind. This, ironically from a terminally ill man who probably had only weeks to live himself. The death tape records his further hectoring:

> *For god sakes let's get on with it. We've lived, we've lived as no other people have lived and loved, had as much of this world as you're going to get. Let's just be done with it.*

According to one survivor-witness, Odell Rhodes, the first to come forward was a mother with a one-year-old baby. She used a syringe without the needle to squirt poison into its little mouth, and then used another one to squirt the poison into her own. But this mother did not die painlessly, or fast. Instead, she died in agony for all to see, out in a nearby field, after being led there by guards to keep the line moving.

In fact, while waiting in line for the poison, many witnessed the unexpected suffering the poison caused, and they "showed a reluctance to die," according to Stanley Clayton, another witness-survivor. A cousin of Black Panther Huey Newton, Clayton had worked in Jonestown's kitchen. This tall, lean chef would be another one of the very few to observe and survive the ongoing massacre. He reported that despite the obvious agony among the poisoned, Jones walked among them, encouraging them to proceed. Clayton stated that "hundreds had to be forced," and that "sometimes the poison was administered intravenously by nurses and sometimes by the doctor."

By now, many members were malnourished, exhausted, and weak. According to Stephan Jones, they had been "hammered" in Jonestown right from the beginning. Furthermore, years of repeated White Night "poison" drills had normalized suicide for many of them: drink fake poison and pretend to fall down. But as ritual and reality now collided, all those years of practice were apparently failing Jones now. During the massacre, which took about four hours, almost all were being forced to kill themselves.

Ever the caretaker, "Mother" Marci dutifully attempted to comfort by saying, "See you in the next life," as if they were leaving on vacation. She gave hugs, trying to ease their fears and hysteria. Nevertheless, Odell Rhodes observed shocked members who "walked around like they were in a trance." At the same time, armed security forces stood along the poison lines, holding down resisters. Up until then, many members may have felt protected by these security guards, but now they were being forced to their deaths by the same people. They were trapped.

It is now widely believed that almost all of the residents were forced to take the poison, but either way, they were, in effect, murdered. They had been trained and conditioned, as well as starved and worn out.

Even so, Jones's security guards pulled resisters and crying children toward the poison tables, where a nurse then squirted cyanide down their throats with a syringe. The poison took only about five minutes to kill children, and even less time for babies. Amid the children's writhing agony, and the piercing wails of grief from mothers holding their dying babies and children in their arms, while kneeling in an open field, Jones admonished:

I tell you I don't care how many screams you hear, I don't care how many anguished cries...death is a million times preferable to ten more days of this life. If you knew what was ahead of you — if you knew what was ahead of you, you'd be glad to be stepping over tonight.

On the same death tape, Maria Katsaris, one of Jones's mistresses, could be heard admonishing the parents who were "inconveniently" troubled by their children's cries, by saying, "It's not painful, they're crying because it tastes bitter."

Odell Rhodes later testified that, at first, some may have thought it was just another White Night drill, but the agony evident all around them soon proved otherwise. Adults took up to 30 minutes to die, so while they were still able to walk, they were led outside the pavilion to facilitate the progress. There, their whole bodies convulsed, and their mouths filled with saliva, blood, and vomit. It was an excruciating death.

Nevertheless, Jones continued to chasten them, scolding: "Die with a degree of dignity. Lay down your life with dignity; don't lay down with tears and agony." These were scathingly hollow words from the man who would soon choose the "dignity" of a bullet for himself, instead of the agonies of the poison.

Overall, it took about four hours for the 909-soul atrocity to end. On my sister's last night on earth, there is no doubt that she, little Mary Margaret, and Peter suffered unbearable agony.

DURING THE MASSACRE, Odell Rhodes, who had worked in Jonestown's school, helped a little boy lie down in a field while the child's eyes rolled during convulsions. Rhodes picked up other children, too, as they suffered, comforting them, then placing them gently down again. While concentrating on helping them, this kind man soon realized that he, himself, was faced with a decision: life or death.

Given an unexpected opportunity, he chose life. When the Temple doctor said he needed a stethoscope to ascertain if people were dead, Rhodes was sent to relay his request to one of the nurses. He then accompanied one of them to the medical facilities, and pretended to search for a stethoscope with her, but then he quietly slipped away. He hid under a building until almost dark. In the meantime, those who could not walk to the poison were given it in their hospital beds, or in the senior dormitories.

While hiding out for hours in the jungle, another escapee, Stanley Clayton, reported hearing the last gunshots at about 10:45 p.m., most likely when Mr. Muggs, the chimpanzee, was shot. However, it would take two days for the beloved mascot to finally die. All the dogs were also shot. After everyone else lay dead, the guards, themselves, took the poison. Then, according to forensic evidence, Jones and one of his closest aides, Annie Moore, died by gunshot wounds to the head.

When it was over, and safely quiet, Odell Rhodes crept out of the compound in the dark, and worked his way through the jungle by using the road as a guide. At about midnight, he reached Port Kaituma where he informed authorities of the massacre. He also reported it by phone to the police in Georgetown. They, in turn, alerted the American Embassy. From there, the following cable was sent to the U.S. White House at 3:29 a.m., November 19, reading, "CIA NOIWON reports mass suicide in Jonestown."

JUST BEFORE THE massacre began, the two attorneys, Garry and Lane, whom Odell Rhodes had seen being escorted from the pavilion, were put under guard in East House cottage. They remained there for some time, fearful of Jones's retaliation for what he considered betrayals. While there, they listened to their lone guard babble excitedly about soon dying along with everyone, apparently believing his two captives shared his euphoria. It was Don Sly, the same person who had attacked Congressman Ryan earlier in the day.

When Sly was later relieved of his guard duty by two other armed men, the attorneys realized the extreme gravity of their situation. They then performed "the best lawyering" of their lives. They pointed out to the guards that someone had to live to tell the story of this "historic" day. The guards agreed. The two attorneys further pushed their luck by asking for directions out of the jungle to make that happen. It was simply over a hill, they were told, and through the jungle to the road. The two attorneys took off literally running for their lives, but there would be nothing simple about it.

Still within earshot of the now ongoing massacre, they overheard Jim Jones's uttering, "Mother, mother, mother, mother, mother, mother," also recorded on the death tape. Lane, the younger of the two men, reported hearing automatic rifle shots, but this may have been a fear-induced hallucination. No automatic weapons were ever recovered from the compound, although looters may have removed them. Other witnesses described hearing only ten or so shots being fired. Whatever the case, unrelenting fear tormented the attorneys' escape as they then navigated a treacherous night in the jungle.

The terrorized men spent most of the night groping about in a darkness so profound, they could not see each other while standing next to one another. But fearing pursuit, they stumbled on, arguing, and getting lost until exhaustion forced them to sleep curled up on the jungle floor. There, bedeviling thoughts of bats, boas, jaguars, and scorpions made for an uneasy rest. In the morning after much backtracking and confusion, they discovered the road out, but stayed hidden along its edge. Finally reaching the guard shack at Jonestown's entrance, they discovered that it was empty. The two men then continued for the last three miles to Port Kaituma and safety, joining other Jonestown folks already there. Tim Carter was one of them.

THAT SAME NIGHT Carter, an able-bodied former Marine who spent three years in Vietnam, had been tapped to carry out a secret mission by Maria Katsaris. As Jones's spindly, dark-haired mistress, Katsaris was also Jonestown's comptroller, and during the final hours of Jonestown, she was busy. Within earshot of poisoned members screaming in agony, this steely woman was now methodically closing out all accounts.

Since Carter had been one of Jones's trusted aides, Katsaris chose him, plus his radio-operator brother Mike, and the Temple's PR man, Mike Prokes, to make a delivery to Georgetown. She handed them three satchels of over $250,000 U.S. in cash, plus documents. They were to deliver them to the Soviet Embassy in Georgetown, as apparently, the USSR was still considered by Jones as their last ally. Katsaris then thoughtfully ordered the men to shoot themselves if caught before completing their delivery.

But for all that, the trusted trio wound up burying part of their load; it was far too heavy to carry the whole six miles to Port Kaituma. Some of it wound up in a chicken coop, and some buried in the sand. Their ultimate destination, Jonestown's boat, the Cudjoe, was supposedly docked at Port Kaituma. The trio left on their mission at about 6:45 p.m., but even in the deepening dark, they avoided the open road. Despite their caution, however, they were detained in Port Kaituma by its police. The three smugglers chose not to shoot themselves, as had been directed, and their goods, guns, and ammunition were confiscated.

The quiet village of Port Kaituma with its 30 families, and a handful of authorities, was about to become very busy.

WHILE THE AIRPORT shootings and the massacre were taking place 150 airmiles away, November 18, 1978, would soon become the worst day of Stephan Jones's life. As some of the Ryan group were bleeding and dying on the airstrip, and the massacre moved along in Jonestown, the Jonestown basketball team was taking in a movie in Georgetown. Considering their spartan existence back in the jungle, it was a rare treat.

Stephan described the capital's lone movie theater as ramshackle, and "decades beyond prudent repair." It had a small balcony, and according to this 6'4" team point guard, sitting in it "felt like being stuffed on the top shelf of a closet." Even so, this intense young athlete with a piercing gaze enjoyed his own space up there, sitting alone behind his teammates. From there, he savored the local custom of loud Motown music broadcast during the theater's opening advertisements. Marvin Gaye was a favorite, and adding to the fun, the rowdy audience would sing along. But on this night, the team never got to see the whole movie. Their hitman-themed entertainment was cut short due to a real-life disaster now bearing down on them.

Up until that moment, the team had avoided the hassles created by the Ryan visit. Their reports of the previous night's successful encounter with the unwanted intrusion had been reassuring. But now, partway through their movie, Stephan's brother and team member, Tim, whispered a message relayed to them there from Lamaha: "We've been ordered to get revenge." It was Jones's secret code ordering them to kill his "enemies," and then themselves. This sudden revenge order stunned Stephan.

He had known that the coded order existed, but considered it to be another one of his father's fantasies. He never thought it would actually be ordered, or worse — taken seriously. To him, his father was a "coward," a big-talker who would never go through with such a thing. Nonetheless, the order had been radioed from Jonestown to the Lamaha staff in Georgetown. As a result, the whole team hurriedly left the theater and headed immediately back to Lamaha, which was now in turmoil.

As Jim and Marceline's only biological son, Stephan was regarded by many as the "crown prince" of Jonestown. As such, he now spoke with authority when he ordered the Lamaha staff not to obey the revenge order. Yet at the same time, his father was serious, even transmitting the exact weapons to be used for the killing, delineating "k-n-i-v-e-s." While struggling with the unreality of the moment, Stephan took charge, nevertheless, by radioing the San Francisco staff to disobey the order. They were contacted again a second time to make sure they understood his no-kill order.

With fear hammering at his brain, Stephan fought to maintain his composure, while trying to organize a plan. There was only one thing he was sure of: There would be no killing if he could help it. Realizing that something must have gone terribly wrong with the Ryan visit, Stephan wisely feigned loyalty to his father, thereby avoiding possible pushback from any of Jones's zealots at Lamaha. At the same time, he tried everything he could to short circuit his father's lethal order. Unaware it was already too late to stop any killing in Jonestown, he went into high gear. The Lamaha staff respected Stephan's command to ignore the revenge order, but there was still much he needed to do, and fast.

Before rushing off to check with the Concerned Relatives at their hotel there in Georgetown, he gave orders for certain members at Lamaha to be closely watched. There were fanatics among them. He entrusted an older male resident, Lee, to keep an eye on one in particular: Sharon Amos. Stephan knew that, at this precarious moment, her rabid devotion to his father could be dangerous. Then, after stabilizing the situation at Lamaha, he sped off to the Pegasus Hotel with some of his team members.

When Stephan arrived there at about 8:00 p.m., he found the waiting Relatives hanging around in its open-air lobby, anxiously hoping for news — good news. One in particular, the once powerful defector Tim Stoen, was among them. In his former position as the Temple's top attorney, he had been privy to sensitive Temple information, including its finances and legal maneuvering. Consequently, he could be a formidable foe; in fact, Jim Jones considered him his greatest enemy. Now, this so-called "traitor" was there in Georgetown to retrieve his young son, John Victor, from Jones's grip. Jones had spirited the boy out of the U.S., claiming him as his own.

Unaware of the deadly events unfolding in Jonestown, yet sensing that something had gone terribly wrong there, Stephan warned Stoen to avoid threatening or harassing his father in any way. The situation at the moment was far too precarious. Then, speaking as the official head of Jonestown security, Stephan assured both Stoen and the rest of the waiting group that they were in no danger. But unfortunately, since he was unable to be more specific, his reassurances turned out to be more alarming than comforting. What had gone wrong?

Neither the waiting relatives, the basketball team, nor any of the staff at Lamaha, knew about the airstrip ambush yet. Even so, they all knew enough about Jim Jones to sense trouble. Thunderstruck by looming disaster, Stephan then raced over to the American Embassy, where unconfirmed reports of the airstrip murders had already been received at about 6:15 p.m. When they informed Stephan of them, he felt "in his gut" that it was probably true, even without confirmation from Jonestown.

Given the severity of the situation and all of the unknowns, the embassy staff could not be sure if Stephan, himself, was trustworthy: he could easily be another hitman for Jones. Thus alarmed, they denied Stephan entry as he stood outside the embassy door, pleading for more information, anything to help him understand the reason for the revenge order. He thought if he could just get to Jonestown in time, he might be able to stop any killing. He might be able to reason with his father.

Still a teenager at age 19, he was frantically trying to manage an active situation occurring far out of his reach. Although aware that he might be viewed by others as an assassin, a leader, or perhaps even a savior, he felt like none of them as he returned to Lamaha. He felt totally powerless.

In the meantime, back at Lamaha, the killing had already begun. A longtime church leader and Jones devotee, Sharon Amos, had been in the radio room when the coded revenge order was received. When the man tasked with guarding Amos was momentarily called away to talk with the local police, there to investigate the airport killings, Amos had excused herself from those present to use the bathroom. According to another staff member, Jordan Vilchez, who was in the room at the time, Sharon then "whizzed out of the radio room clutching the hands of her two youngest children."

In the privacy of the bathroom, Sharon Amos slit the throats of her two youngest children, little Martin, and Crista. Then she and her 21-year-old daughter, Liane, apparently did the same for each other, dutifully obeying Jones's revenge order. Reportedly, Amos had feared that, otherwise, her children would be tortured and killed by the "fascists" that Jones had repeatedly warned about. And they were supposedly now at the front gate; she believed that she was saving her children by administering their mercy killings.

AFTER LEAVING THE embassy, Stephan rushed back again to Lamaha, his mind now racing with fear, somersaulting in all directions. He and his brother Tim walked the last part of the road together, then paused for a few minutes outside on the gravel. They needed to get a grip on the fast-moving situation. They needed to work together to manage it.

But before they could get to the house, a staff member met them outside, delivering the staggering news of the Amos killings inside. Terrified, Stephan bolted to the upper level of the house where he saw blood leaking from underneath the bathroom door. He pushed at the door, but it was blocked by Sharon Amos's now lifeless body. He carefully nudged it open, far enough to see the lifeless eyes of little Martin, age ten, staring upward. His 11-year-old sister, Crista, was lying on her back next to him, her eyes also fixed on the ceiling, seeing nothing. Dead. Their necks slashed from ear to ear, their hair bloody, and their bodies soaking in pools of their own blood.

Stephan then managed to open the door a little wider to see Liane lying on her stomach on the floor, trying to lift herself up while choking on her own blood. She let out a long sigh and died just as Stephan, utterly helpless, witnessed the last seconds of the unthinkable atrocity. Overwhelmed by this tsunami of horror and grief, Stephan went into complete shock, unable to process what had just happened — and what was probably also happening in Jonestown. Even though he had done his utmost to stop it, Stephan was now a helpless witness to his father's carnage.

Stephanie, Stephan's nine-year-old niece, was staying at Lamaha that evening, and had tried to obey the suicide order, too. She may have had help; Charles Beikman, a simple man who lived at Lamaha, and was easily swayed by Jim Jones's authority, was covered with blood himself. He may have dutifully tried to help Stephanie obey Jones's kill order. If so, they had not succeeded with the cutting: Stephanie's knife wounds were only superficial.

When Stephan encountered Stephanie, she was staring off into the distance, being held by two women on staff. She did not respond to Stephan's comforting touch, so he joined other members huddled together in Lamaha's lower level. As they sat together there, wordless and stunned, blood leaking from the bathroom floor right above dripped down through the ceiling, a further torment in their agony.

Lamaha was soon surrounded by the GDF, who blocked off the road out front. Then police arrived to gather evidence from the crime scene. The bewildered members stayed together indoors, now as refugees trapped in a suddenly alien world. By this time, they were aware of the airstrip murders, but not of the Jonestown massacre. Still hoping to prevent that, Stephan wanted to get back to Jonestown, arguing with his captors that he might be able to stop any further killing. But from that point on, the Guyanese authorities were in charge, and they assured Stephan that all that could be done, was being done.

But not quite.

Aerial view Jonestown, 1978. California Historical Society photo

Jonestown cottages, 1979. Jonestown Institute photo

Landing strip, Port Kaituma, Guyana. Jonestown Institute photo

Peter teaching, Jonestown. California Historical Society photo

Peter, accompanying Mary Margaret, Jonestown.
Jonestown Institute photo

Drought bucket brigade. Jonestown Institute
photo

Cassava tuber harvest, Jonestown, 1978.
Jonestown Institute photo

Saw mill, Jonestown. Jonestown Institute photo

Jonestown craft business. Jonestown Institute photo

Cudjoe, Kaituma River, Guyana. Jonestown Institute photo

"Mass transit," Jonestown. Jim Jones, mascot Mr. Muggs. California Historical Society photo

Basketball, Jonestown. Jonestown Institute photo

Henry Mercy teaching high school students, Jonestown. Jonestown Institute photo

US military covering bodies: Jonestown, 1978. Used by permission of Preston Jones/John Brown University

PART IV

LETHAL HARVEST

CHAPTER 12

COURAGE AND COMPASSION

BACK AT THE AIRSTRIP, REITERMAN'S PANTS WERE DRENCHED IN BLOOD. Using his leather belt, he attempted to form a tourniquet on his wounded arm to stem the flow and, after many slippery attempts, managed to do so temporarily. Fearing he could be stalked by more killers as he lay in the tall grasses, he struggled further toward the shelter of the jungle. Once there, he rested for a short while, catching his breath, and trying to process what had just happened. After a period of silence with no more gunshots, he made his way back to the airstrip to ascertain any further threat.

It was eerily quiet there. Some of the survivors were wandering among the carnage in shock. Don Harris had warned everyone to spread out just moments before the shooting began, but it had been too late. The killers had a target-rich crowd near the Twin Otter — easy pickings. Now Reiterman met up there with NBC producer, Bob Flick, who had just lost two of his crew: cameraman Bob Brown and reporter Don Harris. Brown lay sprawled out near the Twin Otter's tail, his brain matter blown all over his camera and the ground. Harris was spread out on his back, lifeless, his boots pointing upward.

Congressman Ryan lay on the runway with half of his head blown off. Reiterman's newfound friend from their newspaper, photographer Greg Robinson, lay dead near one of the plane's wheels. Only a short while before, Reiterman had taken momentary refuge in almost the same spot. Now he could not bear to look at his murdered friend; instead, he carefully removed Robinson's camera and equipment bag, preserving his friend's photos, and keeping the equipment from possible looters.

One of the Concerned Relatives, Carol Boyd, joined Reiterman there. They had chatted earlier during the visit, and were thankful to reconnect now, but with utterly frazzled nerves. Everyone was jumpy, exposed as they were out in the open there. Because of that, when someone at the far end of the runway shouted that the killers were returning, everyone bolted for cover. It was a false alarm. Since Carol was wearing a white blouse, it made her — and them — more visible to shooters in the approaching nightfall. They needed better cover.

The likelihood of the assassins returning to finish them off kept everyone on high alert. For safety, Carol stayed hidden in the bush along with Reiterman, where she helped to secure his tourniquet. Then, the two of them made their way further toward the jungle. As if out of nowhere, a young Amerindian boy suddenly appeared, and then disappeared again after silently leading them into the jungle's dense, dark safety.

While hiding there, the two heard the Cessna's engine running, and scurried back into the open again, hoping to flag it down. They were too late. The small plane was soon airborne, and taking with it all hope of their leaving anytime soon. Their fear was now laced with despair. On the other hand, they could also see a small group of Guyanese gathered around the disabled Twin Otter. Perhaps it was a good sign: the marooned Americans were not completely alone in their calamity. The pair left their hiding place to join them. Soon, two more Guyanese men arrived on the scene, bearing a gallon of water and a bottle of rum, both for drinking and cleansing wounds. They had not been asked to do so — they just showed up.

Meanwhile, the Cessna shooter, Larry Layton, was freely walking about, dazed, but unharmed. After Dwyer took his gun away, the weaselly assailant was soon turned over to local authorities to be held in custody at Port Kaituma. A natural leader, Dwyer then set about making a list of the casualties: four dead, five severely injured, five ambulatory-wounded, and perhaps six more missing, thought to be hiding in the jungle. Monica Bagby, too wounded to move, had been flown out on the Cessna along with the Twin Otter crew. Dwyer carried on, conferring with local officials and soldiers, assessing the rest of the damage, and the help needed. This Army veteran and embassy official turned out to be a natural "battlefield commander" now, too.

While the others were deliberating, Reiterman spoke with a small group of village men arriving on the scene, wanting to know what had just happened. And why. After having been misled as to who the American visitors were, and why they were there, the locals were greatly confused. They had believed Jones's lies about Ryan's group being armed and dangerous CIA.

In spite of that misinformation, the brave Guyanese now gathered there were uncommonly gracious, asking first about the reporter's wounds. Then an improbable, but timely, discussion followed as Reiterman tried to sketch out the actual reasons for Ryan's visit: what they had found in Jonestown, and why the reporters were there. After that, one of the all black Guyanese asked him about racism in America. Reiterman, who was white, as were most of the Ryan group, did his best considering his condition to explain. He said that he and many other Americans did not approve of racism.

The men appeared to accept his explanation, and then courageously offered to help the survivors, despite the possibility of another attack. Evidence of Jones's weaponry, as well as evil intent, lay all around them on the airstrip. Even so, the men's apparent leader, a slight elderly man, declared, "We are with you. We will protect you." Greatly moved, Reiterman was overcome with gratitude for these generous men, whose own children went barefoot, and lived in simple dwellings. They were willing to share what little they had. The men went on to pledge, "We will fight to protect you, and we will hide you. We must get you away from here."

Many of them had either heard about, or witnessed, the suspicious injuries occurring inside Jonestown. In view of that, their offer of protection now was an exceptionally brave gesture when considering Jones's abhorrent violence.

HAVING BEEN SHOT in the flank, Dwyer was one of the walking wounded, but nevertheless, he managed to call on his military experience to take charge. Aided by a naturally calm demeanor, he made a series of good decisions, caring for his stunned and bleeding fellow Americans. Dwyer assured all present that Georgetown had been radioed, and help would be coming, but not until the next day. Right now, they needed overnight shelter.

During the attack, the Guyanese soldiers at the far end of the runway had held back, lacking orders to intervene. But now with their semi-automatic guns at the ready, their presence provided a measure of security. The Americans had no weapons whatsoever, and it was now almost dark — Guyanese jungle dark. With only one flashlight available, Dwyer used it cautiously to save the battery and keep them out of view.

With night descending like a black curtain, fear of returning shooters hastened their recovery efforts. The severely wounded were removed first, carried to the small army encampment there. Its tents became a field hospital in which the first aid kit salvaged from the Twin Otter was soon depleted. The walking wounded helped out as much as they could, but it was the Jonestown defectors who proved to be the most helpful. Some of them had medical experience, having worked in the Jonestown clinic, or from prior training.

Following Dwyer's directions, the severely wounded would stay with the soldiers in the army tent. Everyone else would go into Port Kaituma to shelter in a local pub, "The Rum Shop." Conveniently located at the near edge of the village, it was only a short walk from the airstrip. Compassionate villagers then gently led the survivors through the dark, whispering, "Come this way," while carefully guiding them through the mud and around puddles. Once they arrived at the pub, Reiterman and others put in orders for drinks at the bar, and then gathered around to rest and decompress.

The pub owner, a diminutive, dark-skinned woman named Elaine, took their orders, opening her shop, as well as her heart, to everyone. One of her rooms provided a space for those who needed to lie down, or sleep. The less-injured, and un-injured survivors stayed out in the bar area, huddling together to sort through the trauma, now aided by Elaine's gin and rum.

When Reiterman's wounds needed further attention, Dale Parks, the defector who had tackled Larry Layton in the Cessna, offered to look at them. He had worked in the medical field in the U.S., and in the Jonestown health clinic. By now, more bandages for the reporter's wounds were needed, but none were available. Upon seeing this, Elaine offered them some prized new curtains she had been saving. Over her guest's objections, she immediately tore them into strips for Parks to use on Reiterman's injuries. And she refused to accept any money for them, despite Reiterman's insistence. In fact, he observed that he, and his fellow survivors, did not have to ask for any help, or necessary items. The villagers just came forward with them.

Joining the others at Elaine's bar a short while later, Dwyer announced that there were four seriously wounded people in the army tent who could not be left alone. Because of that, he introduced a care plan for them. Those who were able, would take turns attending them, working in twos during two-hour shifts throughout the night. Jackie Speier's life was on the line, in danger of bleeding out after losing part of her leg and torso. Also critically injured, NBC cameraman Sam Sung had lost part of an arm and shoulder. Both had survived the attack by playing dead while the assassins were walking among them targeting specific "enemies." Anthony Katsaris, a Relative who had failed to extract his sister, Maria, from Jonestown, and Vernon Gosney, shot by Larry Layton, also lay in the makeshift hospital tent.

Throughout the long night, the caretakers were walked by locals to and from the hospital tent. Reiterman and NBC's Bob Flick, who stayed there all night, shared a shift together. They had only aspirin, rum, and rain and river water, to care for their patients. The best they could do was to stay by their sides, offering encouragement, and sips of water or rum. One patient needed his blanket adjusted; another needed help sitting up to breathe better. Reiterman reported that Sung and Speier had suffered the worst injuries, but the two showed tremendous grit, even encouraging one another from their army cots.

Soldiers stood guard just outside the hospital tent, snapping to attention when any vehicle approached. Throughout the night, a truck patrolled the village, and transported Dwyer between Port Kaituma's communications center, the rum shop, and the field hospital.

After his hospital shift, Reiterman struggled to rest back at the pub once again. His attentive host, Elaine, had given him a blanket after he began shivering, but he was too wired to sleep even though he was exhausted. When a loud bang caused everyone who was not already on Elaine's floor to now hit it, the reporter was wide awake again. The noise was from a rain-soaked tree branch hitting the pub's metal roof, but sounded like a gunshot.

The frightful night felt seemingly endless for the jittery group. As they hunched around the pub tables, or stretched out on the dance floor, even the sound of a truck engine scared them. Toward morning, when a train whistle heard in the distance felt threatening, a Jonestown defector assured them that it was, indeed, just a train.

At about 6 a.m., Dwyer entered Elaine's bar again, and despite the troubled look on his face, he had good news. He reported that 20 GDF soldiers had already arrived in the village, and many more would be coming. In fact, all of Guyana was mobilizing to help out, and Washington was fully apprised of their situation, too.

The collective mood in the room brightened, but then the reason for his downcast demeanor became apparent. He announced that Sharon Amos had killed herself and her children at Lamaha in Georgetown. He added that the news out of Jonestown was not good, either. Suicides and murders had occurred. The defectors in the room were shocked, but not surprised. In fact, most of them had almost expected it. One commented that she thought they would never make it past the guard gate when leaving Jonestown. Another believed that even if only one of them had defected, massive suicide and deaths were inevitable.

After Dwyer left again, Reiterman, now wide awake, encountered a heartbroken defector crying by himself in the pub kitchen. Gerry Parks was sobbing uncontrollably as he raged, describing how Jones "would sit there and laugh when twelve beat the hell out of one person." Yet, there was nothing anyone — villager, soldier, or Concerned Relative, could do now to ease his excruciating pain. He embodied the helpless horror of it all as grief and rage engulfed him.

Now too, the Concerned Relatives' mission was tragically irrelevant. They had not only failed to extract their loved ones from Jones's control, their family members were probably all dead. Adding to their horror and despair, their visit may have even helped to trigger the massacre.

BREAKFAST THAT MORNING consisted of milk with rum, lovingly offered to the exhausted guests who were operating mostly on adrenaline by then. At about 8:30 a.m., two uniformed GDF soldiers carrying rifles suddenly arrived inside the Rum Shop, heralding deliverance. It was time for the survivors to leave.

After trudging back to the airstrip now in full daylight, the survivors were treated to a wonderful sight. The runway was bordered all the way around with a line of soldiers. With their weapons drawn, some stood pointing outward toward the jungle, on guard in all directions. No one could hurt the survivors now. What had been a kill zone was now a safe haven. The disabled Twin Otter and the bodies of the dead were also protected by armed guards there.

The injured in the hospital tent had survived the night. When the medivac plane soon arrived, they were given IVs and rushed onto the plane. And just in time. Anthony Katsaris had breathing problems, and Jackie Speier had gangrene in her leg. All of the less wounded then also boarded the plane, except for reporters Reiterman and Javers, who gave up their seats to the distraught Concerned Relatives. When a second plane arrived soon after, there was one more thing Reiterman needed to do before he boarded and buckled his seatbelt.

Ever the newsman, he took photos of the airstrip by using Greg Robinson's camera. He also wanted to check on his lost friend, or rather, his body. It had been turned over during the night, and apparently stripped of valuables. As Reiterman lingered there, others assigned to the second plane hopped into an army jeep to retrieve him, and the dedicated reporter was soon airborne. He was leaving Port Kaituma and Jonestown with the news story of a lifetime.

After overseeing all the departures, Dwyer returned to Georgetown later that day to receive medical care for himself, his impromptu, makeshift field command now over. Mission accomplished.

CHAPTER 13

A SLOW AGONY

ON THE MORNING OF NOVEMBER 19, THE ONLY VOICES IN JONESTOWN CAME FROM JUNGLE CREATURES CALLING OUT, PROCLAIMING ANOTHER NEW DAY. There were no early morning wake-up calls or announcements from Jim Jones. There were no security guards posted on the compound's perimeters, and the kitchen's pots and pans stayed put.

Here in Guyana's rainforests, sunrise reveals a heavy ground-cloud of thick mist. Indigenous peoples acknowledge the importance of this mist by naming it: they call it "Adu." Due to the jungle's high humidity, it forms from condensation during the cool of night. Then, at sunrise as the jungle awakens and begins to heat up, Adu slips away, taking with it the mysteries of the night.

When a local villager walked through the mist into the compound on this November morning, he mistook what he was seeing there for laundry spread over the ground. But as Adu disappeared, bodies—hundreds of them, some placed neatly with arms entwined, came into focus. Other bodies were spread over an open field like windblown trash. There were used syringes, cups, needles, and plastic buckets strewn about and on small tables. Except for the birds, there was no movement anywhere. Even Mr. Muggs, Jonestown's pet chimpanzee, lay still, silently dying in his cage.

From the air, Jonestown now resembled a patchwork quilt made from bits of discarded clothing, and Mary, Mary Margaret, and Peter lay dead, "stitched" somewhere among them. Later that morning, more than 100 GDF soldiers entered the compound after walking the last few miles in. Their train from Matthews Ridge stopped short of

Port Kaituma due to fears of possible booby traps laid by Jonestown hit men.

Entering the settlement on foot, the cautious soldiers were prepared for armed resistance. Instead, they encountered a stillness broken only by the roar of helicopters overhead, the loud chopping of their rotor blades lacerating the deathly silence below. As they swept the area from above, the soldiers searched for survivors on the ground. They found none except for one elderly woman alone in her bed. She had slept through the massacre.

To aid in the search and rescue mission, American special forces were ordered in from Panama. The U.S. military at Forts Bragg and Lee, and air bases in Dover and Charleston, stood by ready to assist. But it fell to the Guyanese police to report to the waiting world what was actually found.

THOUSANDS OF MILES away on that same morning, I was driving my old Chevy to a backroad country bakery, only half listening to the radio. When I happened to hear the word, "Guyana," I pulled over, stopped the car, and turned up the volume. Four hundred Americans had died in a jungle in Guyana. That was it. No details, but I did not need any. I knew.

I turned around and drove straight to my mother's house an hour away. She had sold her farm by then, and lived back in our hometown. I found her at home there, and suggested that we turn on the television together, saying only that I was worried about Mary. Without today's 24-hour news cycle, news was delivered in short broadcasts, with very few on weekends. We sat together with both the radio and television on, desperately hoping that Mary was OK, and not part of the news.

After I called the rest of the family to alert them, Marcia joined the vigil at our mother's house. At the time, Steve was being treated in a residential care unit for his illness, so we decided to spare him until we had more information. But as it was, he was not spared. He saw the unfolding reports in the evening news.

We spent the next day, Monday, hoping that Mary was among the 400 Jonestown members reportedly hiding in the jungle, and not among the corpses viewed from the air. The news was spotty, inconsistent, and wildly inaccurate. One report had survivors in the jungle fleeing Jonestown. Then a second report claimed that these survivors were shooting at the military helicopters swarming overhead. So for now, hope held back our tears, although our mother never cried — ever. But I noticed her eyes were wet when we joked that Mary would be one of those shooting at the helicopters. She could be feisty when necessary, and right now, it was vital that she made her presence known, if not to them, to us.

The news was often conjecture, while rumors seemed to multiply. Yet the gruesome images of bodies flung like broken dolls in a jungle clearing were unmistakable. Confusing preliminary estimates of 200, 300, and then 400 dead, kept our family hoping that Mary would be found among those thought to have escaped. As it was, it took eight days for the ground crews there to uncover the actual magnitude of the catastrophe, accounting for all the dead. Correctly treating Jonestown as an open crime scene, the Guyanese police produced a more accurate report of 800 dead, and even that was an undercount.

Too soon we would learn the terrible truth. Some bodies were layered, one on top of another. There were far more deaths than first reported, perhaps 800 or more. The initial report had been estimated from a flyover; the second report, from the ground. It was then we knew our Mary was dead. And little Mary. And Peter, too.

We kept sinking lower into grief-filled shock, half a world away from those precious bodies.

SURVIVORS TIM CARTER, Odell Rhodes, and Mike Prokes returned from Port Kaituma to Jonestown to help identify the dead. Other members arriving from Georgetown came too, but some were too stunned to be of help. Grief-stricken and in shock, they could only wander among the dead. At first, about 200 bodies were successfully identified and tagged, but the tropical rains washed away the ink on the tags, creating a further setback in the overwhelming identification effort.

In the end, a total of 909 bodies would be found. But due to the delays during identification, the jungle heat and humidity quickly decomposed our loved ones' remains. They were melting away, and because of that, the U.S. military's mortuary unit on the site requested shovels to lift what was left of them.

DURING THIS TIME, I talked with a few close friends who faithfully called to check in on me at my cabin. They did not grill me for details, but just let me talk if I wanted to. Meanwhile, our Department of State and the Red Cross were assisting victims' families in the U.S. My brothers served as liaisons with State and the Red Cross, while I helped with other issues. We were doing what little we could. I kept our mother informed, but carefully so, and Marcia stayed with her most of the time. They were keeping in phone contact with Peter's widowed mother who was living back in York, Pennsylvania, once again.

News in my quiet lakeshore village traveled fast. A stranger stopped me in our small grocery store, wanting to make sure I knew there were far more dead in Jonestown than the original 400. I was shocked by her insensitivity, but it was a harbinger of more to come. On the other hand, friends hid magazine covers of bodies rotting in the jungle to shield me. These small gestures comforted me, yet one friend betrayed our friendship forever.

While working at a large newspaper, he gave out my private phone number to a young reporter new on the job there. The reporter called me early one evening, and proceeded to beg me for an interview, pleading that he could "really impress" his boss with the story. But by now, our family had an agreement to avoid all publicity: no interviews, no press, no TV. I had always had a hard time saying no to people, and it was difficult for me to do so even now with this total stranger. I allowed him to badger me for far too long before I said no, and hung up. I felt violated.

Without unlimited phone coverage, my phone bill skyrocketed as my older brothers and I worked together handling the unfolding situation, working through the logistics. At times, it was often difficult to even think straight. The Department of State, which was overseeing operations, asked families for dental records to identify the dead. I took that job, searching in vain for our childhood dentist, but he was now dead, too. However, his son generously volunteered to search old dental files for Mary. He called back a few days later, apologizing because he could not find them.

When I was a girl, our dentist mentioned that our whole family, including our parents, had "perfect teeth." I had forgotten about that, never thinking to report Mary's "perfect teeth" as a possible identifier for the Red Cross now. As it was, the dental records found in Jonestown had been transferred there from the U.S., and we later learned that Mary Margaret's body was identified from them. It was a small comfort.

For several days during our protracted turmoil of confusion and grief, I also lived in fear. In fact, I was terrified. The State Department requested that families fly to Guyana to identify their dead and retrieve their remains. Newly single, self-employed, and with no children, I was the logical choice in our family to go. The thought of sorting through body bags for Mary and little Mary, robbed me of what little peace, or sleep, I was managing. Plus, I hated flying. Flying by myself in the chartered plane that had been arranged by a family member for the flight to Guyana would be torture, and my grief was now magnified by fear.

Trying to be helpful, an aerospace engineer friend explained the chartered plane's glide ratio, and other statistics, pointing out that it was a safe model. None of it made any difference to me. I was desperate for comfort and found none, vacillating between dread and grief. But as it turned out, Guyana's infrastructure could not handle a large influx of relatives, nor hundreds of additional flights. When our State Department then canceled their request for us to reclaim our dead, I could finally breathe again. The U.S. military would fly the bodies back to Dover Air Force Base in Delaware.

ALTHOUGH I DID not want to think about Mary, little Mary, or Peter, as "bodies," others had to. Hundreds of U.S. servicewomen and men, as well as Guyanese, pitched in after the massacre. Often unnamed and unrecognized, these good people could not escape the horror. Air Force pilot Lt. Colonel Thomas Barrett was one of them. He had flown a U-2 spy plane over Russia, as well as reconnaissance over Cuba. He also flew C-123 planes during the Vietnam War. The "C" in C-123 denotes "cargo," but he never imagined that after hearing about Jonestown, he would be flying some of its "cargo."

His mission was revealed just hours before takeoff from MacDill Air Force Base in Tampa, Florida. He had arrived at the base carrying 110 empty metal boxes requisitioned from as far away as Germany. The boxes were officially referred to as "human remains transfer cases," but they would soon become "coffins." To honor the dead, coffins were not stacked during military flights; however, this mission and its "cargo" to follow would be anything but normal. Barrett's loadmaster had carefully stacked the empty boxes, strapping them in to avoid a load shift, which could be dangerous in flight.

When Barrett touched down at Timehri, Guyana's national airport, in Georgetown, heavy-duty trucks there were busy transferring body bags flown in from Jonestown. Despite crews working around the clock, the crude bags were now leaking odor and liquefied remains, and the stench arising from the backlog in the staging area was overwhelming. To prevent further deterioration of the remains, the bags were transferred to the metal cases flown in by the military, just as Lt. Colonel Barrett had done.

As if this massive undertaking was not enough, the already overwhelmed airport in Georgetown would soon be further impacted by the arrival of the U.S. Joint Task Force. It was an all-hands-on-deck operation.

During the loading process, Barrett was forced to wait amid the chaos for 18 hours. He described the foul odor surrounding the operations as "overpowering," with the smell of rotting death everywhere. Then, later during his six-hour flight to Dover Air Force Base in Delaware, his transfer cases — now coffins — in the aircraft's hold leaked organic gases. Methane, ammonia, hydrogen sulfide, and carbon dioxide could be poisonous for an airborne crew, and they were forced to wear oxygen masks after the cockpit pressure changed with altitude.

Upon landing at Dover, these transfer flights were met by the inevitable press, but also by various religious leaders who performed short religious ceremonies in the planes' holds. Then, after Barrett's loadmaster and the Dover crews removed the metal coffins bearing the "remains," they were stunned. They had to clear out maggots and liquefied remains from the plane's cargo deck.

Barrett carried the stench of decay and death home, where his wife, a nurse, had him remove his clothes. Even seven days after his return to the U.S., the odor still followed him, and frequent showers and laundering did nothing to clear it. Yet, odor did nothing to deter the news media from congregating in his driveway, which the pilot described as a "zoo," for days.

This good man, along with hundreds of unnamed others, performed heroic work after the massacre, but there were no medals or public commendations for them. Their stories have remained largely untold, but not forgotten by the people who lived them. They had spared me from personally sorting through body bags by myself, and then flying home with them in a small plane. They were the quiet heroes who bore the stench of death for the rest of us.

DURING THE SEARCH and recovery efforts, Georgetown's airport continued to handle not only outbound flights transporting remains, but also incoming arrivals of reporters from around the world. They were delivering a feeding frenzy of journalists, eager to peck at every morsel of Jonestown horror. Some even hired private pilots, while still others arrived by boat to get the "story."

Newspapers printed sensational headlines, like UPI's "Jones's SON ADMITS KILLING CULT OFFICIAL, AND HER THREE CHILDREN." The *New York Post* reportedly blared, "400 IN MASS SUICIDE — SMILING CULTISTS LINE UP FOR POISON." It was a feast for the inquisitive, the prurient, and the salacious, with enough "disaster porn" for almost everyone. Within two weeks of the massacre, two paperbacks would be hastily written.

I avoided the news by keeping to myself in my cabin. There, in the woods on the lakeshore, the trees felt like guardians, and the waters, a balm. And even though some of the news coverage may have been respectful, it all felt shaming to me. It was an accusation: we had not saved Mary and her little family. We had ignored or missed too many clues. And as it was, the public had already decided that the Jonestown dead must have been just as crazy as their leader. Since we had not heard from Mary for so long, I myself wondered if that were true. How could she have killed herself? And Mary Margaret? Why didn't Peter intervene? He had attempted escape before.

MEANWHILE, AS THE massacre was being investigated and processed, its surviving members back at Lamaha were struggling. Grief, regret, and horror had flattened them. Living under house arrest, as they were, the ensuing onslaught of legal entanglements and media requests for interviews added to their trauma. Even so, Stephan Jones agreed to meet with reporters from around the world there. Gathering inside a jam-packed room at Lamaha, it was standing room only, and the rapid-fire volley of questions was intense.

With his father's former assistant, Paula Adams, at his side, Stephan was, in effect, asked to explain the horror at Jonestown. This, while he was still struggling to understand it himself. But despite the unrelenting tension in the room, he responded to questions in a thoughtful manner and without resentment, exhibiting a maturity and grace unusual for his young age. By now, he was older than his years, given his unusual history.

Stephan declared, "We never dreamed this would happen," and that his dad "was a very frightened man." Describing Jim Jones as a coward who "feared for his life," Stephan expressed surprise that he had actually gone through with the mass poisoning. He also added that his father "had one of the biggest egos I have ever seen." Then, shifting from his overwhelmed head to his aching heart, he sadly noted, "He has destroyed everything I have lived for."

During the following weeks, 40 or more of the surviving members were kept under guard in Georgetown at local hotels and Lamaha. Some of them just happened to be in the capital during the massacre, like the basketball team. Others, including the defectors, were waiting to be legally processed. A few former members were held longer for possible prosecution, among them Larry Layton. After shooting defectors Gosney and Bagby in the Cessna, he was tried in Guyana for attempted murder, but was surprisingly acquitted. Nevertheless, he was extradited for further prosecution in the United States.

Charles Beikman, the older man covered with blood when the dead Amos family was discovered by authorities, was also in legal jeopardy. As a devout follower of Jim Jones, he had followed his leader with unquestioning devotion. This kind, but easily confused man may have tried to help young Stephanie slit her throat. As a result, he was initially tried for the Amos family murders. However, at his trial in Georgetown, Stephan Jones asserted that he — not Beikman — had killed the Amos family, thereby astounding everyone in the courtroom. It was preposterous, but it spotlighted the guilt and anguish Stephan carried for not being able to prevent that family's deaths, or the massacre in Jonestown, itself. The biblical curse of "visiting the sins of the father upon his sons" threatened to become one of Jonestown's many loathsome legacies.

Ultimately, there was insufficient evidence to support a conviction for Beikman, yet he served time shortened by a plea bargain. Stephan Jones spent a total of three months in a Guyanese jail before being cleared of wrongdoing. According to him, the enforced isolation from the press, and the rest of the prying world, allowed him to decompress. He believed that it "settled" him.

BUT FOR US back home, there would be no "settling." Although I was grateful for the media's updated information, some of it was wrong or cruelly sensational. Conjecture and conspiracy theories began to fill gaps in the evolving story. Murders, looting, escapes, and sinister plots connected with Peoples Temple were exaggerated, or concocted. Then, contrary to our family's mutual agreement to avoid the media, one family member decided to give interviews. Apparently, I had been unreachable when he agreed to do so, which was no comfort when I opened the front page of a large area newspaper to see Mary's high school graduation picture looking back at me. I was furious.

He had gotten the name of her high school wrong. In fact, he had not known much about Mary at all. During a television interview, he claimed that Mary had "lied" to him about her church while having dinner during one of his business trips in San Francisco. Knowing Mary, I suspected that what he called a "lie," was actually an omission on her part, seeking to keep the Temple out of the conversation. Mary was not naturally devious, and would rather avoid than tell an outright lie. Our collective remorse did nothing for what was already our splintered family.

An unstable relative unhinged by the tragedy, misinformation, and gossip, called me to blame us for not rescuing Mary from Jonestown. During that call, I did my best to inform her of her mistaken ideas. But she would not listen. Her call, plus the unfortunate media interview, only added to my anguish. Truth, such as it was, was taking a beating from all directions. We needed to move on from our seemingly endless limbo without bodies to bury, or closure of any kind.

BY THE END of November, all the Jonestown residents that had escaped the massacre had been identified. No further information on that score would be forthcoming from the State Department. In view of that, our family's funeral director suggested that we have a memorial service without "the deceased." It seemed like a good idea, but for me, it turned out to be further punishment.

I met beforehand with one of the two presiding ministers to talk about Mary's life, and her natural goodness. What I wanted others to know about her, beside her now infamous death. I also arranged for a folk singer to perform a hauntingly beautiful song, but our mother wisely vetoed it. She had been born into a musical family, and as a musician herself, she understood the power of music. As a dignified stoic, she understandably wanted to maintain her composure during this public reckoning with our private grief. I had never seen her cry after my father died, nor would I see her cry now. There would be no singer.

We were the only family in the state to lose members in Jonestown, so on a bleak December afternoon, our family arrived at the funeral home with television trucks, sporting ominous antennae, lurking about. The funeral directors dutifully shooed all the media away: they were not allowed on private property. Even so, I walked into that funeral home with our mother, fully aware we were being watched from afar.

When our family entered the service last, we spread out along the front row. I kept my head down, ignoring the large, packed room behind us. I focused, instead, on the two ministers in front of us, framed by a long parade of flower arrangements. Braving the claustrophobic room filled to capacity, our brother Steve joined us there: losing Mary was absolutely devastating for him. Thankfully, he was accompanied by one of his caseworkers from the hospital. So, I stayed focused on our mother sitting quietly next to me, her head bowed.

I was frustrated, and then angry during the eulogies. The ministers totally ignored Mary, the person — our Mary. They preached, instead, about Lazarus and eternal life, employing convenient ecclesiastic dodges, while blatantly ignoring the tragedy that permeated the room like a noxious smog. At least that is how I felt, and my hatred of this same church that had once mistreated our family, flared all over again. Mary and I had loathed it once, and now here "we" were again.

Even so, I hoped that our mother found some comfort listening to them, that is, if she was listening at all. She had become a widow at age 39 with six children. She had a daughter living with a serious brain tumor, and a son battling alcoholism. Her youngest son was burdened with schizophrenia, and now her youngest daughter, and precious grandchild, had been murdered. Our mother was battle-scarred by too much hardship and loss, and there was no protection from this latest catastrophe, either.

Forgoing any reception afterward, I escorted her out as fast as possible without actually running. She was in no shape to accept sympathy, or be burdened by goodwill, or the inevitable questions. One cousin caught my coat sleeve just before we got to the door, and said, "Your poor mother!" Indeed.

Our immediate family then gathered at a relative's large house. With 35 cousins, ours was a large family, but we were not in the mood for socializing. Only a few cousins from out of state were invited to join us. The rooms there were soon filled with cigarette smoke and quiet conversation. But there was not much to say, and I left after a short time. I needed solitude, my cabin, trees, and water. I needed Lake

Michigan. The public spectacle was over, and now another long wait began. For bodies.

THE JONESTOWN SURVIVORS not under Guyanese indictment returned to the U.S. under armed guard, and on commercial flights. When the first of these flights landed at JFK in New York, they had to stay seated before disembarking. After the cabin cleared of all other passengers, they were then escorted out in pairs by federal agents. While walking past members of the public, they were screamed at, with many banging on the other side of the terminal's glass partitions. The arrivals were then immediately debriefed by FBI agents for hours, sustained only by hamburgers in a fitting reintroduction to American cuisine. They were grilled about their participation in, and knowledge of, the massacre while sequestered in secure trailers located in an empty Pan Am terminal.

Later, back in Georgetown, a commercial airline pilot refused to fly Stephan Jones out of Guyana on "his" plane. Other survivors had also experienced the same humiliation. The fallout from the massacre continued to spread far and wide. When San Francisco Mayor Moscone first heard about the massacre, he vomited and cried. Now, Temple members and affiliates in the Bay Area were running for cover. Yet one brave leader stood out in the aftermath of blame and fear: San Francisco Mayor Diane Feinstein. She had just stepped into office after Mayor Moscone was murdered shortly after Jonestown in an unrelated crime.

Seeking to guard against possible violence from, or against, remaining and returning Temple members, Mayor Feinstein reacted with a rare sensitivity for the moment. She reached out to the survivors by setting up counseling and other necessary resources. Yet others were not as kind. Former Temple members were pushed to the margins of society into a pariah status, facing isolation and job denials. Loyal survivors, stunned defectors, and victims' relatives, as well as irresponsible media personnel, all found reasons to hide. They quickly learned to conceal their history with the Temple. As did I.

CHAPTER 14

NO REST, NO PEACE

AFTER JONESTOWN'S CATASTROPHIC DEMISE, A CIRCULAR FIRING SQUAD ERUPTED BETWEEN GUYANESE OFFICIALS, THE GUYANESE AMERICAN EMBASSY, THE U.S. Department of State, and California officials, all attempting to deflect attention and responsibility. Jonestown was political poison.

When the U.S. Secretary of State, Cyrus Vance, suggested that the bodies be buried in Guyana, the Guyanese government would have none of it. The U.S. then agreed to accept the remains. However, following the massive airlift to Delaware, many bodies would ultimately remain unclaimed. Moreover, some American cemeteries, fearing possible grave vandalism, or enshrinement of them, rejected them as well. Jim Jones's legacy endured long after his departure, albeit not the one he had envisioned: it was toxic.

On November 23, the first of the bodies began arriving at Dover Air Force Base in Delaware. There, the Army's mortuary personnel were traumatized by the stench, the numbers, and the tragedy itself. Hundreds more in aluminum caskets, or canvas body bags, soon followed. Yet, information like that was blurred by my grief. Random bits of news occasionally floated past me, but I was just putting one foot in front of the other. On the other hand, for those on duty at Dover, a living nightmare of unthinkable magnitude would continue around the clock for weeks.

After all the remains were transferred to Dover, disorder, and an apparent dereliction of duty by the U.S. government followed. Mismanagement and negligence seemed to rule, as we, the families of the deceased, awaited the return of our dead. Protracted delays left us hanging in limbo, confused, unsettled, and in the dark. Yet one determined family that also lost three members in the massacre refused to remain in that dark. Instead, they went to work.

The Moore family relentlessly pursued the proper handling of two of their dead: Annie Moore and Carolyn Moore Layton. These two sisters had held prominent places in Jonestown: Carolyn was Jim Jones's long-term mistress, and their young son, Kimo, had died with them. Annie Moore was one of Jones's closest personal aides. Their sister, Rebecca Moore, was not a member of Peoples Temple, and was now the only surviving sibling in her family. She lived with her husband, Fielding M. McGehee III, in Washington, D.C., not far from Dover Air Force Base in Delaware.

Working as a team, the Moore family mounted a relentless campaign for information and proper postmortem handling of their kin. The senior Moores, John and Barbara, requested information regarding the manner in which their two daughters had died. News reports mentioned both gunshots and poison in the massacre, and the family wanted clarity to help them better understand their losses. Poison could be swallowed, or forcefully injected. Gunshots could be self-inflicted, or done by others. Hence, autopsies were necessary to ascertain more reliable information for the Moore family.

By U.S. law, autopsies were required for all questionable deaths. But perhaps due to the overwhelming number of remains now under the government's care, that law was ignored, and then ultimately waived. In addition, the Jonestown massacre was an international embarrassment for the country. Why keep it in the news? To make matters worse, it appears that many governmental agencies adopted a "not my job" attitude regarding jurisdictional issues, ducking their official duties. And due to public attitudes dismissing those who died in Jonestown as "nuts," they were able to do so with little complaint.

Government official duties included federal responsibility for postmortem procedures due all American citizens, regardless of where they died, including foreign countries. Mandated agencies included the Department of State (DOS), which was in charge of overseeing the whole post-Jonestown operation. They had contacted our family with information and requests. The U.S. Department of Defense then handled the logistics by using the military to handle, store, and remove the bodies from Guyana, with flights to the U.S. The Armed Forces Institute of Pathology (AFIP) and the FBI were charged with identifying the bodies. Our Department of Justice oversaw money transferred from Jonestown to cover the expense of body removal, and it also investigated the murder of U.S. Congressman Ryan. The Office of Management and Budget kept track of costs, and assisted with further identification of the dead. Nevertheless, confusion reigned.

The state of Delaware attempted to exert its authority by seeking to remove the bodies from Dover as fast as possible. Jonestown was not its "job," either. In addition, hostility between the American and Guyanese governments proved to be a problem. This regrettable mishmash of competing, and frequently uncooperative entities, delayed any kind of resolution for us, the waiting families.

Proper identification and autopsies were of paramount concern, but most were either incomplete, hastily performed, or simply not done. Instead, fingers were cut off to determine fingerprints. Faces were lacerated and teeth removed for dental identification. Many of the remains were so decomposed, it was often impossible to even determine race. Nametags found in clothing were useless because Jonestown residents regularly traded clothes.

The Guyanese government did prove helpful by sending dental records from the Jonestown dental clinic. They also sent fingerprints from their national ID cards, routinely required for all new arrivals in the country. In all, 587 bodies were supposedly identified by fingerprints, or by personal recognition by survivors back in Jonestown.

The mind-boggling identification work was done by Dover crews, working eight-hour shifts around the clock. In the end, Mary's body was not identified by the gold earrings she requested from our mother, or her teeth, but rather by a thumbprint matching her California driver's license. Peter's body was identified by a fingerprint from his personal Guyanese ID card. Mary Margaret's body was identified by her U.S. and Jonestown dental records, but she was also listed among the approximately 300 bodies that could not be identified.

During the protracted effort to identify the dead, California Governor DuPont requested that all the remains be flown to California, the home state for most of the deceased. He believed his state was better equipped to process them due to its experience with handling the fallen from the Vietnam War, as well as his state's numerous facilities. But none of his arguments swayed the federal authorities. The DOS maintained that it lacked the authority, or money, to make the transfers to California. As a result, the work continued in Delaware, even though it lacked enough personnel to handle the unprecedented number of bodies. Experts and volunteers from the surrounding area and other military bases had to be called in to assist.

Rebecca Moore believed that AFIP made a critical mistake when it decided to embalm the bodies, thereby making crucial forensic evidence a casualty of its mismanagement. A postmortem examination without critical body fluids, which are removed in the embalming process, is useless. Physical evidence is destroyed. All morticians and pathologists know this, therefore the decision to embalm meant there would be no reliable autopsy results. Ms. Moore contended that although AFIP could then have saved body fluids for later testing, it failed to do even that. In the end, only seven autopsies were performed, two of them for her sisters, Annie and Carolyn, and only after the family's persistent requests.

The federal authorities' callous debacles led Pennsylvania medical examiner, Cyril Wright, to later declare that the U.S. government's "medical/legal work was inequitable, ridiculous, inadequate, and negligent." Supporting that claim, William Sturner, President of the National Association of Medical Examiners, believed the government's postmortem investigation was "badly botched."

However, due to the tenacity of the Moore family, the U.S. State Department was not able to bury all of its mistakes.

WITH THE CHRISTMAS season now in full swing, our family welcomed a short reprieve from Jonestown dominating the news. An eerie silence from the State Department also prevailed; then we got the call. Two caskets would soon arrive: Mary Beth, and little Mary Margaret.

Accordingly, on December 23, our immediate family gathered for the interment at our family's cemetery. It was the same cemetery that our mother and her sister, Helen, used to run past on their way to school as little girls. But now, instead of being nestled on a quiet country lane, the cemetery's grove of oaks and pines was bordered by a busy road in what had become a commercial zone. Our father's grave was here, too. Our family had also honored him on a wintery day, long before.

On this day, our immediate family gathered around two rectangles neatly carved from the frozen earth. One large, the other small — mother and child. For me, this tragedy finally hit home at that moment, and it hit hard. Up until now, Mary's death often felt like a media event, but the small casket holding little Mary Margaret's body was almost unbearable to see. As was Mary's. Even so, our stoic Dutch family quietly endured the short blessing and prayer. Then it was over and everyone left, but I stayed.

I could not leave just yet, so I sat on a cold headstone off to the side. Unable to cry before, I now wept as the slow torturous roll of this still unbelievable catastrophe engulfed me. After a while, I felt emptied and calmer, and through my blurry eyes, I noticed some gravediggers. Two gray-haired gentlemen were leaning on their shovels, quietly looking my way. When they saw me looking at them, they removed their hats, and I was deeply moved by their gesture. It was a simple, but powerful, gift of unexpected grace. So, with tears now soaking my neck, I left the two caskets. These good men would take care of them, too.

How to reenter a world that was celebrating the Christmas holiday season? How to endure? That night I stayed in town with friends, kind enough to just let me be. I needed time to heal. I needed time alone, time for my own questions — the ones I could no longer escape. Could I have stopped Mary? Why didn't I challenge those White Nights she once talked about? Or her having to ask permission to have dinner with me? Was I negligent?

It was a hard winter with a record snowfall. The drifts were so high that I had to climb up, over, and then slide down the other side of one to reach my cabin. I also risked being crushed when the cabin's roof began to sag under its heavy snow-load. Water was ominously trickling down its inner walls, and I was ordered by a building inspector to immediately evacuate. I stayed with a friend until it was safe to return.

My old car kept breaking down, too — seven times in two months, including once on a lone country road at night. Then, I began to feel unwelcome bouts of fatigue, unable to cross-country ski as usual. Loss was threatening to crush me. I had lost my house, my marriage, and now my sister and her family, and there were no shovels to clear that kind of load. As a result, I processed regret after regret, fingering what felt like a barbed-wire rosary. It was painful. How could I forgive myself for missing so many clues? For making so many mistakes?

And it was not over yet. In mid-January, we got a call from the Department of State. Where did we want the bodies sent? That would be Mary and Mary Margaret? Whose bodies had we buried in our family plot? We had no idea, nor did the folks at Dover Air Force Base, obviously. We decided to spare our mother this new horror. We were unwilling to go through an exhumation, and by now, we had lost trust in Dover's ability to get it right. We let it go.

Our two families had agreed to split up Mary and Peter's family for burial. Peter was "back" with his only living relative, his mother, Margaret, now grieving her only child. When the weather allowed, Marcia and our mother drove to Pennsylvania to meet with her. The trip east was a mission of mutual support for the two mothers, whose granddaughter, Mary Margaret, had died bearing both their names. It demanded courage for them to confront this catastrophic loss head on as they met for the first — and only — time.

In the end, a mass grave would eventually be created in the predominantly black community of Oakland, California. There, the unclaimed, the unidentified, and the misidentified, would include many of the 300 children who died in Jonestown, interred in a mass grave on a steep hillside, on May 11, 1979. If Mary and Mary Margaret's bodies were not in our family plot, then perhaps they would be there among their Jonestown "family."

IN MARCH, SEVERAL months after the tragedy, an unexpected opportunity popped up. A Jonestown survivor would be in my home town for a few days. His shirttail relatives who knew of me had alerted me. Did I want to meet with this survivor? Some of my friends urged me not to. Reports of vigilante "hit squads" involving Jonestown survivors, defectors, and others in the San Francisco area, had kept Jonestown in the news. The information was sketchy but enough to spook me. All the same, I felt compelled to meet with this person and arranged to do so. Consequently, a protective friend insisted on sitting in a parked car outside the restaurant where we would meet in case there was any trouble. I would sit at a window in full view.

Our precautions turned out to be unnecessary and my fears evaporated. Almost immediately I realized this survivor was both brave and generous for agreeing to see me; considering the burden of grief he carried, our meeting was a rare opportunity -- a gift. I had lost three family members in Jonestown. He had lost far more. At the time, I was unaware that Jonestown was comprised mostly of families, and his had been one of the larger ones. Our conversation was rather tentative at first, but soon there was only kindness and goodwill at our table. It was the midafternoon lull in the restaurant, providing us the space and time for my questions. Did he know Mary and Peter? Yes, absolutely.

But first, he explained why he was still alive after so many others had died: he had been in Georgetown on the day of the massacre. And I soon learned that not everyone had worshipped or even liked Jim Jones. He also reported that Jim Jones' wife, Marci, struggled with her husband's ongoing sexual predations and relations with church members. Hearing that, I was uncomfortable when he mentioned that Mary was part of the Temple leadership, which I later learned consisted almost entirely of white, attractive, younger women. That would be Mary. But I was unsure what "leadership" actually meant in Jonestown, and I was too scattered to follow up on it. He talked about Mary's job at the Temple's warehouse in Port Kaituma, which included working with the river boat captains. If I had known at the time how difficult that job must have been considering the lack of infrastructure in Guyana, I would have asked more about it. But as it was, I felt pressured to learn as much as I could in the little time I had with this former member.

In his litany of surprises, the most bizarre one concerned Peter. He said that back in California, Peter had been called out during a congregational "catharsis session," accused of molesting a boy in a high school parking lot. During the session Peter was stripped naked and beaten so fiercely that his penis dripped blood. He had to be hospitalized. I hated hearing this. I hardly knew Peter, and some of our family had never even met him. Yet for those of us who had, Peter was a thoroughly likeable and gentle person. How could this story be true? But then this humble young man sitting across the table from me said, "He child-molested me." The young teenager that Peter had ostensibly abused in that parking lot was now the young man sitting right in front of me. I was speechless. The thought of Peter molesting anyone, and then being openly humiliated and beaten for it, was horrifying. Yet incredibly, this survivor spoke without any ill will toward Peter, or was too kind to say so.

He also reported that Peter had tried to escape Jonestown and was punished for it by spending days underground in something called "the box." I did not ask what that was, but was glad that at least Peter had tried to escape. Then followed the most painful revelation of all: Mary had been beaten after her last visit home. Apparently, she had left a bus tour on her own, breaking the Temple rules by doing so. That was the visit when she had been so angry and bitter that I had not hugged her goodbye. It was devastating to now learn that she had paid dearly for her stolen visit. I realized at that moment that I had completely underestimated her loyalty to us in spite of Jim Jones's diabolical tyranny. She had not been visiting us to collect money: the opposite was true. She was collecting money for the church so her brief escape might be overlooked or forgiven. She had risked a beating for visiting us — she had loved us that much.

Now as we sat together on what would normally be an unremarkable weekday afternoon, this brave survivor's quiet tales of horror fell hard. I was unable to completely process much of our conversation, and I did not follow through by asking enough questions. As it was, I left the restaurant dazed but grateful for the courage he had summoned for even meeting with me.

I later heard that Jim Jones's hit squad, the Angels, were still active in the U.S. Even though Jones himself was dead, they were supposedly targeting defectors whom he had designated as "traitors." Whatever the truth was, the sorrowful survivor I met was anything but a traitor or hitman. And the "hit squads" eventually turned out to be just another media fabrication, part of the perpetual misinformation debris still swirling over the Jonestown story. Lies polluting facts. Sensation feeding ignorance.

OUR FAMILY WOULD never know if the bodies we buried were our kin, or if they wound up somewhere else. Perhaps the Oakland Army base, Fort MacArthur in Los Angeles, or Evergreen Cemetery in Oakland. Learning that Mary Margaret's name was listed in Evergreen's mass grave was deeply disturbing. Peter, whom we thought was interred in Pennsylvania at his mother's request, is listed there, too. Apparently, even in death, there would be no resolution for that little family. Or ours.

Be that as it may, Jim Jones's body was correctly identified and then cremated. Although his ashes were scattered in the ocean, even his name remained toxic for many affected by the massacre. Including it on a commemorative plaque at Evergreen was bitterly contested, and in particular, by Jynona Norwood. She had lost 27 family members in the massacre, and responded to her loss by establishing the Jonestown Memorial Wall and Services foundation, becoming its director. Years later in 2010, while standing in front of her group's newly erected "Wall of Remembrance" at Evergreen, the famed humorist and activist, Dick Gregory, publicly supported her foundation's objection to Jones's name there.

Like almost everything pertaining to Jonestown, reactions were often determined by who, and what, was lost there. A rivalry developed between those seeking to memorialize the Jonestown family, including its leaders and Jim Jones, and others who championed only the innocents, especially the children. Norwood's protest group held that Evergreen would remain forever tarnished by including Jim Jones's name there, likening it to "putting Hitler's name in a Jewish cemetery."

Yet given the gift of time, an evolving kinship grew between many of the Jonestown survivors and defectors. They started meeting regularly, slowly healing together. Having shared experiences unique to Jonestown, they were the only people who truly knew its goodness, as well as its horrors. Many were forgiving of one another.

Larry Layton, the shooter inside the Cessna, would spend a total of 19 years in prison, in both Guyana and the U.S., for his attempted murders. He was also wrongfully convicted for murders he did not commit. Vernon Gosney, who was shot by Layton, understood Layton's misguided devotion to Jim Jones. He had seen firsthand Jim Jones's powerful effect on his vulnerable followers. Because of that, Gosney generously wrote a letter to one sentencing judge, pleading forgiveness for Layton, but without success.

Some Jonestown survivors, including Mike Prokes, one of the three men commissioned to smuggle money out of Jonestown, died by suicide. Others gradually rebuilt their lives. Odell Rhodes, the compassionate man who comforted poisoned children as they lay dying, went on to become a policeman, as did Vernon Gosney. Stephan Jones would begin a long journey of recovery, marked by his name, as well as his heritage. Others returned to their former lives, picking up the pieces after their perilous detour with Jim Jones and Peoples Temple.

Jonestown Memorial, Evergreen Cemetery, Oakland, California. ATLAS OBSCURA photo

Gravestone, Evergreen Cemetery, Oakland, California. Natalia Danesi photo

PART V

PAYING TRIBUTE

CHAPTER 15

HOOKED, DISMEMBERED

WHEN TIM REITERMAN HAD INTERVIEWED TEMPLE DEFECTORS IN SAN FRANCISCO THE YEAR BEFORE THE MASSACRE, THE REPORTER HAD ASKED HIMSELF, "HOW COULD INTELLIGENT, SEEMINGLY WELL-ADJUSTED PEOPLE JOIN AND PUT UP WITH THAT KIND OF ABUSE ... WHO WOULD FOLLOW SUCH A MAN?" I have wondered the same, myself. But hindsight can feel deceivingly clairvoyant when examining the messy tangle of the past. Even so, I still needed to try: what had gone so terribly wrong for Mary?

For one thing, she left home precipitously, lacking the guardrails that college provides with its gradual transition into adulthood. Without that transition, Mary's personal upheavals and the following adjustments occurred in quick succession; Peoples Temple may then have felt like a safe haven. And its fiercely preached ideals of social and racial justice may have been the only kind of "religion" that was still inspiring for her, especially after the cruel and austere one we were used to.

Stephan Jones later described Temple members as being "some of the most lovely, remarkable people I've ever known." I believe that Mary was one of them.

She had a kind heart.

After she left home, she abruptly landed in a burgeoning street culture of recreational drugs and war protests. And she found a lot of company there. As a young idealist rejecting the adult world's "establishment" and power structure, she had already seen enough of that adult world to turn against it by then. But just two years after leaving home, she was then married and a new mother, far from family and friends. She was only 21. In addition, she apparently suffered from postpartum depression with only her husband, Peter, for support. Then Peoples Temple came along.

She needed a home.

Peoples Temple gave her refuge. Her new "family" there reached out with resources and acceptance, eventually replacing the splintered leftovers of what was once our original family. For years, we had experienced our mother's understandable desperation to be free of us, her burdens. Now, Peoples Temple provided her with inclusion and support.

Mary was vulnerable.

But how, then, did Jim Jones win her trust? Although a powerful man, he was also capable of great empathy and kindness. He could read people, find their pain. And Mary had plenty of that. Moreover, Jones's "sexual healing" of her childhood molestation trauma suggests that she may also have been caught in his predator's net.

Back when we were kids, I was extremely fortunate to have a wonderful surrogate father in Mr. A. But Mary had none. At our house, men were either absent, mean, or abusive. As a result, Mary may have felt safer without them. Years later, when I learned that Jim Jones had ordered his members to address him as "Father," it hit me like a brick. Mary and I grew up as fatherless freaks in our closed, little community; fathers were everywhere but at our house. Now she had her own father figure, one who showed her love and compassion, even if only in the beginning.

Considering Mary's gentle nature, another question arises: how did she rationalize all those years of Jones's brutality, lies, and megalomania? No one knows for sure if she ever attempted to escape him, Peoples Temple, or Jonestown. She was easygoing, but she was not stupid. In their excellent book, *Useful Delusions: The Power and*

Paradox of the Self-Deceiving Brain (2022), authors Shankar Vedantam and Bill Mesler help to answer this question.

They discuss the ways in which our brains work; the power of rituals; and the dynamics of group identity. The Peoples Temple and their Jonestown story feel like a textbook study for all three. The authors begin by noting that people cannot function without hope. In Jonestown, while members suffered hunger and abuse, they also clung to the hope that their efforts were helping to create a socialist world.

Also, Vedantam and Mesler contend that we are able to practice "cognitive dissonance," which means tolerating opposing beliefs and contradictory behaviors, even though they clash. Mary did just that by juggling her love for our family, with the Temple's practice of renouncing nuclear families. As a naturally kind person, she also had to somehow rationalize Jones's cruelty toward his followers — including Peter, and perhaps even to herself — with Jones's message of a just society.

The book's authors also maintain that our hopes and expectations powerfully shape what we see, causing our "self-deceiving brains" to sort incoming data accordingly. This can be particularly dangerous. By manipulating our expectations, forceful leaders are able to influence what we think we see by fashioning our expectations. Hence, Temple members who expected to see miracles performed by Jim Jones, believed they did. His repeated harangues about mistreatment by the U.S. government, the press, and the rest of the world, created an expectation among his followers of harm from those entities. As a result, members were fearful and felt in need of his protection. Consequently, on their last day, Jones's warning about the GDF coming to kill their children rang true: they had been conditioned to expect harm.

According to neuroscience referenced in the book, our brain constantly edits an enormous amount of incoming data in order to avoid overwhelming us. Jones assisted with this by ruthlessly editing all incoming data from the outside world, distorting its evils, and curating reality to frighten and control his victims. He "infected" his followers' minds with his own paranoia. As Laura Johnston Kohl, former Temple member and massacre survivor, recounted:

The control was complete. Only Jim and a few "trusted" workers had any outside communication or contact. Jim shunned any intervention or feedback from any source. No one challenged him and although his control was less obvious, he pulled the strings and manipulated the community completely.

In addition, Vedantam and Mesler report that our individual brains are wired to serve our "social brain." They maintain that we are fundamentally wired to be part of a group. Anthropologically, it has been critical for us, as a species, to live with others. Survival rates are higher within a group, rather than as an isolated individual. The authors go on to contend that rituals strengthen these social ties. In an unpredictable world, group membership can assuage anxiety by producing a sense of community, conformity, and even courage. We can see all of this at work in Jonestown.

Throughout his later ministry, Jones was adept at creating layers of ritual, further strengthening group identity — his deadly White Night poison drills being, perhaps, the most dramatic. On a more mundane level, his leadership meetings and church catharsis meetings could also be considered weekly rituals. Vedantam and Mesler add that, the more dangerous or difficult the rituals, the closer the bonds formed. Once again, Jones delivered on that score, too, with beatings, humiliation, and terror.

The authors report that by enduring adversity and hardship together, people often grow closer. And Jonestown did exactly that by providing generous amounts of both — adversity and hardship — right up to its disastrous end.

The authors go on to note that stories, metaphors, and symbols are not only essential to our well-being, but that our brains need them to manage and control its work. As a result, even collective fictions can bind a group by employing a shared narrative, a crucial element for groups committed to something larger than themselves. Sacred causes beyond individual self-interest can endow efforts with a nobility not found in daily living. Jones did this masterfully by selling Jonestown as pure socialism in a promised land; and the Temple exiles there, examples for the world. Socialism was their sacred cause, their new theology. Their suffering, an example for the world; their deaths, a potent message to that world.

The book's authors contend that our hopes and fears — even if divorced from reality — can significantly influence our capacity for both logic and reason. This seems to be fundamental for Jones's hold on his people. Why? Against tremendous odds, they continued with their rituals, endless meetings, and hard work, inside Jonestown. They were a tribe whose devotion to their mission and their community, if not always to their leader, endured.

Jones further cultivated a sense of community by employing an exclusionary mentality. According to him, Peoples Temple was the in-group, the chosen few with a special mission. All others were outsiders. Of course, this was familiar to Mary growing up in the way we did in the 1950s and '60s. Our childhood church was part of a cultish denomination that preached the same kind of harsh exclusivity. Back then, there was "our kind," and then there was everyone else. For Jonestown, this strong sense of community would become pivotal for its survival, and ultimately, perhaps for its demise, as well.

WHEN RICHARD DWYER first visited Jonestown in early 1978, he observed that its community seemed to function as a state unto itself. His first visit there reminded him of an Israeli kibbutz, albeit an overcrowded one. Dwyer officially recorded only a handful of deaths from natural causes there, and in speaking with some of Jonestown's seniors, he learned that they felt safe there. In addition, he observed many "fat, happy, well-cared-for infants" under the care of nurse Marci Jones. He commented on the project's "decent" education system, in which children could advance according to ability, a progressive trend for the times. Children there also enjoyed a homemade zoo of both captive and wild critters, including an anteater, a toucan, a sloth, pet scorpions, several monkeys, and Mr. Muggs, the chimpanzee. Annie Moore, Jim Jones's most devoted aide, would write on the day of the massacre:

What a beautiful place this was. The children loved the jungle, learned about animals and plants. There were no cars to run over them ... nobody to hurt them. They were the freest, most intelligent children I had [ever] known....

Upon reading that, I pictured an exuberant Mary Margaret racing about, happy just to be alive in such a unique setting. Nevertheless, Ms. Moore ignored the children's brutal punishments when she claimed there was no one to "hurt" Jonestown's children. Jim Jones hurt them. He viciously punished them with "Big Foot" and other torments. Yes, the children lived communally, had a zoo and a good school, but at what cost?

Stephan Jones believed that Jonestown residents "had it hard," that they were "hammered with dad's insanity." So, how did they endure? Having a strong group identification can cause vulnerable individuals to lose their sense of individuality. They feel that they exist only as part of a whole, and as such, they live, and sometimes even die, together. Stephan also suggested that many in Jonestown went to their deaths out of loyalty to each other. Not to Jim Jones, to each other. Bonds cemented by their shared mission, as well as their shared adversity, lasting to the very end.

As far as we can know, only a handful of members willingly gave up their lives in Jonestown. Most were forced, one way or another, to die. One survivor, Tim Carter, had time to reconsider when he stood near the line for poison. After watching his wife, baby boy, and sister dying, he changed his mind and bolted. Ever since that day, he has remained adamant about the members' deaths. He contends:

It wasn't suicide, it was murder. There was no choice that day. People say, "Why didn't anyone try to get away?" Well, I had to go and identify bodies two days later, and I know that people tried to get away. The first body I saw, the guy had been injected in the temple. There was a huge abscess. I saw abscesses on necks, arms, thighs. So many that I didn't bother to count. If you had asked people, 'Do you want to die right now for Jim Jones?' I guaran-fuckin-tee you wouldn't have had 918 dead.

Escaped Temple attorney Mark Lane also wrote:

I do not doubt that some, including Jim Jones, voluntarily took their own lives. It appears, however, that many were murdered. In the cases of those who were shot, or injected with the poison over their objections, the crime of murder is apparent.

In fact, the Jonestown death tapes contain clearly recorded cries and screams from children and adults who had not died peacefully, as Jones had promised: it had been his last lie. Employing his heinous practice of "the ends justifying the means," he declared that they would become martyrs for socialism. This tragically mistaken belief blinded him, and perhaps many of them, from common sense; and eventually from reality itself. The world would not understand Jones's protest message so shockingly delivered by mass "suicide." The world would not care. It would dismiss him as a madman, and his followers, equally mad.

IT IS COMMON to refer to those who died that day as "brainwashed." But were they? Some scholars reject the whole concept of brainwashing, suggesting, instead, that "coercive persuasion," or "thought reform" might be more accurate. In addition, other influences, including fear, or deference to authority, can be skillfully employed to control others, even against their best interests. Personal responsibility also comes into play, as does peer pressure. Consequently, brainwashing, as it is commonly understood, may not always be helpful or accurate when speaking of Jonestown, according to author Rebecca Moore, who lost family there.

It can be argued that Jim Jones employed coercive persuasion, thought reform, fear, as well as other means to control his masses. He bound them by separating them from the rest of the world, and from their families. All "others" were contaminated, and he, alone, could provide shelter from an evil and capitalistic world gone wrong.

Perhaps because of this, Mary could easily dismiss our brother Steve's argument that Jim Jones was not God. She could also ignore our mother's offer of her own house if she left Peoples Temple. To a friend, Mary had written that her church was "everything she was looking for in life." Another one of her friends, Jonestown survivor Laura Johnston Kohl, wrote: "We isolated ourselves by feeling superior, and different than those in the world around us. Our family was dismissed as being uninitiated."

The last time I saw her alive, Mary was flattened, her light and warmth gone. But none of us fully grasped, or understood, the changes in her during her last visit home. Our brother Steve had described her as "distraught and dead serious." I had noticed it, too. She was distant and bitter, with none of her inner spark. Had Jones's cruelty, thought reform, and evil double-talk, succeeded in crushing her by then? Or, perhaps she was just worn out, or depressed. Whatever the case, Jim Jones had hooked another good person by then, leaving behind only traces of my younger sister, a little girl's mother, and our mother's youngest daughter.

As CHILDREN, WE used to be horrified by Old Testament stories of God commanding the slaughter of entire cities, including children and animals. This brutal brand of religion with its cruel pieties had been familiar Sunday morning fare for us. Its ugliness helped to turn us away from our church, and from church itself. But then Mary, somehow, put her trust in a self-declared prophet, who then paradoxically turned away from all religion. It had been a twisted path.

So, what exactly was the Temple? A bona fide religion? A cult? Due to its affiliation with the Disciples of Christ denomination, cult status technically could not apply. On the other hand, Peoples Temple had a leader who once claimed to be the second incarnation of God, so, either the Disciples of Christ missed this apparent apostasy, or had turned a blind eye to it. Plus, the term "cult," like brainwashing, can be somewhat contentious. Political, military, and certain religious movements may reject outsiders, but not all of them claim that outsiders are wrong, or dangerous. However, Jim Jones did. He exhorted his followers to be "in the world, but not of the world." This exact mandate, word for word, was often used by our early ministers, an invisible fence for Mary and me, ostensibly keeping us away from outsiders and an afterlife in hell.

We know that relinquishing personal control to an individual, or a cause, can be appealing for some. If a significant amount of uncertainty, or lack of control over circumstances, wounds a child — or even an adult — joining with a "higher power" may feel good. A street gang can become a safe haven. You belong. In a movement with a strong leader, joiners may feel like part of a family with a parent-figure in charge. Still others may be drawn in by ideals, such as making the world a better place. It can be argued that all of these applied to Mary, and perhaps other Peoples Temple members, as well. It is also important to note that the prevailing culture can be conducive to such movements, too.

During the late 1960s, cultlike phenomena included movements like New Agers, quasi-religious groups, and hippie communes, where worshipful followers would sometimes add religious overtones. At the same time, massive cultural upheavals, including anti-war protests, riots, assassinations, and political scandals, served to further destabilize our country. As a result, the combination of new movements and social instability created not only a national identity crisis, but a personal one for many young people. And Mary encountered all of this head on after leaving home.

OVER TIME, PEOPLES Temple evolved from being a religious movement, to a political one. Jones promoted conspiracy theories by painting the world outside the church, and in particular, the amorphous government, as the enemy. It was a soft target, often referred to as "big brother" by others, too, in those days. His message was further enhanced by many of the same government failings and elitist laws that populist leaders everywhere have used to attract supporters.

However, the Temple's touted ideal of a post-capitalist, socialist world was eventually eclipsed by Jones's growing instability and inhumane behavior. He seemed to keep his "human menagerie" in

Jonestown like the one he had kept for his pets as a boy: enclosed and deprived of adequate care. And like those pets, few in Jonestown escaped their jungle enclosure. They, too, were trapped and malnourished. Laura Johnston Kohl wrote:

> ... *Communalism flourished only to be misused, misdirected, and ultimately destroyed by an insane leader. In the end, the survival of the community was dependent on the one person who had inspired the members to break from their pasts and take a chance. Too much power was put in Jim's hands.... [In Guyana] he [Jones] wielded more power over his congregation than he could have in the US. There was no one in Guyana — in Peoples Temple — who would stand up to him, or even get him to reflect on what he was doing, so he was unchecked. The quote 'Power corrupts and absolute power corrupts absolutely' exactly states what happened to him.*

Jones was a master at thought control, persuasive coercion, and ritual. In the proverbial analogy of the frog in a pot of cold water that is slowly heated to a boil, the frog dies before realizing the danger. In Jonestown, only a handful of defectors had jumped out of Jones's "pot" in time. Also, after numerous White Night drills, their suicide ritual had become normalized, with members becoming oblivious to actual danger. Jones even fine-tuned his brand of suicide, declaring that it had to be the right kind. His "revolutionary suicide" was not to be done for personal, selfish reasons. It had to be done for a noble cause, a cause like theirs that advances social and racial justice in an inhumane world.

Most in Jonestown were committed to their communal lifestyle and their mission, suffering great hardships together to achieve them. However, Stephan Jones believed that by the end, many had grown weary of his father's maltreatment. He estimated that perhaps only ten of all those who died on that terrible day took the poison with a clear mind. The rest were exhausted and malnourished, "hammered" by all the hardship. He also indicated that many may have died out of loyalty not to Jones, but to each other.

Furthermore, Jones had not acted alone. He had staff helping out. Sometime before their last day, a small crew of Jones's aides had secured the cyanide poison. They mixed it and tested it on farm animals. Then they killed Jonestown's children and the others with it.

THERE WERE MANY casualties beyond the massacre's tally.

Our broken family teetered and pitched like a kitchen table with a missing leg. Mary's terrible death, and those of Peter and Mary Margaret, weakened our already beleaguered family. This second dismemberment, following the loss of our father, was brutal. Had Mary lived on, I like to believe we might have managed better. But as it was, the twisted contours of our childhoods had not prepared any of us for the adversity that followed us as adults: cancer, alcoholism, betrayals, severe mental illness, and more premature deaths.

Life after Jonestown thus became one of painful questioning. As a family, we had been too splintered to know of, or join, the Concerned Relatives' efforts in Jonestown. Furthermore, had we tried, we might have inadvertently hastened our relatives' deaths, as had happened for the families that did attempt the ill-fated rescues. Moreover, would Mary and Peter even have left with us? We will never know.

I like to believe that had she lived, even phone calls from Mary would have been helpful for Steve. She seemed to ground him, and they had always been close. But now instead, when our mother suddenly died, and Steve needed Mary the most, she was not there. He disappeared for days, unable to bear another catastrophic loss. He had been living with our mother, but now there was nothing, and no one, for him to come home to anymore.

ALFRED ADLER'S QUOTE, "Every child is born into a different family," hits home when it comes to individual childhoods. By chance of birth order, I was positioned to receive our father's whole-hearted affection, but tragically, he died before the children after me — Mary and Steve — could experience him as I had. Steve was still in diapers, and Mary was too young to remember much of him.

Also, Mary and I grew up angry, thanks in part to the pervasive hypocrisy and cruelty from our church and religious schools. As formative institutions, they were utterly devoid of God's love — both preached and practiced. Instead, they provided us with potent fuel for rebellion. Consequently, when Mary later realized that Christians were no better than other people, it freed her. She joined a completely different kind of church family in Peoples Temple, one that initially worked hard to live their beliefs, and emboldened its warriors for racial, economic, and social justice.

To her great credit, as well as peril, Mary maintained a connection with our family, courageously straddling the divide between Jones and us. But I never suspected the price she may have paid for taking time out with me when I had visited her in Ukiah: She had been chancing Jim Jones's wrath by doing so. As it was, she was beaten for making that last, quick visit home during a Temple bus tour. And she risked further punishment, once again, by calling home from the airport before leaving the country for Guyana.

Mary and I also missed out on navigating our adult lives together, as sisters often do; best friends, with an easy understanding that comes from a shared past. Jonestown robbed us of that. We had spent lonely years adrift in the same house, but we never talked about it then. We just lived them — it was all we knew to do. We never got much beyond the teenage years of "borrowing" your sister's clothes when she was not home.

We will never really know what Mary's presence might have meant for our family. No doubt, she would have been worn down by all the troubles; she might even have walked away from them, but not for long. She was made of stronger stuff, and she carried a good heart. Of that, we can be sure.

Our father's premature death had shortened my childhood, functionally ending it at age 13 when I had to step in for our mother. But I eventually gained a surrogate father in Mr. A. Mary lost far more by our father's untimely death: her replacement father figure, Jim Jones, took her with him when he died. She lost her life.

CHAPTER 16

TELLING THE STORY

"We owe respect to the living: to the dead, we owe only the truth." Voltaire

ALL OF HISTORY, BOTH LIVED AND OBSERVED, BECOMES A STORY RETOLD. Those holding the pens, the cameras, and the platforms can wield great power. Because of that, I had to ask myself: Who was I to tell Mary's story? Could I be fair? I risked getting it wrong by painting her as saintly, inserting my own prejudices, or settling old scores. The risks haunted me as I struggled to remain objective, but then, perhaps the concept of total objectivity is itself an illusion.

After Mary died, I thought her story ended at the grave: she was gone. Later, when I wanted to know more about her life and death in Peoples Temple, I discovered that much of her story was being told by others: survivors, scholars, and historians. Her individual story was embedded in a much larger one comprised of many layers. Uncovering it, then, felt more like an excavation, and one without a bottom. One question led to another, and the answers were often painful.

In addition, just as for traffic accidents where accounts of the event often differ, so can the "facts" of Jonestown. Accident "facts" may collide or conflict between passengers, drivers, and even the police. A bystander's point of view can matter greatly, too. The Jonestown story is no different. However, it was a "collision" of enormous proportions.

As a result, life lived under Jim Jones's influence and power demanded careful telling, including the excruciating horror of his final act.

Writing responsibly about our family's history as it pertained to Mary's life was another challenge. For that, I often had to rely on others' recollections, memoirs, and stories, which of course, included their prejudices and personal points of view. Thankfully, immigration documents and ship manifests provided some objective facts to work with.

Since I grew up with Mary, I was more comfortable writing that part of her story, however, the Jonestown massacre threatened to distort even that. Before the massacre, Mary was just my rebellious sister, a member of a revolutionary church. After Jonestown, she was the murder victim of a madman. As a result, I proceeded with caution, aware that my own prejudices, and sometimes even anger, threatened to plague the narrative. Nonetheless, I believed that Mary's story deserved to be told. Others can learn from it, yet will they? Will we?

When a friend initially recommended that I write more about Mary's story, I was reluctant, but since this friend was a professional writer herself, I considered it. Up until then, I rarely thought about it. Mary was dead, so for me, the rest was just details. The story itself did not matter. But as it turned out, it did matter. After checking with other friends, I learned that they, too, wanted to know more, but had not wanted to intrude. As a result, I decided to give it a try, naively thinking that writing the story would not be too difficult since it happened years ago. I was wrong about that, too. I had no idea that it would take years — not months — to write this story, and that learning its truth was harder than I ever imagined.

Most of what I thought I knew about Jonestown was wrong. And even though I had turned my back on Jonestown, the rest of the world had not: documentaries, movies, books, a play, and even a musical have kept it alive. In addition, Jonestown survivors and scholars alike have differing points of view regarding Peoples Temple and Jonestown. Nevertheless, they helped me to uncover information about Mary's life and Peoples Temple, the simplest of which was no apostrophe in the church's name.

The Jonestown story itself is enormous, and at first, overwhelming.

As I worked through astonishing amounts of records, transcripts, inquests, firsthand reports, books, articles, archives, and more, I had to keep returning to the particular path that led Mary to Guyana. I initially avoided reading books written by other family members of the Jonestown dead. This particular story belonged to my family, Mary, and me, and I did not want to be influenced by others. I wanted the world to know that she was a good person, to pay tribute to just her.

But at the same time, as I discovered new horrors, I had to process them myself before writing about them. There were many times when I wanted to stop, yet an increasing desire to know what she went through kept me going. That said, in photo collections spanning almost two decades of material, I saw things I really did not want to see. The image of the crude dirt track tunneling into Jonestown's jungle felt creepy. And no matter how many times I saw them, the aerial and ground shots of the dead wounded me every time. I was looking for Mary, while not wanting to see her; the pictures made the story more real, more painful. I did not want to find her, or Mary Margaret, or Peter, among those bodies. I never did. But I was less guarded while looking through other photos, like those of the church's bus tours, hoping to see a happier Mary in them. I found none there, either.

Much of what I did learn about Mary's story was new to me. For instance, I was unaware that our mother had offered her and Peter her own house if they left the church. It was a generous but shocking offer. I was also unaware that our mother was worried about Mary, except for her being "too thin." And it was yet another surprise to learn from Steve that Mary had considered leaving the Temple at one point.

Why wasn't I aware of all of this? The chasms created by our father's death endured, and before the internet and cell phones, our scattered family remained disconnected. Perhaps, also, because women are frequently the communicators in families, but not in ours. I lost touch living out of town for years, and then during the upheavals of a divorce. Marcia, still unwell, was working hard just to get by with two children as best she could. Our mother, always living in "fast-forward," worked full time, and was busy with house remodels. After Mary left home, she moved to different cities, twice, without notifying me, and I had to search for her.

Before immigrating to Guyana, Mary's Temple life had been carefully shaded, if not completely hidden. Consequently, our family lived with a false reality. Then Jonestown completely slammed the door on even that. Owing to that, it would take a lot of digging to examine all the charades devised for us as outsiders. I was surprised to learn that while still in the U.S., Peoples Temple kept meticulous records of its financial accounts, personal communications, church publications, and sermons. And that this practice continued in Jonestown. Although there were no more sermons given there, other records continued to pile up. Even Jones's rants and announcements on Jonestown's public address system were recorded by its radio room.

Years later after the massacre, I made the mistake of listening to an NPR documentary about the Temple, believing that I owed it to Mary. However, I immediately stopped listening when I heard Jim Jones's high-pitched, ghoulish laughter on it. It was fiendish, and it haunted me even years later as I discovered the terrible suffering he caused. How could he laugh, as reported, when people were hurting right in front of him? When he was hurting them himself? Was it a brain disease, strained nerves, drugs, or just pure evil that triggered his abhorrent reactions?

I wondered, too, about the matching gold earrings that Mary asked be sent to her in Guyana. In hindsight, it was a highly unusual request since, at one time, self-adornment had been frowned upon in Peoples Temple. And she made this request just moments before she boarded her flight to Guyana. It had to be very important to her. But why?

If she was completely under Jones's control as she and little Mary were leaving our country, it was too late for her to turn back. Her eerie passport photo reflected a subdued, hidden Mary, looking off to the side, almost camera shy. Her lovely hair was covered by a scarf, and her face screened by large glasses. No one in our family had worn glasses. She had changed. Yet, in spite of everything, she did let us know that she was leaving the country. Considering the risk involved, her call was both courageous and meaningful. Did she sense their approaching deaths? I think she did. Those gold post earrings could provide a reliable, post mortem identification with her daughter.

THERE WAS FAR much more to process while I wrote. As a mother myself, I still cannot understand how Mary tolerated the Temple's inhumane punishments for children, including hers. By all reports, she adored Mary Margaret, naming her after herself and both grandmothers. Nevertheless, that little girl was murdered only ten days after her eighth birthday. We will never know if Mary or Peter obeyed Jones by killing Mary Margaret themselves, or if they were held back by guards while another guard killed her. These murders, "ordained" as love by a madman, formed a monstrous crime of Old Testament proportions.

Then, after reading how cyanide had convulsed and tortured its victims, I could no longer fool myself by thinking that Mary, little Mary Margaret, and Peter, just fell peacefully asleep after taking the poison — like a sleeping pill — never to awaken. For decades, I had not known, or even wanted to know, that cyanide was an outrageously cruel way to die. But now in writing this book, I learned that precious little Mary Margaret suffered outrageously as she died. But at whose hands, and in whose arms? And did it even matter anymore?

When I read that Jonestown mothers of infants were first in the poison line, squirting it into their babies' mouths, and then led away to an open field to keep the lines moving, I was stunned. And that once there, these mothers knelt on the ground, cradling their babies in their arms, wailing with grief as their convulsing babies died. The mothers then died there, too, having squirted the same poison into their own mouths. After I read this account, I stopped my research. I stopped writing. I could not feel, or function. I was in shock for two days. Numb.

During this grief-stricken stupor, I happened to hear Leonard Cohen singing "Anthem." His words, "There is a crack in everything, that's how the light gets in …," somehow released me, and I wept. I wept as hard as I had at Mary's grave. And then I went back to work, reminding myself that I was doing this for Mary, and perhaps all the other "Marys," and children, and babies who died that day, too.

DURING MY RESEARCH, I came across an enormous online archive of Jonestown information, the Alternative Considerations of Jonestown

H. J. JONES

and Peoples Temple website. It was, and remains, arguably the largest repository of its kind in the world. Through it, I met two experts who would become my "traveling companions" as I worked.

The first was Rebecca Moore, who lost two sisters and a nephew in Jonestown. Twenty years later, she established the Jonestown website, initially at the University of North Dakota, and then moved it to San Diego State University, where it was now housed. Other than my family, I never knew anyone else connected with Jonestown, except for my brief meeting with the massacre survivor. Because of that, I felt an immediate connection with her. When I mentioned that, she responded by saying that there are a lot of us. Logically, I knew that must be true, but this new connection was a turning point for me. It felt like a gift, one I had never considered, or expected — and there were more to come.

She suggested that I contact the webmaster of the Jonestown website, a certain Fielding M. McGehee III, noting that he "has a gentle soul." He would be able to help me with more information. However, she did not mention that he was also her husband, or that he is the world's foremost Jonestown researcher. After contacting Fielding, I asked about his unusual website, and more importantly, why he volunteered to help people like me. He simply said, "This is what we do." Up until I encountered these two people, I had been working alone, and often in the dark. Suddenly it felt like they were walking there beside me.

As a retired copy editor, Mac (as Fielding goes by) provides his encyclopedic archive of Peoples Temple and Jonestown information free of charge. As such, he offered to help me navigate the website, and then, out of the blue, he also offered to help edit my work. I already had an editor-friend working with me, and did not know I needed another editor. But Mac did.

He had worked on several books about Jonestown before, and I soon learned that if he did not have an answer to a question, he probably knew where to find it. I suspect that I turned out to be more work than he expected, due to my limited acquaintance with my old desktop computer. But Mac repeatedly rescued me, patiently showing me how to format my writing, as well as how to tunnel through mind-numbing amounts of Jonestown facts and lore.

Some of my peskiest challenges involved conflicting information. It drove me nuts. For instance, in Jonestown survivor Laura Johnston Kohl's autobiography, she stated that she personally notified Stephan Jones of his father's revenge order; she was on staff at Lamaha when the order was received. But her account seemed to directly conflict with Stephan Jones's own account of that night. He reported that he was watching a movie in the local theater when he received the notice about the revenge order from his brother. I chose his account over hers, but this kind of discrepancy would pop up again. Because of that, I learned to use qualifiers and tread carefully. Jonestown "facts" could be squishy, if not downright maddening.

Another example of conflicting information concerned Mary and the Temple's White Night drills. When I visited her in 1971, she was still open with me, and I remember her telling me about her church's strange practice. This was also when I learned about its surprising doctrine of reincarnation. But then, during my next visit with her in 1973, she said nothing about the church, other than to reveal Jim Jones's sexual healing, and his "protecting" her family from a traffic death.

This timeline concerning the Temple's White Night rituals directly conflicted with Mac's information, unfortunately. He had no evidence of them being practiced before 1973. So, there I was, disagreeing with perhaps the world's foremost expert on most things Jonestown. I had to decide if I was going to trust my memory, or his research. When I finally decided that I had to trust my memory, he graciously stepped aside, sticking with me when others might have quietly slipped away.

I had help from other unexpected directions, too. As kids, we always ranked ourselves according to age, hence every year mattered. I paid close attention to my older sister and her friends: they were the cool ones, not like the "little kids" trailing behind me. Because of that, much of Mary's youth passed by me rather unnoticed, so now, I had to dig for it. Fortunately, help was still available from those who knew her better then — Mary's old school chums. And I welcomed all of it. There was much about her that I never knew, but those friends did.

They still grieved her, and were eager to talk about their friendships with her. To have her in their lives again, if only in memory. They dug into trunks and through old files, looking for her letters. Others just wrote about their memories. They revealed aspects of Mary that were new to me, and at times, disturbing, while at others, quite wonderful. A Mary outside our house, away from its frequent gloom and occasionally empty cupboards. A Mary I wish I had known far better.

Her earliest friend, Carol, wrote that Mary was a "cherished friend" that she "loved dearly," and that Mary's "laughter and bright shining, happy face" live on for her. Mary's friend, Barb (a.k.a. Baboola), shared correspondence with Mary that proved to be highly informative, ranging from 1968 until Mary's first year in Peoples Temple. These letters covered a period of several moves and critical changes within a short time for Mary. Sue, another friend from high school and beyond, had me laughing over their antics together, showing me a side of Mary I never saw much of.

By connecting with her former friends, I learned that Mary's life before Peoples Temple had been enriched in surprising ways. I got to know Mary, the friend. Not only who she was out of the house, but also how greatly she was loved, and is still missed. Her friend Sue had visited Evergreen Cemetery in Oakland twice, noting Mary's name among the hundreds engraved on the granite monuments there. Sue shared Mary's letters and photos with me, as well as answering a host of questions about their times together.

Mary's faithful friend, Barb, had also kept Mary's letters, and sent me copies of them. She had grieved for Mary alone while living out of state. Among other things, she wanted to know the location of Mary's gravesite now, so I agreed to meet her at the cemetery when she came to town. And so it was that on a quiet summer afternoon, I stood back while watching Barb carefully scatter rose petals over two graves: white petals for innocence on Mary Margaret's little headstone, and red ones for love over Mary's. They fell with a tenderness that deeply touched me.

I had never appreciated the healing power of a grief shared. Now it seemed like Mary's friends were gathering around, each embracing her in their own way. And in doing so, they also comforted me. Mary's friend Carol wrote a long, beautiful remembrance of years past with Mary. Meredith, Mary's lone friend from her new high school, as well as coworker at the hospital, gladly supplied me with two important letters from Mary. Sue and I agreed to meet up sometime, and Barb became a new friend, stretching our relationship beyond our ties to Mary.

IN MY SEARCH for former Temple members who may have known Mary, I learned that I was decades late. Many have since died. My timing was off. However, Mac's website was not only a Jonestown encyclopedia, it also served as a forum for survivors, relatives, defectors, and scholars — a virtual gathering place. In his capacity as the site's creator and host, Mac generously connected me with Jim Jones's son, Stephan Jones. I was hoping to find someone who perhaps knew Mary in Jonestown. With Stephan's history and firsthand experiences, a connection like this was a totally unexpected gift, and I was incredibly grateful for the opportunity to ask him about her. That said, I was also quite terrified.

I did not want to impose on anyone living with the kind of trauma that Stephan Jones had endured. Still bombarded by hundreds of interview requests from the media, Hollywood, scholars, and more, the world still wanted a piece of him. His name and history, in addition to the challenges he had faced, seemed enormous to me. To work up the courage to even contact him, I had to keep reminding myself that I was doing this for Mary. Not me.

From what I understood, Stephan kept a low profile, living simply, far away from the media's perpetual searchlights. As an introvert myself, I felt guilty for even emailing him, but I did, and after a few exchanges, we set up a phone date. I dreaded the idea of now actually talking with him, yet I was desperate for some first-person, solid information about Mary. Plus, Mac had opened the door for me, and it would be ungrateful for me to not step through it.

Meanwhile, Mac humored my jitters, assuring me that Stephan was a fine person, and as usual, he was right. In fact, Stephan turned out to be so gracious, I was almost ashamed for having feared my encounter with him. He allowed me to tape our conversation, which lasted not 20 minutes as planned, but an hour, and it was a profound pleasure to think deeply with him.

Stephan turned out to be a gifted conversationalist, easy to connect and laugh with, and I trusted him right from the start. In fact, I had to keep referring back to my notes to make sure I got my questions about Mary in; we kept veering off in other directions. His take on life resonated so deeply with me, I wanted to hear more about him as a person.

From my previous research, I knew that when addressing a group of young people, Stephan once introduced himself by saying, "I owe it to the people I lost to speak well of them and invite the living into their story and learn from them, to identify with their loss." He went on to say that we can "gently" show how anyone can lose their way, and that there is "huge value in the Jonestown story." By saying this, he affirmed one of my reasons for my writing the book.

Stephan also expressed resentment at the media for painting his father as a complete villain, employing binary thinking — all good or all bad. And their take on Jim Jones was almost always, "all bad." He pointed out how one newspaper had edited photos to make his father look like he was scowling, when, in fact, he was not. He was smiling. Disreputable tabloid contrivances such as these had dominated much of the Jonestown reporting, and continues to do so even now.

According to Stephan, it is important to know more about his father to better understand him, including his painful childhood. As a little boy, Jim Jones was cast out on his own. Yet in spite of it, Jim Jones managed to be a gentle and loving father to Stephan, given to laughter, and with a great fondness for both children and animals. Stephan shared that, at one time, his dad had an attractive personality, and that he was kind. He pointed out that if his father had been evil right from the start, his followers would have been crazy to trust in him. It rang true, and I completely agreed: Mary and Peter were proof. They were intelligent, kind, hard-working people.

Stephan also believed that his father had a conscience, and perhaps because of it, he began using drugs to numb himself. At some level, Jim Jones knew he was behaving badly by mistreating people. Stephan also observed that his dad was a very needy person, relying upon others' approval to feel any self-worth as a person. As a result, "He got lost in managing others' perception of him." He also confirmed that his father had been completely devastated when so many members left Jonestown aboard that dump truck on November 18. He had taken it personally.

I wanted to know if Stephan was personally familiar with Mary, even though Peoples Temple had up to 2,000, or more, members. And if he did, perhaps he could shed light on her role in it. However, Mary was 11 years older than Stephan, an adult while he was still a teenager. Consequently, while she was sitting inside the church in Redwood Valley, he was outside it, hiding as best he could. And at about age 12, he "broke" with his father, disengaging, and sneaking out of Jones's long church services, then showing up at the end of them to hide his absence. As a result, he did not personally know Mary while living in the U.S. Then in Jonestown, he spent a lot of time either in the jungle, or with friends his age. He did not know her there, either. But he did know of her.

Stephan was emphatic when he said that Mary was "not anywhere near to leadership" status while in Jonestown, itself. This was a relief. I was hoping that she had at least been spared that. He described the leadership in Jonestown as having many layers, which made sense, given the many challenges they faced there. Providing for 900 people in a jungle while trying to achieve true socialism had soon become a problem from hell.

Then trying to ascertain Mary's level of freedom within Jonestown, I wondered how closely she worked with Jones in any capacity. I asked Stephan if she could have used the river boats to sell handcrafted-goods from Jonestown. He could only say that it "sounds true to me." He added that anyone with that much freedom would have earned Jim Jones's trust. I also asked him about Mary supposedly assisting Jones by faking her death at a revival in Harlem, after which Jones had "healed" her. Stephan indicated that these kinds of ruses were done to "raise the level of faith in the room," but that he had not witnessed that particular one.

Stephen did not personally know Mary, but he did know Peter. He described Peter as "genuinely sweet, sensitive and super smart," and that he had a "light in his eyes." That was the Peter I knew, too. Stephan expressed "nothing but compassion for" Peter after he was savagely beaten for the sexual molestation incident, stating that Peter then "suffered horrible abuse treated as therapy" for it. I mentioned research about pedophilia (or to be exact, ephebophilia, an attraction to fifteen-to nineteen-year-olds), being currently studied as a possible brain disorder. Stephan listened, adding that knowing Peter, it "must have torn him up" to have done something like that to another person.

When I wondered why Peter was allowed to stay in the church after the incident and beating, Stephan confessed that he did not know. He offered that his father had acted out sexually, too. Jim Jones "preyed on 18- and 19-year-old girls." Mentioning this felt like a generous gesture on Stephan's part, perhaps softening any anguish about Peter's behavior, or affliction.

Stephan revealed that he spent as much time as he could away from the Jonestown "village," exploring the jungle, instead. When we talked, he had recently returned from Costa Rica, and indicated that it was the same latitude as Guyana. Yet, according to him, its jungle could not compare with the rainforest jungles of Guyana. Clearly, Guyana's had set a high bar for him, and it was comforting to learn that, for him, the jungle had been a sanctuary.

When I asked about his mother, Marci, he said that they had been very close. He added that, "she lost her way trying to manage" his father. As he was talking, I could hear the love softening his voice, describing her as "beautiful inside and out." According to him, she had been Jim Jones's salvation by "validating" him as a person for decades. And that during Jonestown's final days, she struggled mightily to keep him from "going off the rails." He also reported that when his maternal grandparents, the Baldwins, visited Jonestown just weeks before the massacre, his grandmother had encouraged Marceline to leave Jim Jones. Exasperated after so many years of sticking it out with him, Marci responded that it was too late. She was trapped there in the jungle, too far from home.

Stephan noted that, by the end, "most people were hammered in Jonestown with Dad's insanity." Even his base of supporters within the leadership were arguing among themselves. He also believed that most who wound up dying in Jonestown had stuck it out from loyalty to each other, not to Jim Jones. Their sense of community bound them together, and only a very small number had taken the poison willingly.

As he talked, Stephan exuded a strikingly generous empathy, and I became more interested in him as a person, not just his place in history.

When he expressed guilt at not being in Jonestown "when they really needed me," I pictured him as a 19-year-old, severely traumatized, bereft of family. I asked how he had coped after his return to the U.S., bearing the sorrows and trauma of the massacre, plus burdened by his name and lineage. He had lost his parents, his family, and his whole world.

He talked about taking time to decompress in Hawaii, where his family had once spent an extended vacation. Thus, it was familiar and it had jungles, too. While recuperating there, he met with a wise, elderly man who counseled him, declaring that, "It does not matter what the world thinks of you — what matters is what kind of man you are." This wisdom opened the way forward for Stephan as he sought to build a whole new life.

He was now so open and approachable, I felt comfortable broaching the subject of good and evil head on with him. His unique experiences seemed to be a gold mine for both. He responded elliptically, first by observing that it is important to know where actions originate: "Fear or love?" Who was "running a [head] game, or running on heart?" He believed that Mary, for example, worked from her heart as a true "servant." When we went on to discuss Jim Jones's operating principle of, "the ends justifying the means," Stephan declared it to be the "most pernicious" contrivance in the world, a rationale for doing wrong.

Upon my mentioning forgiveness regarding the massacre, Stephan offered this: "Forgiveness is not a useful concept. Compassion is." It was an epiphany that not only hit home, it released me. And it surprised me, too. Considering the murders of Mary and her little family, I had no room for forgiveness. Jones's evil means for his twisted ends had left no room for it, whatsoever. Accordingly, Stephan's take on compassion managed to ambush me. In addition, after learning about Jim Jones's appalling childhood of sustained, severe neglect, it was impossible not to feel pity for him as a lonely child.

After my conversation with Stephan, I suspected that if that wise old Hawaiian who once counseled Stephan was still alive, he would be proud of the man Stephan had now become. Stephan spoke with great empathy and hard-won wisdom. And by actively rejecting bitterness and hate, he was instead using his world-famous platform to promote compassion and truth. Once an angry teen living under a father gone mad, then trapped into witnessing, and sometimes even committing violence himself, apparently Stephan had become a wise man himself.

CHAPTER 17

REVELATIONS

EVEN THOUGH I DESPISED JIM JONES'S ACTIONS, I COULD NOT LEAVE MARY'S STORY WITHOUT KNOWING MORE ABOUT THE MAN WHO CUT HER OFF FROM US; THE MAN SHE FOLLOWED INTO THE JUNGLE. In view of that, it was unsettling to discover things that softened my view of him. It was easier just to hate him, but there was a lot more to know about this infamous leader.

By any measure, the big picture of Jim Jones and Peoples Temple can be muddled and confusing. And why wouldn't it be? Good and evil often dance together in the same ballroom. Nevertheless, we can still ask: Was Jones exceptionally good, or was he exceptionally evil? Or both? He was a complicated, but powerful leader: at one time, he was widely praised by Californian community leaders in San Francisco, Los Angeles and statewide.

He could be tenderhearted with babies and animals, once admonishing a little boy for removing the wings from an insect. As a boy, Stephan had experienced his father as loving, supportive, and even gentle. Was Jones a good man? Ask the multitudes of his black followers, astounded by a white man that actually understood the scourge of racism. A man who devoted his life to fighting it. On the other hand, he had also ordered many of them to their agonizing deaths.

Before writing this book, I did not want to hear anything good about Jim Jones, or Peoples Temple. Nor did I want to consider the question of personal responsibility among his followers, especially those who worked closely with him. Ultimately, he was the one who ordered and committed unimaginable evil acts. Yet, he also did great good by calling out racism, sexism, and economic and opportunity inequality, long before many others.

That "ballroom" where good and evil dance their tangos and waltzes, presents a conundrum. Is the rapist who faithfully mows an elderly neighbor's lawn all bad? The embezzler who volunteers at a food bank? And how about the pedophile physician working in a refugee camp? Do we judge him knowing that his brain may be abnormally wired? Could Jim Jones's brain have been impaired by an untreated brain disease, like schizophrenia? It was important for me to understand more about Jim Jones, the person, if possible.

We know for sure that he had a hard start, subjected to a desolate childhood, abandoned by both of his parents; one by illness, the other by absence. His father, James Thurman Jones, was a veteran of World War I, and had been injured by mustard gas in that war. Because of it, he was too weak to hold down a steady job. His hard-charging wife, Lynetta Putman Jones, wound up supporting the family. James Warren Jones, their son and only child, was born in 1931 to a mother who had to work long hours. She worked all through the Depression in the 1930s, and for decades afterward.

Lynetta had doted on her little "Jimmy," despite her long absences from home. She also prodded him to become "somebody," while openly despising her sickened husband, a "nobody." She considered him to be a weak man. Consequently, as a child, Jimmy often heard her berating his father. The boy soon learned to bury his own shortcomings by compensating with braggadocio and grandiosity, and they became a shield.

Meanwhile, his feisty mother, who preferred pants to skirts, defied many social conventions of the day, including traditional roles for women. Providing her only child with a nurturing homelife did not register with her. As a result, even as a toddler, little Jimmy often wandered around their rundown neighborhood alone. There was no one at home to care for him.

At the same time, his father frequented the local pool hall, and even though he picked up menial jobs, the family remained poor. Their ramshackle house next to railroad tracks had little furniture, and lacked comforts of any kind. Moreover, the family did not eat meals together, nor did Jimmy's parents show up for family functions at his school. As an adult, Jim Jones still carried the fury and shame he had experienced back then, witnessing how other parents cared for their children, including showing up at school.

Over time, the boy's almost relentless misery created a fundamental loneliness in him, and his early humiliations would dog him for the rest of his life. His childhood had scorched him; he grew up angry. He described his family as "white trash," which perhaps sensitized him to the evils of class discrimination, and racism. On the other hand, these wounds enabled him to later speak from his heart to others' wounds as a forceful leader, whose fiery sermons attracted throngs. Yet, tragically, his followers would ultimately pay a price for his rage: Mary and her family, and countless others. And those of us they left behind, too.

It may also be that he was suffering from more than a childhood of bruising neglect.

BECAUSE OF OUR family's long experience with my brother Steve's brain illness, the more I learned about Jim Jones's behavior, I wondered if he, too, might have suffered from paranoid schizophrenia. But if that were the case, how could Jones have survived on his own without proper medication and treatment?

To begin with, he was not really on his own: he had a devoted nurse-wife, and dedicated support staff to see him through the worst of times. In addition, during Jones's short life span an accurate diagnosis for schizophrenia was frequently missed. As a poorly understood illness, schizophrenia had often been misdiagnosed as a "nervous breakdown," depression, or schizoaffective disorder.

Reportedly, in 1961, Jones had been hospitalized at age 30 for hearing "voices from outer space." In addition, Jones was hospitalized again while in San Francisco. Perhaps if he had been observed for longer than one week while there, his diagnosis of "paranoid personality disorder with delusions of grandeur" might well have been "paranoid schizophrenia with delusions of grandeur," instead. Furthermore, Jones may have eluded proper diagnosis and treatment by self-medicating with drugs and alcohol, which continues to be a common coping mechanism for untreated mental illnesses still today.

In the 1950s and '60s, schizophrenia was still a poorly understood brain illness, difficult to diagnose without an adequate history of symptoms. Far more is known about it today. According to current mental health experts, some of its most common symptoms include delusions, hallucinations, and disorganized speech. As far as we know, these particular behaviors were often observed by those close to Jim Jones.

His delusions of persecution and impending disaster were readily apparent to anyone who spent much time with him. In fact, he moved his whole church to California partly to avoid nuclear war. And he, himself, reported hallucinations, both auditory and visual. He heard voices. He "saw" a nuclear blast in California. In fact, his disorganized speech remains evident still today in his recorded rants and sermons. And significantly, there appears to be no evidence that neither his delusions, nor his hallucinations, upset him. On the contrary: They convinced him further of impending peril. His paranoia was unyielding, right up to the end.

With his claims of being the second incarnation of God, and then God himself, Jones's delusions of grandeur were strikingly apparent. His hallucinations of nuclear explosions; disorganized thinking — despite his high intelligence; relentless paranoia; fixed suicidal thoughts of revolutionary suicide; rambling, disorganized speech; and self-medication with drugs, all might suggest an undiagnosed, and untreated brain illness.

Of course, no one knows for sure, but a debilitating brain illness like schizophrenia could help to explain his extraordinary behavior, and catastrophic downfall. This once powerful leader, with his electrifying oratorial skills, may have struggled with far more stressors and burdens than anyone realized. His tormented life, once hidden in obscurity, was then exposed by a tragedy of historic proportions.

WE KNOW NOW that, as part of Jones's habitual paranoia and secrecy, he often employed codes: his massacre order was triggered in code. He also gave certain members code names. When I later learned that Mary had been given the code name of "Aleisha," it was not welcome news. Did having a code name mean that she held an important leadership role? We don't know, but any leadership roles were likely confined to her Temple work in the U.S.

Leadership in Jonestown was far more demanding than back in the U.S. During its final days, Jones's small inner circle was bedeviled by difficult decisions, poor sleep, and diminishing supplies. And according to Stephan, his father purposely incited disagreement among them to prevent coalitions from forming against him. He would stand aside after conferring favors and stoking rivalries, apparently a master at controlling the few, as well as the many. I hope that, at least, Mary had been spared that.

REVELATIONS KEPT POPPING up as I wrote, opening my eyes to a much wider reality, one that included our childhoods. Mary and I grew up hearing our mother say that she liked us kids when we were sleeping. But it was a different story when we were awake; at least it was for me. I was a lightning rod, rebelling and speaking out, and Mary witnessed the consequences of that. My anger got me nowhere. She, on the other hand, was naturally humble, and even quiet — good survival tools, especially after seeing the trouble I got into. Considering the perils in Jonestown, where absolute obedience was the rule, Mary already had the tools to survive, using what she had done best: keeping her head down.

There was more. For years, my storms of anger and grief over our father's death collided head on with our mother's refusal to grieve, or even talk about him. She used to say rather proudly that she "didn't have time for it." But she was angry, often at me and perhaps at our dad, too. Theirs had been a turbulent marriage according to relatives, but with typical Dutch reserve, our mother never talked about that, either. Instead, it remained a festering undercurrent as I muddled through a bewilderment of forbidden grief, and my mother buried hers.

Our childhoods had been split in two: before and after our father's death. After, we could not talk about him, or much of anything from the "before" times. And in those days, children's lacerating grief was rarely acknowledged. Even adults were left to their own devices, save for their religious faith or useless bromides. My mother kept pushing me with my bothersome grief, and then anger, away. But had I told any grownups this, they would not have believed me. She was well-liked by everyone, and greatly admired for the way in which she managed to carry on. My friends appreciated her easygoing ways and earthy humor: they would never have believed me, either.

As I write today, a fatherless family would be considered normal, not "broken." In fact, records show that in 2019, the United States had the highest rate of children living in single-parent households in the world; almost a quarter of children under the age of 18 lived with only one parent. Yet, when Mary, Steve, and I were growing up in the 1950s and '60s, we were trapped in a restrictive religious community with no "broken families" whatsoever. As a result, we lived as functional orphans, shamefully hiding in plain sight while our mother worked full time. Years later, Peoples Temple was also a restricted community, but at least this one provided a welcoming family. And a "father."

LOOKING BACK, STORIES of our mother's childhood always felt like a flickering, vintage black-and-white movie, and just as irrelevant. So, when I was 13, I never thought about her being removed from school against her will, to save on school tuition. And then work in the barn while all of her older brothers attended college. In those days, daughters were more easily trimmed from family trees than sons. As if that was not bad enough, her mother had emotionally abandoned her and her siblings after losing five others to early deaths. Our mother used to say, "I never knew my mother." I had never appreciated the gravity of that.

As a teenager, I got to live at home. When our mother was 14, she had to leave home to work for a wealthy family of seven children. Her wages as a nanny and housekeeper there were needed to support the farm. Still a child, she missed her home and family, but regardless, her life was now suddenly elsewhere. I never considered what it was like for her to miss out on both middle and high school, in addition to losing her home. She was just a child. Later, when I was in college,

I failed to appreciate that, at that age, my mother was still a live-in servant, with almost no free time. Her teenage years were all spent in servitude.

Later, as I accrued graduate degrees, I never once thought about all that she had missed out on, in part because she was a girl. I also callously ignored her lifelong wish to get her GED. She never had the time while working so hard. In fact, I never even thought of her as anything other than the adult we kids knew. Compared with her lack of opportunities, our young lives must have looked easy. Realizing this now was another gift: I was not to blame for all her unkindness, but neither was she.

When I was a teenager, I hated hearing grownups exclaim, "You look just like your mother!" But I never stopped to wonder if my mother saw herself in me, too. Or if she envied me because I had something that she never had: an education. Even as a mother, myself, none of her painful past registered — until writing this book. Life stories take time to be appreciated. Like small mosaic tiles fitting together, the whole picture, or story, has to be seen from a distance. Or in my case, while writing a book. I only wish Mary and I could have discovered our past together.

And more of that past kept surfacing. With just her sixth-grade education, our mother must have felt like an imposter as a nursing student among her younger, educated classmates. Yet, she stubbornly managed to stay in nursing, just not as an LPN but as a nurse aide. Despite the obstacles, she had forged ahead, and with a completely different mindset than mine. Through the lens of her past, her kids' lives looked privileged. But seeing all the stay-at-home moms caring for their children, I thought Mary, Steve, and I had been cheated.

Decades later when I asked our mother what my father's death had meant for her, I was prepared to be sympathetic. How terrible it must have been being marooned at age 39 with six children, one still in diapers, and with no vocation herself. It had to have been a living nightmare. In view of that, it came as a shock when she answered my question with a satisfied smile, simply saying, "I got to be a nurse." Our loss had been her gain.

Old-world patriarch that he was, our dad would never have allowed her a nursing career. Accordingly, his death had freed her, but not us kids. It had deeply wounded us. I regarded her nursing uniform with resentment, especially when I had to iron it for her when she was running late. That uniform took her away from us, but it had fulfilled her.

When she suddenly died at age 86, her death drew mourners from all over, including neighbors from 40 years back. The large parking lot at the funeral home was full. When some of the cousins gathered around her casket confided that she had been a better mother to them than their own mothers, it stung, but I got it. She was that special.

LONG OVERDUE RECKONINGS accompanied these revelations. I began writing to honor Mary, but soon realized that in doing so, I also had to face my own grief for her. After that, coming to terms with our mother's childhood of servitude was downright humbling. But more than anything else, reading about the torture and suffering my sister had endured was the most devastating. I had never done so before.

I also had to recognize my position of white privilege. It was unsettling. Even though I knew about Jones's ministry to black Americans, I always pictured both the Temple and Jonestown as primarily white, with a small minority of black members. When I had visited Peoples Temple in 1971, this seemed to be the case. But while that changed when the church expanded its reach into more of California, my image of it had not. As a Caucasian, my "white as normative" bias had held firm. As a result, learning that the church was actually 80–90% Black in San Francisco, and only slightly less so in Guyana, made my head spin.

I realized then that my gutsy sister had dedicated her life to a black church, led by a white minister. This combination was highly unusual back then, and I suspect it remains so, even now. I also failed to appreciate what her church's choir, which performed across California, and eventually cut their own record, may have meant to her. Mary had sent their record to our mother, but I never bothered to listen to it. When I considered doing so later, knowing that Mary Margaret was part of the children's choir made it too painful. Her jubilant little voice had been brutally silenced by then. As a result, I forgot all about the Temple choir, that is, until one day when the Edwin Hawkins Choir reminded me of it. That choir's triumphant joy had always moved me, but upon listening to it now, it also delivered an epiphany. I realized that Mary's "soundtrack," in both California and Guyana, included a choir like the Hawkins choir. Her life was not joyless.

Inspired by this insight, I finally listened to the Temple's album, "He's Able," online, and it was quite wonderful. Like a benediction from the past, I realized that Mary's difficult and complicated life was also graced with music. Peter played his guitar and sang in performances, and he taught Mary Margaret how to sing while accompanying her. Logically, I knew Mary's life must not have been all hardship and pain, but now I actually felt it, too. She had joy and inspiration, music, and dancing, and I was comforted realizing that.

Former Temple member and saxophonist, Mike Cartmell, remembers their choir this way:

> It's difficult to appreciate the transformative appeal of the choir in person and in full voice. We came at our audiences like a soulful all-consuming wave of sound, and we swung like (what I imagine would be) Duke Ellington's own heavenly chorale. We were invited to perform all over California. And it's never far from my thoughts that little more than five years after the children sing the opening number, "Welcome," they were all gone. More than anything else, that breaks my heart.

WHILE EXCAVATING THE past, still another revelation surfaced. As the stand-in "enforcer" at home after our mother became a nurse aide, I always felt resented, and sometimes even hated, by Mary and Steve. Those were hard years for all of us. Because of that, I was thunderstruck when Barb (Baboola) reported that Mary did not hate or resent me; in fact, she really looked up to me. I refused to believe it, but Barb insisted that it was true. Upon hearing that, six decades of my buried guilt and regret seemed to lift a little. Still skeptical, I checked in with our brother Steve, asking him about my enforcer role in the family. Surprised by the question, he said he had not resented me, either, and actually thanked me for looking after Mary and him. Hearing this, my "villain's cape" seemed to float away, yet another gift from beyond the graves.

IN ADDITION TO telling Mary's story, I came to believe that telling the larger story of Jonestown, itself, is important. Invisible "Jonestowns" continue to spring up around the world, forming wherever a dangerous gap between the rich and the poor separates people. Within those spaces, autocratic demagogues, and media personalities, alike, spew pretty lies and empty promises. They fill their listeners with false hope, as well as hate. And hungry people everywhere will consume lies like these just to feel better.

Starving for deliverance, believers become captive to an us-against-the-world, siege mentality. While thus separated from everyone else, they also become easier to control. Meanwhile, their self-proclaimed saviors elevate themselves by using their followers' pain as a platform. But in the end, their followers ultimately pay the price for their misbegotten trust. Communities, cities, and whole countries can, and do, fracture.

Jonestown holds a lesson.

But perhaps its lessons will go unheeded, and Mary's story will be repeated. As long as people are suffering from ruinous inequality, racism, and want, there will be room for demagogues, dictators, and false prophets — more Jim Joneses.

I REGRET THAT in the past, I had failed to appreciate Mary's pluck and dedication, even if misguided, at almost every turn. I may also have gotten some of her life story and history with Peoples Temple wrong. But even so, I seek to honor the Mary that I did know: a good person who deserved far better than she got. And although I may have underestimated my younger sister, others had not:

What I remember of her is that she was a gentle, warm and quite loving person. She had red cheeks and seemed to smile a lot. (Jordan Vilchez, Jonestown survivor)

She was a Light — in every setting, her cheer and calmness were like a sweet balm. She handled great responsibility with ease, and was a caring and utterly dependable friend. We had many riotous times in our outings with her patients from her care home. She was always thoughtful and I [miss] her. Her parenting of her darling daughter Mary was wonderful to see. Mary worked so hard to make a better world for her daughter Mary. She would have had a great impact on the world had she survived. (Laura Johnston Kohl, Jonestown survivor)

During the last few hours of Jonestown, several suicide notes were hastily written. Among them, an unsigned one pleaded:

Collect all the tapes, all the writing, all the history. The story of this movement, this action, must be examined over and over. We did not want this kind of ending. We wanted to live, to shine, to bring light to a world that is dying for a little bit of love ... If nobody understands, it matters not. I am ready to die now. Darkness settles over Jonestown on its last day on earth.

It is my hope that Mary has now been lifted up and out of that darkness, and that she will continue to shine once again.

ACKNOWLEDGMENTS

WHAT BEGAN AS a short story, eventually became a historical narrative spanning three continents and many decades. Blindsided by its scope, I needed a lot of help. Fortunately, it was not only available, but readily given. Friends and strangers, alike, pitched in. Over time, some strangers became friends — and friends more appreciated.

Many writers leave their family for the end of their acknowledgments; however, I must begin with mine. They put up with my absence, both mental and physical, for almost three years, enduring my frustration and disappointments along the way. At times, the contagion of the massacre and its story infected our family life: In effect, they were "living with" Jonestown, too. My husband generously offered on-the-spot editing, and my daughter, razor-sharp editing and a keen eye for design. For their patience and support, I will ever be grateful. In addition, my son-in-law, a mainstream minister, was always ready with biblical references if needed.

My brother Steve, who knew Mary better in some ways than I, was an invaluable source of information. Despite decades of living with numbing psychiatric medications, he was able to pull from memory facts I had long forgotten, plus many that were new to me. To my profound sorrow, he died of accidental injuries before publication. He had so wanted to hold this book in his hand, even if his brain illness would have prevented him from actually reading it himself. He was always glad to answer questions, and often said, "I like helping out."

A hero straight from a fairy tale, and one with the equally appropriate name of Fielding M. McGehee III, deserves top billing. Thankfully he goes by Mac. Living on an off-shore island clear across the country from me, he stayed close nevertheless. Countless emails, impromptu phone consults, chapters read and edited, and facts checked or provided, were all freely given. And this man, courted by CNN, Hollywood, and many other venues for his expertise, refused all payment for his work with me. His declaration that he "refused to make money from those dead bodies" further opened my heart, and I soon came to not only respect Mac, but to love the guy. His generous heart and capacity for organizing data have been a gift, not only to me, but the rest of the world. And no doubt, many scholars would agree.

Mac and his wife, Rebecca (Becky) Moore, have spent decades preserving the Jonestown story, as well as its records, and done so with respect and dedication. In addition, they actually visited Jonestown just five months after the massacre. It had to have taken tremendous grit and love to walk into that jungle, witnessing remnants of the massacre, and sensing its horror firsthand.

These two dedicated scholars, and flat-out good people, provided me with the courage I needed to face what I had turned away from for so long. Becky opened doors to my Jonestown education by referring me to both Mac, and the Jonestown Institute which they created and maintain. On a more personal level, Becky felt like rare company in my private grief. Having carried the shame of Jonestown in our family for far too long, I felt supported after finding another "grieving sister."

With these solid new connections, I was refreshed, able to plow ahead and reach out. The first stranger I then contacted was a member of the First Presbyterian Church of York, Pennsylvania. Before then I had known almost nothing about my brother-in-law, Peter Wotherspoon, or his family, but this church's librarian did. Lucinda Lobach generously sent me a large packet filled with newspaper articles and church records regarding the Wotherspoon family, its former members. Thanks to her, I came to know my long-lost brother-in-law and his birth family a little better.

Despite my early successes, as an introvert, I dreaded contacting Mary's friends for information about her. They might resent the intrusion so long after her death. And yet they were glad for the call, eagerly sharing information and memories of their beloved lost friend.

I first found Mary's friend, Sue, through Mac's Alternative Considerations of Jonestown & Peoples Temple website, where she had posted a remembrance of her. Sue and I were soon talking by phone, laughing, and tearing up while remembering Mary together. Sue eagerly provided me with letters and photos saved all this time, introducing me to a different Mary than the one I had known. And she mentioned in passing that she felt closer to Mary just by talking with me. I experienced the same, myself, and then with all of Mary's other friends.

Sue led me to Meredith, a.k.a. "Maude," another of Mary's other friends from high school. Meredith was surprised but happy to be contacted, and she, too, shared letters from Mary. Their brief correspondence revealed important changes in Mary I never knew, or even suspected.

When I found Barbara through her high school alumni office, I held my breath. Would she resent the intrusion after all these years? Would she even trust me? But as I was leaving her a voice message, "Baboola-Barb" picked up the phone immediately, actually grateful for the call. She, too, had kept treasured letters from Mary and sent many copies.

Through Barb, I found Mary's earliest childhood friend, Carol. Carol and Barb had been early school chums along with Mary, and later, those two were college roommates. Carol sent me a long letter, lovingly remembering Mary along with decades-old photos.

Barb, a retired book editor, then offered to help with the book early on. Her suggestions landed easily, and were almost always spot on. Counting Mac, I then had three editors: the first was Linda, also a retired editor and friend. Linda wielded a fearsome "red pencil," originally busting me for using too many commas. After pinpointing other punctuation sins, she presented me with a copy of *The Heath Handbook*, which she had edited. I needed it: my last and only grammar lessons were from 9th grade.

Editor number four, Sandy, was a longtime friend, but until now, I had never fully appreciated her moxie and skill as an acquisitions editor for a major publishing house. She read the whole book through and suggested critical changes in the format. Another old friend, Sheri, suggested that I write more about my last visit with Mary, and after that, to keep going. So, I did, never suspecting it would consume not months, but years. Looking back, it seems like I was surrounded by "book" folks, unaware that I would need their help, myself, someday.

Just when I thought I had enough editors, a fifth one popped up. Kate, a graduate of Princeton with a PhD in history, greatly improved my relationship with colons and semicolons. She generously worked through the whole manuscript patrolling for needed changes and rewrites. I owe this fine grammarian my new familiarity with "track changes," and a keener eye for dangling modifiers, adverbial phrases, and garbled — if creative — syntax.

Another longtime friend, Valerie from the A family, generously contributed to publication costs. And she did so with the same glad heart that her parents had when they welcomed me into their lives long before. Valerie is still "that kind of friend."

My phone visit with Stephan Jones marked the high point of researching and writing. As both a generous and kind person, he was open with me, and to his credit, made me feel comfortable within minutes of "Hello." Stephan's redemptive grace felt like a gift as we spoke late one Friday during his commute from work. It would be presumptuous to say we were kindred spirits, but I felt a deep connection with him, as well as awe and gratitude for his hard-won wisdom.

Two California institutions also deserve recognition. Together, they house an immense repository of Jonestown data and materials, enabling scholars and others, like me, access to Jonestown's history. I spent countless hours searching through hundreds of their documents, tapes, photos, and other ephemera. I chanced first upon San Diego State University's Special Collections of Library and Information Access. It hosts Mac's website, *Alternative Considerations of Jonestown and Peoples Temple* anf I mined its mother lode of information almost daily. Created "to give personal and scholarly perspectives on a major event in the history of religion in America," it did, indeed.

I was also thankful for the California Historical Society in San Francisco. Since 1871, they have been stewarding an immense, and continuously growing, collection of historical data pertaining to their state. As such, the Jonestown Institute has entrusted this society, which is run mostly by volunteers, with thousands of photos, ephemera, and other materials related to Peoples Temple and Jonestown. One staff member in particular, Debra Kaufman, deserves recognition for patiently enduring my repeated requests for materials, and guiding me through their seemingly endless archives.

My thanks also go to Mission Point Press, where Heather Shaw shepherded me through the self-publishing process. Her steadfast support, good nature, and committment to this book were an unexpected but greatly appreciated gift.

NOTES

ABBREVIATIONS:

Alternative. *Alternative Considerations for Peoples Temple &*
Jonestown, https://jonestown.SDSU.edu

West. *"Inside Peoples Temple"*: Kilduff, Marshall, and Tracy, Phil.
New West magazine, August 1, 1977.

Raven. Reiterman, Tim, with John Jacobs. *Raven: The Untold Story*
of the Rev. Jim Jones and His People. E.P. Dutton, 1982, New York,
reprint 2008, New York.

Understanding. Moore, Rebecca. *Understanding Jonestown and*
Peoples Temple. Praeger, 2009, 2018.

PART I — UPROOTED

CHAPTER 1: THE NEW LAND

5— "Back in their home province of Friesland:" Farmland was
usually inherited by family. Until about 1800, the family had
"niaarrecht," the right of niaar being the right of the next. A seller
was obliged to offer the land to a family member at first, before
he could sell it to a third party. When selling a piece of land, the
sale was announced in the church three Sundays in a row. If no
one applied to the right of niaar, the seller was free to sell. Of
course, this led to a lot of legal processes, which are nowadays
used for genealogic research, not easy to read in the early days.
Information provided by Melle Vander Heide, Genealogist, The
Netherlands, 2021.

PART II — TRANSPLANTED

CHAPTER 6: A TEMPLE IN THE VALLEY

Reiterman, Tim, and Jacobs, John. *Raven*. Unless otherwise noted, the historical information in this chapter can be credited to these authors' magisterial history of Jim Jones, Peoples Temple, and Jonestown. I am deeply grateful for their work.

74— "clairvoyance": *West.*

75— "Mind": Peoples Temple newsletter, July 1971, https:// jonestown.sdsu.edu/?page_id=14097

76— "25% of members' incomes": *West.*

80–81— "every other weekend, Mary rode," "Communal sharing within the church," "some 30 individual properties," "others reportedly rode underneath": *West.*

81— "vacation... $200", "large cans of tuna": *Alternative,* https:// jonestown.sdsu.edu/?page_id=102275

82— "overflowing bus toilets," "Jim Jones's private quarters": *West.*

86— "elitist behavior": *West.*

87— "misinformed bigot": Stuckart, Emerson Maureen. "Rev. Jones provided the only information members needed, while simultaneously suggesting that all outsiders were wrong or misinformed bigots." *Never Heard A Man Speak Like This Before: Reverend Jim Jones And Peoples Temple. Alternative,* https:// jonestown.sdsu.edu/?page_id=61794

87— "hand-in-hand": Peoples Temple newsletter, July, 1971. https:// jonestown.sdsu.edu/?page_id=14097

89— "regularly beaten": *West.* " …the belt was replaced by a paddle dubbed 'the board of education', and the number of times the adults and children were struck increased to 12, 25, 50 and even 100 times in a row. Temple nurses treated the injured." Kohl, Laura Johnston. Remembrance of Mary, *Alternative,* https:// jonestown.sdsu.edu/?who_died=wotherspoon-mary-beth

91— "hundreds in attendance," "board of education," "knocked out": *West.*

102— "Peter beaten so badly": Personal communication with survivor.

CHAPTER 7: CROSSING THE GOLDEN GATE

Raven, unless otherwise noted.

94— "had never seen a black person": Moore, Rebecca. *Understanding,* 24.

97— Moscone mayoral race: *West.*

99— "I am a nigger": *Alternative,* https://jonestown.sdsu.edu/?page_id=62874

100— "I am an atheist": *Alternative.* https://jonestown.sdsu.edu/?page_id=27498

101— "Jim Jones praised": Transcript of a taped church service with Jones mediating a disagreement between Judy Merriam and Mary Wotherspoon, who worked together in the same eldercare home in Ukiah, and also lived communally in this same home. *Alternative,* https://jonestown.sdsu.edu/?page_id=27463

102— "being beaten": Personal communication with former member, Garrett Lambrev, 2022.

102— "too thin": "[Jim Jones] likes thin people. You have to be thin to please him. But thin does not apply to him. He associates fat with being capitalistic and having a love of worldly things." *Alternative,* https://jonestown.sdsu.edu/?page_id=18869

CHAPTER 8: EXODUS

104— "all men are latently homosexual": Wise, David. "Sex in Peoples Temple," *The Jonestown Report 6,* October 2004.

Kinsolving, Lester. Unpublished report *San Francisco Examiner,* 1972.

113— Long weekend bus trips: *West.*

Reiterman, Tim, and Jacobs, John. *Raven,* 328—321.

PART III — SOWING LIES

CHAPTER 9: AN UNPROMISING LAND

124— **"hell…heaven":** Jones, Stephan. "Death's Night," *Alternative*, https://jonestown.sdsu.edu/?page_id= p 40172

129— **"labeled as "concrete":** Kohl, Laura Johnston. *Alternative*, https://jonestown.sdsu.edu/?page_id= 81246

129— **"split up families":** Just ten days after the massacre, Gosney gave an interview to U.S. government officials from an American hospital bed. Gosney, Vernon. FBI affidavit: *Alternative*, https://jonestown.sdsu.edu/?page_id= 64894

135— **"Peter has an astonishing":** Roller, Edith. A 62-year-old former college instructor, Roller arrived in Guyana on January 27, 1978, to head up the Temple school programs. A longtime member, she kept a journal in San Francisco, and continued to do so in Jonestown. *Alternative*, https://jonestown.sdsu.edu/?page_id=35694

137— **"Jonestown even had a basketball":** Reiterman, Tim, and Jacobs, John. *Raven*, 468.

CHAPTER 10: THE JUNGLE WINS

142— **"Big Foot":** Lindsay, Gordon. *Alternative*, https://jonestown.sdsu.edu/?page_id=18869

142— **"Mary Margaret…endured this horror":** Personal conversation with survivor.

142— **"snakes crawling":** *West.*

143— **"Jim wants her worked to death":** Roller, Edith. *Alternative*, https://jonestown.sdsu.edu/?page_id=35696

146— **"Edith Roller," "hot sauce":** *Alternative*, https://jonestown.sdsu.edu/?page_id=35694

146— **"theft":** Moore, Rebecca. *Understanding*, 48.

147— **"hatred of nuclear families" "treason":** Ibid., 73.

Stephan Jones and the jungle. Personal conversation, 2022.

148— **"siege"**: Moore, Rebecca. *Understanding*, 67.

148-149— **"most meals...rice," "rules were relaxed"**: Ibid., 47. Author's note: Temple's net worth ranged wildly before a final tally in receivership.

149— **"his father had once been loving...tormented by the cruelty"**: Personal conversation Stephan Jones, 2022.

151— **"staggering around"**: *Alternative*, https://jonestown.sdsu.edu/?page_id=29478

151— **"unfit to practice"**: "Dr. George Baird, chief medical officer for Guyana, wanted to rescind Schacht's licence to practice, as Schacht's only real experience (other than school) was a five-week internship programme. This was not nearly enough to act as the sole monitor of 1,000 malnourished people who were not used to Guyana's humid climate." *Alternative*, https://jonestown.sdsu.edu/?page_id=81646

CHAPTER 11: IT WAS MURDER

155— **"needed help walking"**: Condition reported by his in-laws visiting Jonestown shortly before the massacre. Reiterman, Tim, and Jacobs, John. *Raven*, 468.

156— **"get the fuck out"**: Moore, Rebecca. *Understanding*, 73.

The narrative of the landing and following events, unless otherwise noted, are described by Reiterman, Tim, and Jacobs, John. *Raven*, 107-114.

161— **"like a dying man"**: Reiterman, Tim, and Jacobs, John. *Raven*, 493.

162— **"barbed wire"**: Ibid., 494.

Vernon Gosney FBI affidavit, *Alternative*, https://jonestown.sdsu.edu/?page_id=64894

169— **"hundreds' actually wanted"**: FBI affidavit, *Alternative*, https://jonestown.sdsu.edu/?page_id=64894

170 —**"his father's self-worth"**: Personal communication Stephan Jones, 2022.

171— **"His nose was being rubbed"**: Reiterman, Tim, and Jacobs, John. *Raven*, 515.

173— **"Gosney simply replied":** FBI affidavit, *Alternative*, https://jonestown.sdsu.edu/?page_id=64894

176— **"They're killing everybody!":** Ibid.

181— **"hundreds had to be forced":** Odell Rhodes, survivor-witness inquest, December 1978, *Alternative*, https://jonestown.sdsu.edu/?pagei=id 13675

181— **"hammered":** Personal communication, 2022.

184— **"this 'historic" day':** Lane, Mark. The complete story of his escape from Jonestown is covered in *Alternative*, https://jonestown.sdsu.edu/?page id 71542

Jones, Stephan. "Death's Night," *Alternative*, https://jonestown.sdsu.edu/?page =id 40172

PART IV — LETHAL HARVEST

CHAPTER 12: COURAGE AND COMPASSION

The events surrounding the airport shooting were reported by Tim Reiterman and DCM Richard Dwyer, both of whom were wounded there. In addition, Vernon Gosney relates his experience of being shot trying to escape. (Reiterman, Tim. *Raven*, chapter 54, "Holocaust," 521: Dwyer, Richard DCM, Gosney, Vernon. FBI affidavit, *Alternative*, https://jonestown.sdsu.edu/?page =id 98908)

CHAPTER 13: A SLOW AGONY

212— **"shovels":** Personal communication, Fielding M. McGehee, 2021.

"Air Force Pilot Tells of Experiences in Jonestown Bodylift," by Chris Knight-Griffin. *Alternative*, https://jonestown.sdsu.edu/?page =id 40221

215— **"two paperbacks":** Moore, Rebecca. *Understanding*, 120.

Live interview with Stephan Jones. https://www.youtube.com/watch?v=IXhb0YYOWds

220— **"Dianne Feinstein":** Moore, Rebecca. *Understanding*, 137.

CHAPTER 14: NO REST, NO PEACE

The events surrounding the handling of the bodies at Dover Air Force Base were investigated and reported by Rebecca Moore, who lost two sisters and a nephew in Jonestown. (Moore, Rebecca. "Last Rights," *Alternative*, https://jonestown.sdsu.edu/?page =id 16585)

PART V — PAYING TRIBUTE

CHAPTER 15: HOOKED, DISMEMBERED

Reiterman, Tim, and Jacobs, John. *Raven*, 330.

Vedantam, Shankar, and Mesler, Bill. W.W. Norton and Company, 2022.

239— "When DCM Richard Dwyer first visited": *Alternative*, https://jonestown.sdsu.edu/?page_id= 64894

240— "What a beautiful place": Moore, Rebecca. *Understanding*, 100.

Stephan Jones's quotes, personal communication, 2022.

240— "It wasn't suicide, it was murder.": *Alternative*, https://jonestown.sdsu.edu/?page_id=64894

241— "the crime of murder is apparent.": *Alternative* https://jonestown.sdsu.edu/?page_id=71542

241— "brainwashing": Moore, Rebecca. *Alternative*, https://jonestown.sdsu.edu/?page_id= p 80836

242— "We isolated ourselves": Kohl, Laura Johnston. Jonestown Survivor, iUniverse publisher, 2010, p 50.

Kohl, Laura Johnston. Jones's power. *Alternative*, https://jonestown.sdsu.edu/?page_id= 30283

245— "hammered" by all the hardship": Personal communication Stephan Jones, 2022.

CHAPTER 17: REVELATIONS

262— "voices from outer space": Reiterman, Tim, and Jacobs, John. Raven, 262.

269— **"Mike Cartmell, remembers":** *Alternative*, https://jonestown. sdsu.edu/?page_id= 30796

271— **"gentle, warm":** Vilchez, Laura. Personal email, Rebecca Moore.

271— **"a light":** *Alternative*, https://jonestown.sdsu.edu/?who_ died=wotherspoon-mary-beth

271— **"collect all the tapes":** Suicide note. Moore, Rebecca. *Understanding*, p. 101.

www.ingramcontent.com/pod-product-compliance
Lightning Source LLC
Chambersburg PA
CBHW021612120626
46545CB00001B/186